300 Questions
And Answers
On the Catholic Faith

Msgr. Charles Pope

ISBN:151233040X
ISBN-13:9781512330403

DEDICATION

To all who have taught me. And To God who taught them.

CONTENTS

ACKNOWLEDGMENTS

Our Sunday Visitor

Holy Comforter- St. Cyprian Parish

Mount St. Mary's Seminary

Introduction

Life is filled with questions. In a way, our faith begins with a question. On the day of your baptism you were asked a question: "What do you ask of God's Church?" And you (or your sponsor) answered, "Baptism." Adults who are baptized are asked further, "What does Baptism offer you?" And again, an answer came forth: "Eternal life."

Yes, life is filled with questions, from the very beginning. Question, from the Latin *quaero*, meaning to seek or search. Answers, too, when rooted in the truth are very precious things. And the National Publication "Our Sunday Visitor" Answers Column has long been a faithful guide for Catholics throughout the country.

I was recently asked by "Our Sunday Visitor" and agreed to write the Question and Answer column. I am herewith publishing my first 50 columns, each with two questions covered. The questions are of a random nature, and appear here in the order I received them and published the answers.

"Our Sunday Visitor" (OSV) has a long legacy in this country of informing and encouraging Catholics. I remember OSV as a regular fixture of the periodical rack in vestibules of all my parishes going back to my youth. Even as a pre-teen I would often be asked by my mother to make a donation and take a copy home so we could read it during the week. Many fond memories!

Hence, it is a great honor to be able to contribute to such a long-standing and informative Catholic Newspaper.

The questions and answers that follow are from a wide variety of areas such as liturgy, the moral life, marriage and family issues, bioethics, culture and faith, Church history, apologetics, and so forth.

Msgr. Charles Pope

1. OUR LORD GOD

Q1: Did Satan know Jesus was God, or was he just tempting His human nature to fail? – *Ann*

A: It would seem that Satan and other evil spirits *did* know Jesus was God, at least in some general way. Scripture reports: *Whenever the evil spirits saw him, they fell down before him and cried out, "You are the Son of God"* (Mk 3:11). Another time a demon cried out: *I know who you are--the Holy One of God!"* (Mk 1:24). There are similar passages (e.g. Mk 1:34 and Luke 4:41).

That said, we ought not to conclude that Satan had a comprehensive or flawless knowledge of Jesus, and the full plan of salvation. Had Satan such a complete knowledge, especially of the plan of God, he would not have inspired the crucifixion of Jesus, the very means by which he (Satan) was defeated.

Hence, there is evidence that Satan had a basic understanding of Jesus' divinity, and plan, but one that was limited, and likely flawed to some extent, due to his intellect being darkened by sin and rage.

However, when Satan tempted Jesus, it was only to his human nature and his human will that he could appeal, even though he knew Jesus also to be God.

Q2: To me, the Holy Spirit is an Enigma. Please teach me how better to understand the Holy Spirit – *James*

A: Scripture comes to mind, that when St Paul went to Ephesus, he inquired if they had received the Holy. They replied, "We have not even heard that there is a Holy Spirit." (Acts 19:2). You of course have heard, but like many, are not sure of His role in your life, and wonder how better to experience Him.

Within the Blessed Trinity the Father beholds the Son, and the Son beholds the Father. And there flows from them both, and between them, a divine love that is so perfect, and of such infinite ardor, as to be a living Love, and a divine person (for it is the very nature of God to exist), and we call this Love, the Holy Spirit.

To have the Holy Spirit living in us, received at Baptism, is to be caught up into the very love and life of God. The work of the Holy Spirit is, first, to sanctify us, to make us holy and pleasing to God. The Holy Spirit also bestows on us countless graces and charisms to transform us and make us a blessing to others.

It is no surprise that one image of the Holy Spirit is that of fire. For as tongues of fire came to rest upon the first disciples, so too for us does the Holy Spirit light the fire of God's love in us, purifying and refining away impurities, and instilling in us, with increasing perfection, the life, love and glory of God.

Another image of the Holy Spirit is that of the rushing wind that came upon the disciples at Pentecost. The word "Spirit" means "breath." Yes, God, the Holy Spirit breathes new life into us. And by his power we become more, and more alive, in the new life Christ purchased for us, a new mind, by the Spirit's inspiration, and new heart by His love, a growing transformation and a share in every good and perfect gift by his grace.

What does the Holy Spirit do for you? Consider the transformation of the first disciples at Pentecost. Anxious individuals gathered in an upper room were suddenly transformed and, throwing open the door, went forth with love and confidence to boldly proclaim Christ. This, the Holy Spirit offers you as well.

Q3: I was taught that the persons of the Trinity are all equal. But Jesus says, somewhere, that the Father is greater than him. Is this so, and does this mean I was taught incorrectly? – *Edwin, OK*

A: You were taught correctly. The three person of the Trinity are all equal. Regarding their equality and oneness, the preface of the Holy Trinity says of our Triune God: *In the confession of the true and eternal Godhead there is adored a distinctness of persons, a oneness in essence, and an equality in majesty.*

So what does it mean when the same Jesus who said, "The Father and I are One" (Jn 10:30), also says, "The Father is greater than I" (John 14:28)?

Theologically it means that the Father is the source in the Trinity. All the members are co-eternal, co-equal, equally divine, but the Father is the

Principium Deitatis (the Principle of the Deity). Jesus proceeds from the Father from all eternity. In effect Jesus is saying, "I delight that the Father is the principle of my being, even though I have no origin."

Devotionally, Jesus is saying I always do what pleases my Father. Jesus loves his Father, is crazy about him, is always talking about him and pointing to him. In effect he says, by calling the Father greater, "I look to my Father for everything and I do what I see him doing (Jn 5:19) and what I know pleases him (Jn 5:30). His will and mine are one, and what I will to do proceeds from him and I do what I know accords with his will, whom I love."

It says in Luke, that Jesus was subject to his Father and Mother, Joseph and Mary. Where they superior to him? No. And neither is Jesus less than equal to His Father by looking to him for everything and being of one will with Him.

Q4: We teach that God is changeless. But at some point the Second Person of the Trinity became man. How is this hypostatic union not a change in God? - *Tim Hart*

A: Among other things, the answer to your question is caught up in a very deep mystery of God's relationship to time. In fact, many of our questions about God, and our struggle to understand Him, go back to this mystery.

The fact is, God does not dwell in time as you and I do. Rather, He dwells in the fullness of time, a mystery we call "eternity." The word eternity does not simply mean a long, long time. Rather, eternity means "the fullness of time." That is, past, present and future are all experienced at once.

To illustrate eternity, consider a clock. Let us say that the current time is 12 noon. For us who live in serial time, that means that 3 PM is in the future, and 9 AM is in the past. But now move your eyes to the center dot of the round clock face. At that center point, all three times 12 noon 9 AM and 3 PM, are equally present, and have the same relationship with that center dot.

This is an analogy of what we mean by eternity. Thus, for God, who is eternal, the future is just as present to him as the past. God is not waiting for things to happen, neither is he reminiscing on things past. All is present to him in a comprehensive "now."

This is mysterious to us but helps illustrate why our questions about God are often wrong, even in the way we ask them. Thus, your question about whether God "changed" when Jesus became incarnate, presupposes that God lives in time as we do. But he does not.

While this approach may seem to be avoiding an answer to your question, we do well to meditate on the truth that we do not even know how to word our questions properly, let alone get simple answer. Change, as we define it, presupposes serial or chronological time. But God is not there. God is beyond such categories.

Thus we are right to conclude, as you observe, that God does not change. And yet He is able to interact with us who do change. But how exactly this is accomplished is mysterious to us and is caught up in our limited capacity to understand the mystery that we call time. In no sense is God waiting around to do things, like becoming man, nor is He changing as time goes along. All is present to him in a comprehensive now. God simply Is.

Q5: Major religions address God by Different names. Are we all praying to the same God? And since most in the world do not acknowledge Jesus, what can they expect in terms of judgment?
- *Ed Eddy, Ft. Myers, FL*

A: Whether we are praying to the same God, is assessed on a case-by-case basis. A special understanding is given to the Jewish people. Of them, the Catechism states, *The Jewish faith, unlike other non-Christian religions, is already a response to God's revelation in the Old Covenant. To the Jews belong the sonship, the glory, the covenants, the giving of the law, the worship, and the promises* (No.839). They direct their prayers to God the Father, as we do though they do not understand God as Trinity, or accept Jesus or the Holy Spirit as God. And yet, it is fair to say they *do* direct their prayers to the same God, though imperfectly understood, to whom we direct our prayers though more perfectly understood.

As to the Muslims, they are monotheists, and, as a Catechism notes, *"These profess to hold the faith of Abraham, and together with us they adore the one, merciful God, mankind's judge on the last day."* (No. 841.)

The Church's relationship with other non-Christian religions is less certain and variable. Of these the Catechism says that God is clearly the common origin and end of the whole human race (*cf* No. 842). Further, *The Church recognizes in other religions that search, among shadows and images, for the God who is unknown yet near since He gives life and breath and all things and wants all men to be saved.* (No. 843)

As to what the majority of people can expect, especially those who do not know or obey Christ, the Church expresses hope, but also warns that though their salvation apart from Christ is possible, that does not mean it is probable. For the Catechism also reminds that sin requires the remedy of faith, *"But very often, deceived by the evil one, men have become vain in the reasoning, and have exchanged the truth of God for lie, and served the creature rather than the creator."* Thus unbelief or imperfect belief is a form of darkness that hinders salvation and needs the healing of true faith.

So, in the end, there is only one God and all yearning for God is somehow directed to him. But there are often errors in the ways people of the world understand him. And thus it is essential for the Church to correct errors, and draw everyone to the one, holy, Catholic and apostolic faith in which there is the best hope for salvation.

Q6: Is there an appropriate name for our Savior in the context of certain situations? Should we refer to him as Jesus, Christ, Jesus Christ, Christ Jesus etc.? - *name withheld, Norwood, MA*

A: As your question suggests, exactly how we address Jesus will vary in certain contexts. Perhaps it is most important to distinguish at the outset that "Christ," is not part of Jesus proper name, but rather, it is his title. In this sense, it sometimes helps to put the definite article "the" in front of Christ, saying, "Jesus the Christ," to remind us that "Christ" is not his surname. Jesus is "the Christ," Which means, "the anointed one" and translates the Hebrew word "Messiah."

His proper name, "Jesus" means, in Hebrew, "God saves." To put all of this together in English, his name and title might be rendered "Anointed Lord and Savior."

While it is certainly fine for us to call him simply by his proper name, "Jesus," in the formal liturgy of the Church we often speak of him more fully, such as, "Christ our Lord," or "Our Lord Jesus Christ," and so forth.

All this said, it must be added that there are over 100 titles of Jesus, and ways of referring to him in the Scriptures which can also be appropriate ways of referring to him in certain circumstances. For example he is called" Alpha and Omega, Author and Finisher of our faith, Son of David, Son of Man, Good Shepherd, Emanuel, I AM, King of Israel, the Way the Truth and the Life, Light of the World, Redeemer, Teacher, Rabbi, Son of God, Son of Mary, True Vine, and so forth. There are more than 100 other such titles.

Thus, we do well to remember that the magnificent truth of Jesus Christ, our Lord, often requires us to speak of him in many ways, pondering his glory from many different perspectives through these titles.

Q7: Why is Jesus called "Son of Man" in the Gospels? What does "Son of Man" mean and why is it used so often in the Gospels?
- Arlene Farrell, Huntington Station, NY

A: In the scriptures, the title "son of God" is used in many different senses and is, paradoxically more vague that the Title "Son of Man." "Son of God" can be a title of Israel itself (Ex. 4:22; Hos 11:1), of the Davidic King (Ps 2:7) and of the angels (Gen 6:2), all humankind, all the just and peacemakers are called sons of God (Mat 5:9), and so forth.

In view of the ambiguity of the term, this is why Jesus did not simply say, "I am the Son of God." Rather, he spoke more clearly, saying for example, "The Father and I are one… to see me is to have seen the Father," etc. Indeed, the anger and charges of blasphemy by many of the Jews at Jesus' time show that Jesus claim to divinity was far better accomplished this way than to us a more ambiguous term of that time "Son of God."

Paradoxically, "Son of Man" is a clearer profession of divine transcendence that can be traced to Daniel 7:13 which Christ appropriated to himself. That prophecy speaks of one, like a Son of Man coming on the clouds to judge the earth, who has a Kingdom that shall never end.

Jesus' preference for the term is shown when Caiaphas the High Priest said: "I put you on oath by the living God to tell us if you are the Messiah, the Son of God." Jesus answered, *"The words are your own. Moreover, I tell you that from this time onward you will see the Son of Man seated at the right hand of the power and coming on the clouds of heaven."* (Mt 26:62-66)

Thus, "Son of Man" is a more clear and lofty title, which Christ prefers for himself.

Q8: The Catechism in paragraph 460 says, "that man might become God." Please explain. *– Jim Jeson, Milwaukee, WI*

A: The catechism here references a quote from St. Athanasius, and also a clarification by St. Thomas Aquinas. It is true that Athanasius speaks boldly, as Saints often do! But as both St. Athanasius and St. Thomas were careful to do, distinctions are necessary.

The exact quote from the catechism is *For the Son of God became man so that we might become God. The only-begotten Son of God, wanting to make us sharers in his divinity, assumed our nature, so that he, made man, might make men gods.*

Note that the second sentence, a comment by Thomas on Athanasius' statement, the word "gods" is not capitalized. And this is to make it clear, as Athanasius would agree, that we do not become a god as separate and distinct from the one, true God. But rather, that we "partake" or "participate" in the Divine nature.

To partake, or participate comes from the Latin Word *particeps*, meaning to take up a part of something, but not the whole. Thus, though we come to share in aspects of the Divine nature, we do not do so in a way that is separate from being members of Christ's Body, through baptism. We access this "share" in a part or aspect of divine life and nature only in union with Christ, only by entering into communion with Jesus at baptism, and thus receiving divine sonship.

Q9: Since every human child receives half of his chromosomes from his Father and half from his mother, where does the Church teach Jesus got the other half of his chromosomes, since he had no earthly father?
- *Peter Stein, Everett, WA*

A: I am unaware of any official Church teaching in this regard. Knowledge of DNA etc., is very recent and still deepening. Hence one would not expect a thorough theological treatise on a matter of this sort now.

However one principle must surely apply, namely the teaching from both Scripture and Tradition that Jesus, as a Divine person also had a complete, intact human nature and was like us, in this regard in all things but sin. Hence he had the complete and proper number of chromosomes. How exactly God supplied the part usually supplied by a human father is not revealed.

Speculation though always a human tendency, would remain only speculation. We are dealing with miracle and mystery. But this truth remains clear, Jesus, though one person, is fully divine, and fully human.

Q10: I never understood the Baptism of Christ, since he is sinless and born of a sinless mother. Please explain. - *Lydia Volpe, Oneeda, NY*

A: It is clear, that Jesus was without sin (e.g. Heb 4:15). Even as Jesus approaches John for baptism, John instinctively protests. However, the Lord explains, saying, *Let it be now so in order to fulfill all righteousness* (Matt 3:15).

Jesus is referring to the righteousness (justice) of God. God's justice is his fidelity to his promises. And God had promised to send us a Messiah to go ahead of us and lead us out of sin, and into righteousness.

At the River Jordan, Jesus is like Moses, who did not just tell the people to cross the Red Sea, he went ahead, courageously leading them through the stormy waters. Jesus does no less. And does not tell us merely to go to the waters of baptism; he leads us through baptism, out of slavery, into freedom.

The liturgy of the Church, speaks of Jesus not being made holy by the waters, but making the waters holy to bless us.

Jesus also does this with the "baptism" of the whole Paschal mystery. He does not merely tell us to take up a cross, he takes up his cross and bids us follow him. He does not merely point to the hill of Calvary; he leads us up over that hill and unto glory.

This is God's righteousness, his justice, this is his fidelity to his promises.

Another aspect of Jesus' baptism is the remarkable fact that he identifies with sinners, though he himself is not a sinner. He is *not ashamed to call us his brethren* (Heb 2:11). He who was sinless, was seen as a great sinner, and crucified publicly. Such love, such emptying, such humility. For the Lord conquers Satan's pride, and ours, by astonishing humility. And in this too, Jesus "fulfills all righteousness" by being Baptized, going into the waters ahead of us.

Q11: What does the I.N.R.I. mean on the top of our crucifixes mean?
— *name withheld, Palm Beach, FL*

A: It is an abbreviation for *Jesus Nazarenus, Rex Judeorum* — Jesus of Nazareth, King of the Jews. In Latin the "I" and "J" are usually interchangeable and ancient Latin did not use the "J" That is why it is INRI not JNRJ.

It was common for the Romans to hang a "titulus" or sign above the crucified to indicate the charges against him. Scripture says that Pilate put the charges in Latin, Greek and Hebrew.

Pilate placed this title above Jesus in scorn and mockery rather than faith. He also likely knew it would irritate the Jewish leaders, which it did (see Jn 19:21).

Yet even in his ridicule, Pilate spoke truth. Jesus is King, not of the Jews only, but of all things.

Q12: You Catholics pray to Saints but the Bible says there is only one mediator, Jesus. How can you justify this? -*Jason, via email*

A: Jesus of course mediates a relationship with the Father in a way no one else can. No one comes to the Father except through Him. However, in terms of our relationship with him, Jesus has established things and people which help mediate our relationship with him: apostles, evangelists and teachers and roles of service to build up the body of Christ. Faith comes by hearing, hearing by the word of God. Therefore, our relationship with Jesus is mediated by both Scripture, and those whom the Lord sends to evangelize us.

You seem to understand "one mediator, "in a completely univocal, and absolute sense. If so, then you should never ask anyone to pray for you. Neither should you listen to a sermon, or even read scripture. For these are things and people which mediate Christ to you in some sense.

Catholics do not hold that the prayers of Saints substitute for Christ's mediation, but rather is subordinate to it, and facilitated by him. For, as Head of the Body the Church, he creates a communion of all the members, allowing, and expecting that all the members of the body assist and support one another. This does not substitute for Christ's mediation, but rather, presupposes it.

Q13: Jesus tells Mary Magdalene in one of the resurrection appearances, "I am ascending to my God and your God" (Jn 20:18). This has always confused me since I thought Jesus is God. –*Mary Taylor, Sarasota, FL*

Yes, Jesus is God. But Jesus is also one person with two natures, divine and human. When he speaks of "ascending to my God" he does so in terms of his human nature. As God, he cannot ascend to God, there is nowhere for him to go. But in terms of his humanity he can use expressions such as "my God" and he has the capacity to ascend.

It is important to realize that the resurrection accounts place heavy emphasis on Jesus' human nature. For it does not pertain to Jesus' divine nature to rise from the dead, since God cannot die. Only as man can he rise from the dead.

Not only is his human nature raised up, but it is transformed. We speak of his resurrected humanity is a glorified humanity. And in this sense he is ascending. That is, he is taking up his glorified human nature to dwell forever at the Father's right hand.

Q14: Please explain how Jesus can be God as well as man at the same time. – *Anthony Retnam, via Facebook*

A: If I could explain it, I might be a heretic. There are mysteries here, which caused the ancient Church to fall to its knees when the words of the Creed in this matter we said. How can the infinite enter the finite, How can Mary's creator, be born of her?

The Mystery is described by the term "Hypostatic union," which states that Jesus, though one person, has two natures, divine and human. These natures are united in his one person but not mixed or confused.

Your question, "how can this be" can only be answered by an appeal to God's omnipotence and will to save us. Jesus had to be God to save us, but had to man to represent us. Hence, it is fitting that Jesus be both, but How this is done is left to God.

Q15: I was speaking to a friend about the "Angel of Death" in Exodus and she responded that she couldn't believe in a "killing" God, only a loving God. How do I explain passages like this? *-James Cayea, via email*

A: Pope Benedict in the Post-synodal exhortation "Verbum Domini" referred to events like this as the "dark passages" of the Bible. And while they are hard for many modern people to digest, they do speak to times where modern forms of conflict resolution were little known. God had not yet led these ancient cultures to a clearer grasp of justice and the dignity of the human person. That would take centuries of sending the Law, prophets, and finally his Son to teach us in these ways and deepen our grasp of justice and mercy.

As such, warlike solutions were rather common in the ancient world and conflicts were often "resolved" with one side winning.

As for Pharaoh, it took the death of the firstborn to finally secure the release of the Jews from slavery. One can argue that God acted in a way that was necessary in those conditions to secure the common good. Your friend may wish to ponder if she has the scales to measure what is worse: the tragic death of a certain number of firstborn Egyptian children, or the cruel enslavement of the entire Jewish nation for 400 years. How does one weigh the common good of action by God or continued inaction? Remember too, none of the previous plagues were enough to secure the release of the slaves.

In addition, your friend might wish to recall that God, who gives life, has the right to take it when and how he sees fit. God numbers all of our days. Some of us will live long lives, others not. Some of us will die in bed, others by violence. Only God knows what is best for us an for the common good.

Q16: I have always understood that the baptized are members of the Body of Christ. But in Bible Study last month the Deacon taught from Colossians that Jesus "holds all creation together in himself." So how can we Christians claim any special status? -*Geraldine Kramer, via email*

A: The quote from the Colossians hymn is an accurate though older rendering of the New American Bible from 1970s. The more current version reads: *In [Jesus] all things hold together. He is the head of the body, the Church.* Col 1:17–18

So, Christ does hold all things together in himself, but only the Church is his Body.

Perhaps by analogy you and I could have something in or associated with our body that is not our body per se. For example, I could have food in my stomach that is in me, but not of me.

The analogy falls short however (like all analogies do) since I do not cause the food in my stomach to exist or "hold together." But Christ, as God, is the ground of all being and is "being itself." Thus, St. Paul rightly says that in him all things "hold together" (the Greek is *synestēken*, meaning to be sustained, consist, or to stay together) for without the Lord they would not exist at all.

However, despite this immanent (close) relationship of Christ to all of creation, only the Church, consisting of baptized members is the Body of Christ. For by grace, a baptized Christian becomes one with Christ, *becomes a 'son of light,' indeed, becomes "light" himself* (Catechism 1216, 1267; see also Jn 1:9; 1 Thess 5:5; Heb 10:32; Eph 5:8).

Therefore the Christian is not only sustained or held together by Christ, but becomes one with him, a member of his very body, dying with him and rising with him, ascending with his entering the Holy of Holies in heaven. Only the baptized are said to receive this glory and to be a member of Christ's body.

Q17: When the crowds hailed Jesus as "Son of David" and "King of the Jews" wasn't that enough for Pontius Pilate to crucify him?
– *Robert Bonsignore, Brooklyn, NY*

A: No. Pilate was aware of these attestations, but was not particularly impressed by them. He did interrogate Jesus about this matter and Jesus had said, "My kingdom is not of this world." (Jn 18:36). Even if Jesus had claimed to be a King in a rival sense (which he did not) Pilate had him under arrest and Jesus seemed quite "powerless." Pilate might have been more alarmed if Jesus seemed to wield political power and influence but his "own people" had handed him over and the religious leaders and the crowd were saying "We have no King but Caesar!" (Jn 19:15).

With all this in mind, Pilate wanted to let Jesus go after some sort of punishment.

What Pilate *did* fear was the crowds and a riot if he did not accede to their demands to crucify Jesus. This appalled his sense of justice (e.g. Lk 23:16) and went against a warning he had received from his wife who told him of a dream she had that he was innocent (Matt 27:18-19).

Pilate thus violated his own conscience out of fear and this weakness is more the cause of his actions.

Q18: The Catechism says in # 460: *The Word became flesh to make us "partakers of the divine nature": "For this is why the Word became man, and the Son of God became the Son of man: so that man, by entering into communion with the Word and thus receiving divine* *sonship, might become a son of God." "For the Son of God became man so that we might become God."... Does the Catholic really teach that we can become god?* — *Douglas Austin, Boise, ID*

A: The phrase "that we might become God" is meant in a qualified sense, not in an absolute sense. The Catechism is quoting St. Athanasius.

But you will note that prior to quoting St Athanasius, the Catechism sets the context by referencing 2 Peter 1:3-4 which says, [God's] divine power has granted to us all things that pertain to life and godliness, through the knowledge of him who called us to his own glory and excellence, by which he has granted to us his precious and very great promises, so that through them you may become partakers of the divine nature, having escaped from the corruption that is in the world because of sinful desire.

Hence the Catechism, in setting the same context from which St. Athanasius reflects, is not teaching that we become our own "god" but that we participate in, and become sharers in the divine nature of God. We do this by grace, and because we are made members of the Body of Christ through Baptism.

Saints and preachers often use hyperbole and other techniques for memorable impact. However it is important to understand the mode of speech that is being used. Frequently we do not use words in an absolute sense, but rather in a qualified or sometimes metaphorical sense. We do so for impact.

If I were to praise you and say, "You're the man!" Despite my use of the definite article "the", I do not mean to state that the there are no other men in existence, or that you are the only one among all other existing males worthy of praise. Rather it is a kind of "flourish" or exaggeration meant to single you out for something in the moment. I speak in an absolute sense, but I do not mean it in an absolute sense.

And so too for the memorable saying of St. Athanasius: We share in the divine nature as Scripture says, but we do not become separate little gods unto ourselves.

2. SCRIPTURE

Q19: I don't understand why Judas' betrayal of Jesus is so important. Surely the Chief Priests and others who wanted him dead knew who he was and could have found him without Judas. And didn't Peter also betray Jesus by denying him three times? Was his betrayal less harmful than Judas'? – *name withheld*

A: Practically the Temple leaders could have found and arrested Jesus when he was out in public but, as Scripture says, they feared the crowds who might riot upon such an act (e.g. Matt 21:46). To find Jesus at a more private moment would surely have required more "inside knowledge," which Judas could provide.

Theologically, no one could lay a hand on Jesus until his "hour" had come. He was always able, until he freely chose to lay down his life, to evade their attempts at arrest (e.g. Jn 8:20). This may also have caused the Temple leaders to conclude they needed inside information.

And while God could have allowed another way for Jesus to be turned over, Judas fulfills Scripture, which says: *Even my close friend, who ate my bread, has turned against me* (Ps. 41:9).

Betrayal and denial are fundamentally different. Through betrayal Judas handed Jesus over. Denial, while surely sinful, is to deny association with Jesus, and does not amount to handing him over. Thus it is less harmful to Jesus than what Judas did.

Q20: I am a convert from the Evangelical Church and my RCIA teacher told me that the seven days of creation in Genesis is a primitive mode of speaking and does not really mean seven days. Is this true? – *Shelly*

A: The catechism discourages the word "primitive" (eg CCC # 304) in reference to scripture. A better Catholic approach is to describe the creation account as a poetic account, rather than a modern, scientific account.

If we try to hold to a literalistic reading of all the details, we have difficulties. For, if a "day" is a 24 hour cycle of the sun, it is surprising to read that the sun and moon are not even created until the 4th "day".
Further, if the account is purely a literalistic, scientific account, there is the problem that there are two accounts of creation in Genesis 1-2:3 & 2:4ff. They are both *very* different.

What is essential for us to hold from these accounts is that God made everything out of nothing, He did so in wisdom and love, guiding every step. And though transcendent, remains present and active in all he has made.

So, seven days is likely more poetic than scientific.

Q21: In Luke 23:44, the writer states that an eclipse of the sun took place at the time of Christ's crucifixion. Is there a basis of fact as to its occurrence? And, if so, was this solar eclipse coincidental and in accord with the laws of science? - *Chick P*

A: I am not sure why you call it an "eclipse." None of the Gospel writers use this term. Matthew, Mark and Luke use the Greek term σκότος (*skotos*), which means, simply, "darkness."

As a general rule we should avoid applying certain meanings to texts that are more specific than the author intends. That there was darkness over the land from noon till three is certainly attested in the sacred text. But the cause of that darkness is unexplained. Perhaps God made use of natural causes, such as an eclipse or very heavy clouds to cause the darkness. But it is also possible that the darkness was of purely supernatural origin and was experience only by some.

Hence, trying to explain the darkness simply in terms of "the laws of science" risks doing disservice to the text by missing its deeper meaning, namely, that the darkness of sin has reached its height. Whatever the mechanism of the darkness, its deepest cause is sin and evil.

Jesus had said elsewhere, *"This is the judgment: Light has come into the world, but men loved darkness instead of light because their deeds were evil."* (Jn 3:19). He also said referring to his passion; *"Night is coming, when no one can work."* (Jn 9:4). And when Judas leaves the Last Supper to betray Jesus, John observes simply and profoundly, *"And it was night."* (Jn 13:30). Yes, deep darkness had come upon the world.

You ask if there is a basis in fact that this darkness actually occurred. Though some modern scholars consider it a mere literary device, there seems little reason to doubt that it actually occurred. While some refer to a purported *Letter of Pontius Pilate to Tiberius* that verifies it, the historical value of the document is highly disputed. Yet, three of the gospels record it, and most of the Fathers of the Church treat the darkness as historical.

That said, how widely experienced, and how deep the dark, is not specified. We should balance accepting its historicity with an appreciation that the texts are restrained in terms of precise details.

Q22: Somewhere in Scripture it is written that a naked man was seen running from the scene of Jesus arrest. Where is this and what does it mean? – *Joan Beaulieu, Titusville, FL*

A: It is in Mark: *A young man, wearing nothing but a linen garment, was following Jesus. When they seized him, he fled naked, leaving his garment behind* (14:51-52).

Who this young man is, and the exact meaning of this passage, are rather debated and uncertain. Most modern scholars think the young man is Mark himself who is describing a humorous story of when his faith was not strong.

Note he is described as a young man, possibly less than 12, which may explain why he was lightly clothed. Like today, youngsters might be permitted to wear fewer clothes. Others see the image of youthful virility in this description, since the description of the clothing points also to gym clothing.

The meaning of the text is much debated. However, two explanations seem most likely. First, there is the link to Gen 39:12 described by several Fathers of the Church. In that passage Joseph, seeking to escape the seduction of the wife of Potiphar, flees naked. Thus the Christian, must be prepared to leave everything behind to avoid the snares of the sinful.

A second explanation focuses on the youthful strength of the young man and ties the event to a prophecy of Amos: *And he who is stout of heart among the mighty shall flee away naked in that day, declares the LORD* (2:16). Thus the text indicates the weakness of even strong men and the need for God to save us.

Q23: Regarding Matthew 24, it would seem Jesus' predictions on Jerusalem's ruin were fulfilled. However what of His descriptions of alterations in the sun, moon and stars? Where these fulfilled?
- Paul Forester, Clinton, MD

A: Biblical scholars have differing opinions on what elements of the Mount Olivet discourse relate to the destruction of the Jerusalem in 70 A.D., and what might refer to the end of the world. Some of the details quite clearly relate to the events of 70 A.D., such as wars, Jerusalem being surrounded by armies, etc. Even some other details such as earthquakes, and famines occurred around at that time.

Other details may be references to the end of the world, (e.g. the sun and moon darkened, signs in the heavens, and the Son of Man coming on the clouds), or they may also have occurred in 70 AD. Josephus an historian at that time, describes clouds of smoke as Jerusalem burned, which dimmed the sun and eclipsed the moon and stars. He also describes strange wonders in the heavens, possibly a comet, and strange lights near and above the Temple at night.

A balanced approach would be to acknowledge that all the signs had an historical reference, rooted in 70 A.D., but also symbolically point the end of the world, of which Jerusalem is a sign.

As for Christ "coming on the clouds" it is a prophetic language describing judgment on ancient Israel for lack of faith. It is also clear that Jesus will come in judgment on this world as well.

Q24: I am aware that when we say in the Creed, Jesus *descended into Hell*, we do not mean the Hell of the damned, but merely the place of the dead. But do we have any idea what that place was like? Also, were the justified and the condemned in that place together?
-Leonard Loftus, Geneseo, IL

A: You are correct in your distinction between the Hell of the damned, and the "Hell" that refers to the place where all the dead were until the Messiah came. It is an unfortunate fact, that in English, "Hell" is used to refer to both places. But the Jewish people clearly distinguished between "Sheol," were all who had died were detained, and the Hell of the damned which Jesus often called "Gehenna."

As for what Sheol was like, we are, unfortunately, left to a great deal of conjecture. Generally Scripture describes it as a place of darkness, as the pit (Job 17:13–16). The state of the deceased there is described as a place of utter inactivity. The souls there would seem to be in a sleep-like, semi-comatose state. No one there is able to thank the Lord, or praise him (Isaiah 38:18), there is no work, no thought, no knowledge, no wisdom expressed there (Ezekiel 9:10). It is a place from which no one emerges and is sometimes conceived as a kind of fortress with gates and bars (Isaiah 38:10).

It would seem that both the just and the wicked went there, prior to the coming of Christ, though some are said to go down there "in peace" (1 Kings 2:6 etc.), and some go down there "in sorrow" (Genesis 37:35 etc.).

Further, in this sort of suspended state, there does not seem to be any mention of punishment of the wicked, or reward for the just. Rather, it would seem that all waited until the Lord, who alone can deliver from Sheol, would come (1 Samuel 2:6; Psalm 16:10 etc.). Mysteriously, God is present to those there (Psalm 139:8) but how the dead might experience that presence, is not described.

It is to this place, that the Lord descended. As Scripture implies, he awoke the dead (Ephesians 5:14) and preached to these "souls in prison" (1 Peter 3:19–20). And while we have no complete biblical description of what took place, we can reasonably speculate that some among them, in particular the just, rejoiced in him and accepted him, while others, the wicked and the self–absorbed, rejected him even in death, and from there descended to the Hell of the damned.

Q25: Please explain why Nathanael (in John 1:49) is not considered to be the first disciple to recognize Jesus as Messiah and Son of God when Scripture has him say, "Rabbi, you are the Son of God, you are the King of Israel." We discount his statement and accept Peter's

statement in Matthew 16:16 "You are the Messiah, the Son of the living God." - *name withheld, Houston, TX*

A: When you ask why "we" do this, it is important to note it is actually Jesus who does this. At some level we will have to wait and ask Jesus why he responded with great solemnity to St. Peter, and yet seems little more than amused with what St. Bartholomew (Nathaniel) says. That said, permit the following provisional answer to your question.

At one level, the two responses *do* seem similar. But in analyzing the texts we must first notice some linguistic differences. Nathaniel refers to Jesus as the "King of Israel," whereas Peter calls him "the Christ." And though some scripture scholars think that first century Jews would have use these terms interchangeably, they are nevertheless not identical. The term "Christ" (Greek for Messiah) is more theologically precise.

Secondly, we must remember that context is important. Nathaniel makes his comment as an early, and almost ecstatic claim. Peter however makes his declaration after Jesus has spent time teaching and leading the apostles. And though the Father inspires his utterance, it is also rooted in the formation he has received from Jesus.

Further there may be many other factors that are unknown to us simply in reading a written text. For example, there may significance in the tone of voice, or the look on the face of Peter or Nathaniel that adds shades of meaning. There may also have been discussions or events prior to the utterances that influence the moments.

We can only trust that the Lord Jesus not only experienced all of these contextual things, but also knew the mind and heart of those who spoke. And thus he reacts one way to Nathaniel, and in a more solemn way to Peter.

At times, this is the best that we can do. Biblical texts supply us with what we need to know, not necessarily everything we want to know.

Q26: The priest told us recently at Mass that Jesus did not actually multiply the loaves and fishes, he just got people to share, that this is the real miracle. Is this so? - *name withheld, TN*

A: No it is not so. Jesus actually multiplied the loaves and fishes. The "spin" given in the sermon is a rather tired and dated notion that developed in the 1970s. It has a seemingly clever insight with a moral imperative, that if we learn to share, there will always be enough.

But denying that a true and plainly described miracle took place is not respectful of the text. Jesus says plainly, they have no food (*cf* Matt 15:32). The Apostles observe the same and offer as evidence a mere five loaves and two fish. Further the texts are clear that it is from *these* five loaves and two fishes that Jesus feeds the multitude miraculously. The Apostles take and distribute the food from these very sources. There is no indication whatsoever that people started taking out other food that they had been hiding and learned to share.

Q27: I was talking with a Protestant friend who scoffed at the literal interpretation of "This is my Body" by saying, Jesus also said, "I am the door." How should I answer this objection? - *Emma Simthson, CO*

As with any written text, some sophistication is necessary when reading the Scriptures. All or nothing approaches which hold that the Bible is to be read in an entirely literalist way, or that it is all merely symbolic, must be avoided. The more authentic question is, which text are to be read and understood literally, and which texts employ metaphor, simile, hyperbole, or other literary techniques?

Thus, the site your friends example, it would be strange to read Jesus literally when he says, "I am the door." This would require us to think of Jesus as a large wooden plank, with a doorknob. It is reasonable to conclude that Jesus is speaking metaphorically when he says this, since the specific context of the saying, and the wider context of the overall Scriptures, in no way encourage us think that Jesus spoke in a literalistic manner here.

When it comes to the Eucharist, however, there is a very different conclusion to be reasonably reached. When Jesus says over the bread, "this is my body," and "this is my blood," we are on good grounds to conclude that he is not speaking metaphorically, but literally. This is because, the wider context of Scripture supplies, and insist upon a literal interpretation.

In particular Jesus insists in John 6 that the bread he gives, is this true flesh for the life of the world. The Jewish people, listening to him that day, understand him to be speaking literally, and most of them scoff and murmur in protest. Though Jesus could have corrected their interpretation, and insisted he was only speaking metaphorically, he did nothing of the sort. Rather, he intensifies a literalist interpretation by insisting that they must eat his flesh, and drink his blood. Many, horrified at this, left him and would no longer walk in his company.

Thus, Jesus pays a rather high price, for a literal, but a metaphorical understanding of the fact that Holy Communion is in fact a receiving of his true body and true blood.

St. Paul also teaches that Holy Communion is a partaking of the body and blood of Christ and goes on to insist that those who receive it unworthily, sin against the body of the Lord.

A final bit of contextual evidence is supplied by the fact that the early Church, as seen in the writings of the Fathers, universally understood these words in a literal way.

Hence we are on good ground and insisting, that the utterances of Jesus, this is my body... This is my blood" are to be interpreted literally. This also illustrates the kind of sophistication necessary when approaching sacred Scripture.

Q28: I have heard that Chapters and Verses were not part of the bible until much later. Who added these? -*Addy Thomas, Neptune, NJ*

A: You are correct. Modern and very helpful devices such as the enumeration of chapters and verses are not part of the original biblical text. These helpful conventions were added much later.

The setting of the biblical text into chapters occurred the 13th century when the Catholic Archbishop of Canterbury, Stephen Langton assigned chapter numbers in order to make the reading of the Bible easier. The enumeration of the text into verses did not happen until 1551 Robert Stephanus, a Protestant former Catholic, classical scholar and also a printer, published the first such Bible in Paris.

Q29: Why does the Catholic Church and Catholic Bibles fail to use the upper case, that is capitalize, pronouns referring to the persons of the Trinity? Does not the Lord's Prayer say, "hallowed be Thy name?" — *Joseph Krueger, Divide, CO*

A: Capitalizing pronouns (e.g. he, him, his, you, your etc.) referring to the Blessed Trinity has not been a widespread practice in Christian tradition. In fact, these pronouns are never capitalized in the source documents. They are not capitalized in the Greek text of the Scriptures. Neither did St. Jerome capitalize them we he translated these texts into Latin Vulgate.

Even as the biblical texts were translated into English, the pronouns remained in the lower case. This is true of both Catholic and Protestant translation to the Bible. The Douai Reims Bible did not use them, neither did the King James. Neither do over thirty current or old translations that I consulted online.

Outside the Scriptures, official English translations of Church documents and texts do not use the upper case for the pronouns either. For example the English translation of the Catechism of the Council of Trent used lowercase, as does the current Catechism of the Catholic Church.

Thus we see that the use of the lowercase for pronouns, even pronouns referring to the Divine Persons are always in the lowercase, beginning with the very biblical text.

Some years ago, at least in English-speaking countries, there was a pious practice that set up, of using the upper case for pronouns referring to members of the Trinity. However this practice was neither widespread nor ancient.

As for God's name being holy, this is absolutely true. When referring to God by name, or proper title, we should capitalize these proper nouns. Thus, Father, Son and Holy Spirit are capitalized, as is the name of Jesus. But pronouns are not proper names, they are by definition, words that stand for, or point back to proper nouns.

One may well argue that such pronouns *should* be capitalized, but given the widespread and ancient practice to the contrary, one ought to be careful not to impugn motives of impiety for those who do not do so.

Q30. Why do some of the gospel accounts of the resurrection say three women went to the tomb and others say only one? There also seem to be other differences that I can't recall. If these contradictions are real how can I deal with them? *-Ben Acton, via email*

A. The resurrection accounts in the gospels do have some differences in detail. How many women went out to the tomb that morning, one (Jn 20:21) two (Matt 28:1), or three (Mk 16:1)? How many angels did they see that morning, one (Matt 28:2; Mk 16:5) or two (Lk 24:4; Jn 20:12)? Did the women run to the disciples and tell what they had seen (Mt 28:8; Lk 24:9) or did they say nothing out of fear (Mk 16:8)? Did Jesus see them first in Galilee (Mk 16:7; Mt 28:9) or in Jerusalem (Lk 24:36)? Among the Apostles, did he appear to Peter first (Lk 24:34), all eleven at once (Mt. 28:16), or the eleven minus Thomas (Jn 20:24)? Did Jesus appear to them in a room (Jn 20:19) or a mountaintop (Mt 28:16)? Lastly, did Jesus ascend on Easter Sunday (Lk 24:50-53; Mk 16:19) or forty days later (Acts 1:3-9)?

Most of these apparent discrepancies are not actual conflicts upon closer examination and are easily explained. We cannot look at them all in a short column. But as to your specific question, it would seem most likely that several women went out that morning. That John only focuses on Magdalene is not a denial that others were there. Matthew and Mark, in saying two or three may not be engaging in a headcount per se, but engaging in generalization, such as when we say words like, couple or several.

We should not be surprised that there are some differences in the accounts. Even today, eyewitnesses of an event often emphasize certain details and have different recollections as to the particulars. People often summarize longer stories as well and speak only of essentials. This does not mean that the event did not happen or that unmentioned details by one person is in conflict with details mentioned by another. Given the numerous times Jesus appeared and the many people who saw him, we should not be surprised to find certain differences in the accounts. In this light the differences actually lend credibility to the gospel accounts, which do not try to paper over them, but realistically report them. (See Catechism #s 642-643)

Q31: I was told Jesus is without sin. But on Easter, at Mass I heard a reading that said, "Jesus died to sin." Which is true?
- *Alan Smith, Jackson, NE*

A: You are quoting Romans 6:10 which says, "the death he died, he died to sin, once for all." In saying that Christ "died to sin," St. Paul is not saying he died on account of his own personal sins. The Greek word *hamartia* (Sin), Is often used by St. Paul to refer to our own personal sins. But it is also used to refer in a more collective sense to the sin of the world. For, this fallen world of ours, is immersed in sin, in an attitude of rebellion pride, greed, lust, and so forth. And this climate of sin, is like a force, a mindset, initiated by Satan, and connived in by human beings. It is to this world of sin that Christ died. He broke its back, by dying to it, and rising victorious over it. And he defeated it in the most paradoxical way: he conquered pride, by humility, disobedience by obedience, and death, by dying and rising.

It is to this regime of sin, that Christ died, not his own personal sins of which scripture is clear, he had none. (*cf* 1 Peter 2: 22)

In the same chapter (6:2, 11), we are taught to realize that we too have died to sin, and that this world of sin is to have no more power over us. We must come to experience increasing power, authority, and victory over the influence of this world of sin. We are to lay hold of the life, which Christ offers us wherein this world of sin has no more power over us.

Q32: The Old Testament mentions that many of the Patriarchs, like David, had numerous wives. The Lord even says to David through Nathan: I gave your master's house to you, and your master's wives into your arms (2 Sam 12:8). How are we to understand the permission of polygamy and when did God forbid it?
—*Teresa Thompson, Des Moines, IA*

A: When God first established marriage, it is clear that his vision was that: *a man leaves his father and mother and clings to his wife, and they become one flesh* (Genesis 2:24). Hence there is one man, with one wife, and the two are stably united by "clinging" to one another as the text says. Hence divorce and multiple wives were not part of God's design of marriage.

However, on account of human sinfulness, and out of fear that men would kill their wives to be free to marry another, Moses allowed divorce. It is also clear that the customs of the Ancient Near East also infected Israel's notion of marriage and that many, at least wealthier men and patriarchs, did often take more than one wife. Thus we see that sin corrupted what God intended and that, for a time, God overlooked this sinful behavior.

However, we ought not equate the mere reporting of sinful behavior with approval of it. For, while the polygamy of the Patriarchs is reported, so is all the trouble it caused wherein brothers of different mothers contended and even killed one another. For example, there are terrible stories told of the sons of Gideon, and also the sons of Jacob, to mention but two. The well-known story of Joseph being sold into slavery by his brothers emerges from the internecine conflicts of brothers of different mothers. Hence while reporting polygamy, the Bible also teaches of the evil it brings forth.

Gradually God led the ancient Jews from approving of polygamy such that, by the time of Jesus, it was rare. As for divorce, Jesus sets it aside by teaching the people at that time although Moses allowed divorce due to their hard hearts, it was not this way at the beginning and it was now time to return to God's original plan (*cf* Matt 19:4, 8) and that we should not separate what God has joined.

As for Nathan saying that God gave David his many wives, this can be understood as the ancient tendency to stress God as the primary cause of all things. It does not necessary mean that God actively wanted and approved of polygamy, only that he is the first cause of everything that exists and happens.

Q33: Original sin is based on the belief that Adam and Eve are the parents of all mankind. Where and when did they live?
- *Rex Gogerty, Hubbard, IA*

A: The nature of your question asks the Genesis account to be what it really is not, namely, a scientific and strictly historical account of creation. It proposes to be neither of these. Rather it is more of a poetical account of God's creative act.

Hence the chronological dating of Adam and Eve to, say, 6,000 BC, based on Genesis is not possible.

The account *does* seem to locate the Garden in Mesopotamia, but here too we need not presume this is meant as a precise map but could be more allegorical.

What we must hold is that God created everything out of nothing and guided all the stages of creation, even unto this day. Catholic teaching does prefer to see Adam and Eve as directly created by God and as actual, historical persons.

Q34: I was recently reading this passage from the New Testament at Luke 14:25-33 where Jesus says, *"If anyone comes to me and does not hate his father and mother, wife and children, brothers and sisters he cannot be my disciple."* I am shocked by this wording, especially since the Spanish Bible renders it, *Si alguno viene a mí y no sacrifica el amor* (if anyone comes to me and doesn't sacrifice the love...") instead of "hate..." How could Jesus ask us to hate anyone?
– *Peter Kinghorn, Danville, CA*

A: In this case the English renders the Greek word *miseó* (hate) more accurately. Jesus is using a Jewish manner of speaking in which hyperbole (exaggeration) is used to emphasize the point being made. Jesus is teaching that we are to prefer no one to him and what he commands.

However, simply to render it as "prefer" in English would not deliver the full impact of what Jesus says. Thus the English translators properly retain the literal meaning, "hate." For Jesus is not merely asking for some preferred place in the world of loyalties and ideas, He is asking for a radical preference. Jesus is not just part of our life, he IS our life.

The impact of what he is saying is that we must so strongly love and prefer him, that others might think at times that we "hate" them by comparison. Thus, "hate" here does not mean to despise, condemn or harbor grudges. But it *is* a call for a radical preference that the use of the simple word "prefer" does not capture. Jesus uses hyperbole as a way of emphasis. We do this a lot in English as well when, for example, we say things like, "There must have been a million people there." There may not have even been a thousand, but our emphasis is a hyperbole that means there were a LOT of people there.

Q35: In St Luke's Gospel, there is mention of the Good Thief on the cross near Jesus who repents. No name is given him, but most say his name is "Dismas." Is this true? – B. *Quinn, Philadelphia, PA*

A: We don't know. The story itself is very moving and there is naturally a human tendency to want to know more. Thus traditions and legends often set up in cases like these. But the historical accuracy of such things is often difficult to assess. "St. Dismas" is a name that tradition supplies us in the Western Church. However other names have also accrued to him in the East and in other eras such as Titus, Zoatham, Demas, and Rach.

Interesting though these traditions are, we sometimes miss the main point when biblical figures are not named. For, if you are prepared to accept it, *you* are good thief who "steals heaven," if you are willing to repent, take up your Cross, be crucified with Jesus and persevere to the end, asking God's mercy and admission to his Kingdom.

The "good thief" was not so much good as he was smart. He knew that he was a sinner, justly condemned, and that his only hope was grace and mercy. Having repented, he turns (which is what "conversion" means) to Jesus and in faith seeks his salvation. Jesus says, "No one who comes to me will I ever reject" (Jn 6:37). And thus he is saved. Smart!

Q36: I heard a Protestant Minister say that the young boy Jesus drove demons out of near Mt Tabor wasn't really possessed, he just had epilepsy. Is this true? - *Mel Johnson, via email*

A: Well, Jesus, who was on the scene and a rather smart, seems to have concluded differently than the preacher you mention.

That said, we do not usually bring people with seizures to an exorcist, but seek always to rule out natural causes first. In rare cases, what manifests as seizures may have demonic causes, but not usually. So rather than second-guess Jesus, or consign biblical insights to "primitive" thinking, we do better to assess what is before us, humbly realizing that there are often many levels to human struggles. And while some ailments are simply physical in origin, some may include other dimensions as well.

Q37: Our parish priest asked us at Mass which book of the New Testament was the oldest. Most of us said, Matthew. He said we were wrong, and that First Thessalonians was the oldest. This doesn't seem right does it? - *Donald Wilde, Warsaw, MO*

A: When we speak of the age of a particular Book in the Bible we can speak about its age in terms of the events it describes, or of the likely date it was put into the written form we have today. Usually when scholars speak of the age of a Book they refer to the time of its appearance in final written form. And in this sense, it is largely accepted that the First Letter to the Thessalonians is probably the oldest book, the first of St. Paul's letters, and written between 51-52 AD.

The writing of a letters in the New Testament was a fairly straight-forward process and, while St. Paul and others may have had made some final edits, or even a second draft, it is likely he dictated it a scribe, who wrote it and then had it sent within a matter of days. Other copies may also have been made a circulated.

The emergence of the Gospels in written form was a much more complicated process. And while the events they detail are older (from the early 30s AD), the writing out of these events went through several stages.

Obviously the first stage of the Gospels was the actual events themselves, the words and deeds of Jesus. But it will be note that Jesus did not write a book, or even say to the Apostles, "Go write a book." Rather, he sent them to preach, teach, and baptize disciples into the life of his Body, the Church.

Thus, the second stage was the oral stage wherein the Apostles went forth proclaiming what Jesus taught and did and who Jesus is. During this time the teachings began to be written by scribes, collected and circulated.

And thus, we begin to see the written stage. The idea that Matthew or John just sat down and wrote the gospel is probably inaccurate. Recall that most people could not write in the ancient world. Scribes and others acted as secretaries for the author who helped refine and edit the final product. Some think that Mark was Peter's assistant and scribe.

Gradually the gospels were collected and edited in what came to be their final form, as we know them. The exact dates and order of their final form are hotly debated topics among scholars. However, it is safe to say that the four gospels took their final form between 60 and 90 AD, some time after St. Paul had sent his letters.

Q38: I recently heard an author interviewed, who denies that Jesus was born in Bethlehem, and even seems to wonder if he existed at all. I forget all the details, but what are we to make of this?
- Arthur Johns, Sacramento, CA

A: A lot of modern skepticism regarding Jesus, and details of the Scripture, center around a rather stubborn refusal to regard the Gospels as an historical source. This a-priori assumption about the historical reliability of the Scriptures, is a kind of skepticism that surrounds almost no other historical documents.

More has been recorded about Jesus, than almost any other person in history. There are four rich essays depicting his life, which we call Gospels, and over a dozen epistles. These combine both eyewitness accounts, and credibly collected accounts by others who lived at or very near the time of Jesus.

Some modern scholars like to dismiss these accounts because they are written from the perspective of faith. But all history is written from some perspective. Simply excluding Scripture as an historical source, is neither reasonable, nor does it comport with approaches we use in studying other historical figures and events.

Q39: Why does Matthew in his gospel list the ancestors of Jesus, when they are really those of his stepfather Joseph, with whom he shares no genes? *– Salvatore Leone, Tampa, FL*

A: The purpose of a genealogy for ancient Jews was more complex and rich than to simply demonstrate physical descent. The modern science of genetics, chromosomes and the genetic code were unknown in the ancient world.

But even among us moderns, relationships are set up both by blood, *and* by marriage. That is to say, two people can be related either by direct physical descent, or "legally" through the marriage of themselves or others in their family. And thus, while Joseph and Jesus shared no physical genes, Joseph's family and Jesus are one through Joseph's marriage to Mary. So, Joseph's family tree "matters" to us and to those in ancient Israel because, through Joseph and his marriage to Mary, Jesus relates to many others in Israel.

In ancient Israel, Genealogies existed to show that one was in fact a member of the nation of Israel. They located them in a particular tribe, and also to show their in relationships with others.

These are Matthew's main purposes; namely, that Jesus belongs to the family of Israel both as a son of Mary, and through his relationship to Joseph, the husband of the Virgin Mary.

Matthew also has other complex purposes in mind in the names he highlights and the way he groups them in patterns of 14, all laid out according to different periods of salvation history. There are also other numerological details too complex to lay out here.

So, as you can see, there is more than a question of physical descent involved in the recitation of ancient Genealogies. Human beings relate in more than physical ways, but also through a complex network of relationships we call families, tribes, and nations.

Q40: It seems logical that many others than Matthew, Mark, Luke and John wrote the life of Jesus. Why then were these four Gospels chosen to be the accepted ones, especially since Mark and Luke where not Apostles? When and how was this determination made?
- Robert McBride, Cheswick, PA

A: While there certainly are other reputed accounts of Jesus life, and some of these have the names of apostles attached to them, (for example, Thomas, and James), the evidence seems pretty clear that these Gospels were written long after the death of these apostles.

As for Mark and Luke not being apostles, yet having Gospels, St. Mark was likely the assistant to St. Peter, and so his gospel is largely held to be St. Peter's account. As for Saint Luke, he is very clear to state that he carefully analyzed eyewitness account in preparing his Gospel.

Which books ended up in the canon (a word which means "list") of Sacred Scripture was a complex process that developed in the early years of the Church under the guidance of the Holy Spirit. Even through the late Fourth Century there were some disagreements among believers as to which books belonged to the Canon. The Book of Revelation, and some of the epistles were disputed. Likewise some for inclusion in the canon proposed some other edifying writings from the early years, such as the Epistle of Pope St. Clement and the Didache.

The resolution of the final list or canon of Sacred Scripture was largely resolved in a series of Councils in the late fourth century: The Synod of Rome in 382, The Council of Hippo in 393, and the Council of Carthage in 397. These Councils, in consultation with Popes Damasus and Pope Innocent gave us the list of books in the canon of Sacred Scripture that we have today in the Catholic Church. This canon, was largely undisputed until the 16th Century when Martin Luther, removed a number of Old Testament Books and certain other Protestant denominations followed his unfortunate and unauthorized move.

The primary standards used by the Council Fathers and Popes was liturgy and doctrine. Did a particular book have widespread use and acceptance in the liturgy of the Church? Did a particular book comport well with the faith and received doctrine of the Church? These standards, along with some particulars too numerous to mention here, produced the list that we have today of Sacred Scripture. Surely, by faith, we know the Holy Spirit inspired this process as well.

Q41: In the finding of the child Jesus in the temple I have always had trouble with two things. First that Joseph and Mary would not have kept watch over him and went a whole day before they knew he was missing. Second that Jesus seemed to care little for their feelings at having lost him. Please explain. – *Rich Willems, Big Lake, MN*

A: Two factors need to be kept in mind to understand the loss of Jesus. At age 12, Jesus would have been considered almost an adult in that culture at that time. Perhaps it would be like a 17-year-old in our culture. It does not pertain to parents to keep as close a watch on a much older child as with a very young child.

Secondly, pilgrims making the journey from Galilee Jerusalem and back, a walk of over 70 miles, often walked in fairly large groups. It was common for people to divide out, women walking with women, men with men. Older children might also walk together; the younger children would stay with their mothers.

As an older child, reaching adulthood it is easy to understand how Jesus might have walked with a group apart from his parents. And this would go unnoticed until the evening when families would reunite. Immediately upon noticing Jesus' absence and inquiring among other relatives, they rushed back to Jerusalem to find him.

With these two factors in mind, they were not negligent. The temporary separation from him was understandable, and immediately upon noticing it they saw him out.

As for Jesus' reaction, it is mysterious. But we need to remember that we cannot hear his tone of voice. Further it could simply be that he was surprised in terms of his human knowledge at their wonderment in a genuine way, figuring they knew where he was.

Q42: My Husband who is not Catholic tells me the Church used to discourage reading the Bible. Is this true and why?
- name withheld, Detroit, MI

A: Reading the Bible is of course to be encouraged. The problem is not reading, it is interpreting. If in the past priests once encouraged the faithful to be cautious in reading the Bible, it was only to protect them from the Protestant tendency of private interpretation, which leads to a lot of divisions. That priests ever did discourage the faithful from reading the Bible is exaggerated in terms of its extent and severity.

However, any such warnings ought to be seen in the light of what private interpretation has wrought: namely some 30,000 different denominations of Protestants all claiming biblical authority for their differing views.

Today, Catholics are strongly encouraged to read and pray with their Bible but to strive an conform their understanding of the text to Church teaching and norms of Catholic Biblical interpretation articulated in the Catechism.

Q43: In Bible study we recently discussed Jesus saying from the cross "My God, my God, why have you forsaken me?" Was Jesus merely reciting Psalm 22, or was he crying out in pain and giving voice to a kind of despair? – *Paul Hummel, Bowling Green, FL*

A: With Sacred Scripture, there are many levels of meaning at work. You are correct in observing that Jesus is quoting from Psalm 22. And many argue, with good merit, that quoting the first line of Psalm 22 Jesus intends the whole of Psalm 22 for himself, and us.

In Psalm 22, we are alerted to the many ways in which prophecies are being fulfilled. The Psalm speaks of an afflicted man who feels downcast, but also mentions others who divide his garments among them, and cast lots for his vesture; who pierce his hands and feet; and who ridicule him in his suffering. And all these prophecies are being fulfilled almost exactly as Jesus is on the cross.

Psalm 22, is also an important catechism for us about suffering because, considered as a whole, it is not a Psalm of despair and grief, but also of trust and hope in God's deliverance. It recalls how God has delivered devout men and women in the past, and asserts that God never spurns those who cry out to him in their misery. The psalm writer confidently expects God's help, and to be able, one day, to tell his descendants of the glorious things the Lord has done. And thus, while Psalm 22 surely gives voice to the pain and grief that we experience in our suffering, it also reminds us to call on the Lord and trust that he will deliver us.

And so we see, first of all, that Jesus, in quoting Psalm 22, is a great teacher, even from the pulpit of the cross. We are taught to revere prophecy, and also to trust God in our afflictions.

And yet we ought not to wholly exclude that Jesus is also quoting the psalm for his own sake as well. Surely, as man, he suffered great anguish, both physical and mental, emotional and spiritual, on the cross. And thus he, for his own sake, has recourse to Psalm 22. Indeed, how often have many of us in our sufferings found in Scripture great consolation and vindication. Perhaps we will say, "This scripture text expresses exactly how I'm feeling!" In this there is a kind of consolation that God knows what I am experiencing and that others have endured similar trials. We also experience consolation as Scripture teaches us how God has delivered others and will in due time deliver us too. Surely, at the human level, Psalm 22 consoled Jesus in these and other ways.

Q44: In the garden of Eden God said to the serpent, "I will put enmity between you and the woman, between your seed and her seed, he shall crush your head while you lie in wait for his heel." There are many details her that puzzle me. Could you explain this?
– *Helen Schulte, St. Louis, MO*

A: The text you cite (Genesis 3:15) is often called by theologians the "protoevangelion" (meaning "the first good news") since, after all the harm caused by Original Sin, God announces the good news that he will send a savior to rescue us through the woman, that is, through a descendant of hers. And that is what the word "seed" means here.

The "enmity" spoken of here is an older English word meaning hostility, adversity or even hatred. In effect God indicates that Satan and "the woman" would be particular enemies, or by extension that she would be his greatest enemy.

The Genesis text would seem to indicate that Eve was the woman. However she died and none of her direct children rescued us from Satan. Thus "the woman" came to be regarded as and symbol of a woman who would one day come. In John's Gospel Jesus indicates that his mother Mary is in fact that woman for Jesus calls his mother "Woman" John also speak of her in this way in Revelation 12 when he speaks of the "Woman clothed with the Sun" and goes on to describe a woman who is historically Mary, for this woman gives birth to a Son (Jesus) who is destined to rule the nations.

The image of striking at the heel and being crushed is drawn from the image of what snakes and humans will often do. A snake will strike at the heel of a person since that is the part closest to the ground. A human being will often seek to defend himself trying to crush the head of the snake. And all of this is used as an allegory of the spiritual battle which takes place between the "seed" (son) of the Woman and Satan.

An interesting sidebar in this discussion was the practice of older Catholic translations which rendered the pronoun as "she." Hence the text read, "She will crush you head while you strike at her heel." Many older statues of Mary show her standing on a snake for this reason. The Hebrew pronoun "hu" is ambiguous and can be rendered "he, she or it." St. Jerome in the Latin Vulgate rendered is "she" (Ipsa) and this influenced later translations.

However, theologically it is more apt to render the text "He shall crush" since it is Jesus, who is the "seed" the Savior who crushes Satan. Thus most modern translations render the pronoun as "He." Thus, while Satan has a special hostility for Mary and she has a special power him, her power is derived from the fact that it is her Son, Jesus who conquers Satan.

Q45: I was telling my daughter that the Bible teaches against Homosexual acts and thus Same sex marriage. She dismissed the Bible and said it once approved slavery and thus carried no moral authority for her. What can I say? – *name withheld, via email*

A: There are several problems in the both the logic and the understanding of Scripture involved in this objection.
The first problem involves equating what is a definitive precept with what is at best a tacit tolerance. Homosexual acts (as well as all heterosexual acts outside of marriage) are explicitly condemned throughout the whole of Scripture, from the early pages of the Old Testament right through the closing pages of the New Testament. We are commanded to refrain from any such acts. But nowhere are we commanded to own slaves.

The Scriptures treat of slavery as part of the existing social structure of the ancient world and set norms so as to avoid the excesses that sometimes accompanied it. But the mere tolerance of questionable practice should not be equated with supporting it let alone prescribing it as something good. An argument from silence does not connote approval.

The second problem is the term "slavery" itself. While the same word is used for the ancient reality and the practice of the colonial period, there are important differences that made the condemnation all the more necessary and ultimately required. In the ancient biblical world slavery resulted from essentially three sources: one owed debt they could not repay, one had been a solider in a defeated army, or one may have committed certain crimes. As such slavery was an alternative to death or imprisonment. It was not without its questionable dimensions, but neither was it intrinsically evil. Even today we often seek alternatives to imprisonment (such as probation and house arrest) wherein one forfeits some of their rights, are forbidden certain freedoms and must report to an State Official.

But the slavery of the colonial period exploited and enslaved people who had no debt, had committed no crimes and had not waged war. This is a very different situation, morally speaking from the slavery of biblical times. It required the condemnation and rejection it received.

Finally, even if one were to insist that Scripture once approved slavery (a point not conceded here) and this discredits it as a source for moral teaching, then we ought to ask what would happen if this same standard were applied for example to the US Constitution. Is the Constitution fully discredited since it once remained silent or gave tacit approval to slavery? Is your daughter's right to free speech discredited because the US Constitution was once imperfect or even wrong on another topic? Most would find this notion too extreme. And neither does Scripture does not lose its value even if it was once less severe on slavery than we would wish today.

Q46: In bible Study I learned that Matthew and Mark do even mention Jesus appearing in Jerusalem (as John and Luke do), and have the angels tell the brethren to go to Galilee where they will see Jesus. This seems like a major discrepancy. Did Jesus Appear in Jerusalem or not?
— *name withheld, via email*

A: Yes, he did. To not mention something, is not to deny that it happened. Consider for example if someone would ask you to recount your summer vacation, you might not include every single detail in your reply. Perhaps, for the sake of brevity you will omit some aspects of the vacation. Further, you might choose to include or exclude certain details based on the audience or person you are addressing. Perhaps to one group you would include certain aspects, and to another group you include very different aspects. This is just a nature of human interaction and there is nothing necessarily dishonest or problematic about it.

Thus, for theological and pastoral reasons of their own, Matthew, Mark, Luke, and John treat of different aspects of the resurrection stories. Luke and John treat of the Jerusalem appearances as well as others, while Matthew and Mark skip right to the Galilean appearances. Perhaps they do this to keep things brief, or perhaps they know that most readers have already heard other recounting from other sources. Perhaps to Matthew and Mark use the Galilean appearances in order to use Galilee is a symbol of heaven, or as a return to where the disciples were first called.

As for the instruction of the angel to the women that the brethren should go to Galilee where they will see him, here too, Matthew and Mark are likely truncating longer instructions by the angel. And they do this, likely, for the sake of brevity, and to draw our attention immediately to Galilee where they choose to focus the recollections.

Rather than destroying the credibility of the resurrection accounts, such differences actually serve to underscore the credibility. It is clear through the variations, and selection of material, there were no attempts to control the message. Rather, the ordinary human modes of communication are retained as people joyfully recount the events. It makes a lot of sense that people, in recalling such stunning events, would report differences in details, or talk about only selected aspects, lest they overwhelmed the listener.

Q47: The Catholic Bible contains the books of Maccabees, The King James version does not. Why? – *Robert Bonsignore, Brooklyn, NY*

A:Interestingly enough, the original 1611 version of the King James Bible *did* have these, plus other disputed Old Testament books in it. Later, they were removed.

In addition to the issue related to the Book of Maccabees, there are a number of other omissions that make Protestant Bibles shorter. The following Old Testament books were deleted from Protestant Bibles: Tobit, Judith, Baruch, Wisdom, Sirach, First Maccabees, and Second Maccabees. There are also section of the Book of Esther and Daniel that are omitted.

Why these differences exist is complex, but the central facts focus on ancient Christian tradition, and the departure from this by Martin Luther.

The most widely used version of the Old Testament at the time of Jesus, was a Greek translation of the Old Testament called the Septuagint. This remained the case with the emergence of the Church in the apostolic age and going forward. The earliest Church documents, and the Church Fathers all make widest use of this version, which included the books that Protestants later rejected.

The Fathers of the Church often referred to disputed books, and the Book of Sirach was widely used in the early Church as a first book of instruction for catechumens and converts to the faith.

By the mid-fourth century, the Church settled on the definitive list of sacred scripture, which now included the New Testament books. Three Synods (or Councils) of Bishops at Carthage, Hippo, and Rome largely settled debates about the New Testament books, and also included the Old Testament list from the Septuagint, which contained the disputed books and passages the Protestant Bibles later removed.

And thus, we see that the Bible emerging from antiquity is the Bible that Catholics still have today.

In the 16th century, Martin Luther, removed a number of books from the Bible. Originally, he also wanted to remove New Testament books such as James and First and Second Timothy. However friends prevailed on him to leave the New Testament list untouched.

But he *did* remove the books listed above largely because they supported a number of Catholic teachings that he rejected, such as praying for the dead etc. He claimed that the Jewish bibles of his day did not contain most of these passages. And that is largely true. However, it is a serious matter set aside 1500 years of Christian tradition, rooted in apostolic authority, in favor the opinions of Jewish rabbis of his time.

From this perspective therefore, Protestant Bibles are deficient by failing to include significant sections of the Old Testament that nourished the Jewish people of Jesus time, and have been part of the Christian Bible for 2000 years now.

Q48: At a recent Bible study, the Deacon said that Satan is the prince of this world, so he's in charge down here. That didn't really sit right with me. Is this really what the Bible teaches? - *name withheld*

A: As your question implies, we need to be careful. It is true that in John 14:30 Jesus in describing his passion, death, and resurrection to his disciples, concludes by saying *I have told you before it happens, so that when it happens, you may believe. I will not speak much more with you, but the prince of this world is coming, but he has no hold over me.*

And thus, Jesus does use the phrase "prince of this world," thereby indicating that Satan has some power and influence here. However, whatever influence the prince of this world has, Jesus remains the King of the universe, and thereby limits Satan's power and overrules it.

Jesus says elsewhere that, as a result of his being lifted up from the earth, *the prince of this world will be driven out* (John 12:31). He also says, *The prince of this world now stands condemned* (John 16:11).

All these texts must be carefully balanced. The title "prince of this world" is fundamentally limited to the hearts of those who have refused the Kingship of God and accepted the practical authority of the evil one. Sadly, through them, Satan exerts influence in this world. And though Jesus has cast him out and made clear his condemnation, the Lord mysteriously allows Satan to wander through the ruins of the world he once had greater authority over. But Jesus, who is King, limits Satan's power and influence.

Though Satan's activity at times seems intense, it always remains under God's power who permits his influence only to obtain greater good from it in the end.

We ought not so exaggerate Satan's power that we forget God's grace, which is greater. Scripture elsewhere says that, for now, Satan's power is limited (see Revelation 20:1–3) and that at the end of time, he will be released for a brief time, and then utterly cast into the lake of burning fire forever. (Revelation 20:7-10)

Be assured of this, Satan, whatever power he may seem to have just now, is the loser. His plans are going nowhere. Christ has already conquered and we ought to be clear of the final victory for the Lord and all who chose and trust in him.

Q49: You wrote recently about the dates in the Genesis text and said it is not a requirement of a Catholic to accept a very literal reading of the Bible. I have always understood that it IS a requirement that we accept the bible pretty much as written, i.e., a literal interpretation. — *John S, via email*

A: The principle stated applies to the early Genesis texts (and the references to "days" and other time indicators). It is not to be understood as a sweeping principle for all of Scripture. Certain biblical texts describe people and events in very literal ways. Other texts use parables, poetic images, allegory, metaphor, hyperbole and other genres and modes of speech.

Thus we must rightly attend to the nature of a text by determining the genre and mode of speech used, view it in context and relation to the whole of Scripture and Sacred Tradition, and defer to the Judgment of the Church which exercises the divinely conferred commission of watching over and interpreting the Word of God. (see Catechism 108-119).

Some texts are understood literally, others metaphorically, but always conferring Divine Truth.

Q50: I hear a lot about the love of God but then I also see a lot in the bible about his wrath and anger. I don't know which view of God to believe in. — *James Westenholmer, Seattle, WA*

A: The biblical concept of the wrath of God must be understood with a good degree of sophistication. It does not simply mean that God is mad. We do not have a God who is moody, grouchy, or prone to fits of temper. God's anger, or wrath must be understood in the light of his love. From this perspective, one good definition of God's wrath is his decisive work to set things right. God, out of love for us must level the mountains of our pride and fill in the valleys of our despair and neglect. In His bold action it may at times seem to us that he is angry, but it is more true to say that he loves us, as well as truth and justice and is seeking for our benefit to establish them more firmly.

In another sense, it is proper to say that the wrath of God is an experience that is more in us than in God. From this perspective, the wrath of God is our experience of the complete incompatibility of our sinful state before the holiness of God. That which is unholy, simply cannot endure the presence of God who is utterly holy. It is like wax before fire.

Consider too the image of fire and water. They do not mix or coexist in the same spot. One hears the conflict between them as a kind of sizzling and popping. One element will win; the other must depart. Unrepentant sinners before God also experience this conflict within themselves. Though they may attribute the problem to God, calling him wrathful, the problem is really in us, not in God.

Think of how at night we will often have lights on in our room. But then the lights are put out and we sleep. Early the next morning the lights are put back on, but now the light seems obnoxious. Yet the light has not changed at all, is the same 100-watt light bulb it was the night before. It is *we* who change. But notice how we say the light is "harsh." Yet the light is not harsh; it is what it always is. It is we who change.

It is like this with God, who does not change; of whom the book of James says there is *no variableness or shadow of turning* (1:17).

Therefore, as you can see, wrath is a notion, which must be balanced with other truths about God: that he is love and that he does not change. Neither is he given to irritableness or arbitrary outbursts of anger etc.

Q51: I remember the Bible describing the Holy Land as flowing with milk and honey. When I visited there recently, I found it dry and more desert-like. Was the Bible exaggerating? – *Richard Evans, Tampa, FL*

41

A: Probably not. There is good evidence that the Holy Land as we know it today is somewhat warmer and drier than in Biblical times.

For example, in Genesis 13 the region of Sodom and Gomorrah is described as being well watered, and like a rich garden. But the text makes it clear that this was its appearance "before the Lord destroyed Sodom and Gomorrah." (Gn 13:10) Today that region, likely the area around the Dead Sea is deep desert.

Other areas of the Holy Land seemed to have featured more trees and agriculture in biblical times than today. For example, in 1000 BC Solomon is described as being able to harvest prodigious amounts of trees for his building projects. Land-use studies and archeology also provide evidence of the prevalence of crops and forests, which were suited to cooler, wetter climates.

In Jesus' time too there is evidence of a bit more rainfall than today, given descriptions by Josephus and others who lived at the time.

Over time however, due to many wars and poor land management, the area has been gradually deforested. This, plus other climatological factors over two millennia, has contributed to a process of moderate desertification. The result is that the region is likely somewhat warmer and drier than in biblical times.

Israel currently has a program attempting to reverse the desertification by planting trees, a program that has received large financial support. This is an attempt to partially reforest Israel.

Your visit many also have been affected by topography and season. Israel has a wet season from October to April, and a dry season from June to September and this affects the greenery a great deal. Further, the region up north around the Sea of Galilee is far more green and lush than the areas South near Bethlehem and Jerusalem. To the East the elevation drops and the Dead Sea and the Jericho are very dry and deep deserts.

Therefore, the Promised Land known in Biblical times likely did flow with "milk and honey." This expression speaks to abundant livestock and the rich crop life of an area more green and lush than today.

Q52: Jesus relatives are identified as brothers and sisters due to language variables. In Luke 1:36 the word relative is used in regard to Elizabeth: *And behold, your relative Elizabeth in her old age has*

conceived.... **Did the original word in the Greek use "sister" for Elizabeth? But if there was a word for relatives, why did the Gospels use brother and sister and not relatives when speaking of Jesus' "brothers and sisters"**
—*Leonard Loftus, Geneseo, IL*

A: The Greek word used in Luke 1:36 is *suggenes* and does mean "relative" or "kinsman." It is from the Greek roots *syn* (with) + *genos* (seed or offspring). Thus the word refers here to Elizabeth as being related to Mary, in some physical but unspecified way. The Greek word for sisters (*adelphai*) is not used in Luke 1:36.

Why certain words are used or not is a complex question. Our modern ears tend to crave a kind of specificity in written texts that they do not always give. This is likely because they did not begin as written texts, but as oral stories.

Even today we are often flexible in our use of terms like relative, brothers and sisters etc. when speaking. For example, when it comes to the word "brother" in its most technical sense, there are only two men on this planet who are my brothers, in that we physically share the exact same father and mother. However, on any given Sunday, I stand before hundreds of people and call them "my brothers and sisters." But here I am using the terms in a broader sense of our shared humanity, and in the spiritual sense of our shared Father in heaven.

In Jesus day things were similar, people use terms in both the strict sense, and the wider sense, freely interchanging terms like brother, cousin, relative, etc. Many Protestants today seeing references to Jesus' brothers and sisters, simply presume these terms were meant in a very strict sense, and that such references therefore disprove that Mary was ever-virgin.

But in this matter, the Church would argue that they have fallen into a linguistic fallacy by insisting that the terms can only be interpreted in the strict sense. The early Church was not unaware of these references, nor troubled by them as she handed on the sacred Tradition of Mary's perpetual virginity. Rather the terms brothers and sisters were understood by the Church more broadly to mean cousins, and this is the ancient sense of those texts.

Q53: Why did Jesus say, "If you don't believe me, believe my Father?"
—*Rita Schroder, Eddyville, KY*

A: You likely refer to John 5 where Jesus presents four proofs of his status as Messiah and Lord: *You sent emissaries to John, and he testified to the truth...But I have testimony greater than John's. The works.. that I perform testify on my behalf that the Father has sent me. Moreover, the Father who sent me has testified on my behalf.....Search the scriptures, ... even they testify on my behalf. But you do not want to come to me to have life.* (John 5:32-40)

And thus Lord points to his miracles, to the testimony of John the Baptist, to the Witness of God the Father in their hearts, and to the Scriptures as witness that he is Lord and Messiah. As such he effectively accuses them of stubborn disbelief and sends them away to reconsider.

Q54: My wife, who is not Catholic, says that in her Protestant denomination they count the Ten Commandments differently because we Catholics eliminated the Second Commandment forbidding graven images so we could worship statues. I know she is wrong but not sure how to answer. — *name withheld, via email*

A: It is true that there are two different numerations for the Commandments, but it is not as simple as saying Catholics and Protestants have different ones since Both Catholics and Lutherans follow the same numerations which is based on the Jewish Talmud and St. Augustine. . Baptists, Presbyterians and Evangelicals follow a different numbering system based largely in the classifications of the Jewish Philosopher, Philo and the Greek Septuagint.

The difference is based in the fact that the original biblical text does not assign numbers to the Commandments and some of the Commandments go on for several verses, especially the commandments against worshipping other gods and keeping holy the Sabbath. There is a further difficulty since the reciting of the Commandments is given twice (in Exodus 2:1-17 and Deuteronomy 5:4-21) and the wordings are close but not exactly alike. Thus, how to divide the 17 verses into Ten Commandment's is a matter that has two traditions.

The Calvinist/ Baptist/Evangelical tradition takes the First Commandment in our traditional First Commandment and breaks it into two: one forbidding the worship of other God's, and a second about not carving images and worshipping them. But the Catholic/Lutheran numerations see the worshipping of graven images as part of the first commandment forbidding worship of other gods. We do not worship statues, which would be a grave violation of the First Commandment. It is also silly to worship statues or trust in them since they cannot see or hear us and have no power. Perhaps your wife mistakes us for fools. We are not.

At the end of the Commandments the Calvinist/Baptist/Evangelical tradition brings our final two commandments about coveting into one commandment against coveting. The Catholic/Lutheran numbering however, sees these as different Commandments, since the English word "covet" is actually translating two different Hebrew words. The text (especially from Deuteronomy) most literally says that we ought not "desire" our neighbor's wife, neither shall we "covet" his goods. And this permits us to distinguish the coveting (desire) rooted in lust from the coveting rooted in.

Either numeration in fine at the end of the day so long as we remember that our division of the 17 verses in 10 commandments is not part of the original biblical text but is merely a traditional break out of them.

Q55: In one of the Gospels Jesus talks about leaving ninety-nine sheep to go in search of one stray sheep and he says the ninety-nine have no need to repent. But I thought we were all sinners. What does Jesus mean that the ninety-nine don't need to repent?
– *Ben Johnson, Birmingham, AL*

A: According to a well-established tradition among the Greek Fathers of the Church such as St. Irenaus, Gregory of Nyssa, Gregory Nazianzus, St Cyril of Jerusalem and others, the ninety-nine who have no need to repent are the angels. The straying or lost sheep is wayward humanity.

The verse you reference is Luke 15: *I tell you, in the same way there will be more joy in heaven over one sinner who repents than over ninety-nine righteous who have no need to repent.* Note that the verse refers to the rejoicing "in heaven." And this would seem to strengthen the notion that the ninety-nine are the angels, who at that time, would have been the sole occupants of heaven other than God.

And so too, on this account, it can be said that Jesus "leaves" them and goes in search of the one straying sheep (us). And this refers to his incarnation and to his saving work among us.

Finally, Angels do not need to repent since their "yes" to God is once, and for all. Thus they do not sin or need to repent.

Q56: Scripture says that Joseph had no relations with Mary "until" she bore a son and named him Jesus (cf Mat 1:25). Does this imply that they had relations afterward? – *Rosemary Easley, Catonsville, MD*

A: The word "until" can be ambiguous without a wider context of time. It is true, in English, the usual sense of "until" is that I am doing or not doing something now "until" something changes and then I start doing or not doing it. However this is not always the case, even in Scripture.

If I were to say to you, "God be with you until we meet again." I do not mean by this that after we meet again God's blessing will cease or turn to curses. In this case "until" is merely being used to refer to an indefinite period of time which may or may not ever occur. Surely I hope we meet again, but it is possible we will not, so go with God's blessings, whatever the case.

In Scripture too, we encounter "until" being used merely to indicate an indefinite period whose conditions may or may not be met. Thus we read, *And Michal the daughter of Saul had no child until the day of her death.* (2 Samuel 6:23). Of course this should not be taken to mean that she started having children after she died. Likewise Paul says to Timothy *Until I come, attend to the public reading of scripture, to preaching, to teaching* (1 Tim 4:13). But this does not likely mean that Timothy should stop doing these things when and if St. Paul arrives.

Thus, "until", while it often suggests a future change of state, does not necessarily mean that the change happens, or even *can* happen. Context is important. It is the same in the Greek language where *heos*, or *heos hou* (the terms are used interchangeably and translated "until") require context to more fully understand what is being affirmed.

The teaching of the Perpetual Virginity of Mary does not rise or fall on one word. Rather a body of evidence such as Mary's question to the Angel as to how a betrothed virgin would conceive, Jesus entrusting Mary to the care of a non-blood relative at this death, and also the long witness of ancient Tradition are some other sources.

Q57: You stated in a previous column the 99 sheep who need no repentance are the angels, who at that time would have been the sole occupants of heaven other than God. What about the Transfiguration, which describes Jesus speaking with Moses and Elijah? Where did they come from? - *Richard Juetten, via email*

A: The tradition about the ninety-nine sheep being angels is the common explanation of the early Fathers of the Church. As for Moses and Elijah, (and we might add Enoch who scripture says was taken to God without dying (Gen 5:24; Heb 11:5)), where exactly they were prior to Christ reopening the gates of heaven is not clear.

Scripture uses the word "heaven" in different senses. Sometimes it means areas above the earth, where the clouds and the rain are. Sometimes a higher or second heaven is referred to where the stars and planets are. At other times it refers to the abode of God, sometimes called the third heaven.

When St. Paul speaks of being caught up into the "third heaven" (2 Cor 12:2) he is most surely speaking of the very abode of God, and speaks of such glory as cannot be described.

The layout of the ancient temple also had a threefold dimension. There was the sanctuary where the Priests and Levites ministered the animal sacrifices just outside the temple building. There was the holy place, just inside the temple building where the showbread and the menorah were; and there was the Holy of Holies, where God had his dwelling and the Ark of the Covenant was.

When Moses, Elijah and Enoch are taken up to heaven we cannot be certain exactly where they abided. However it seems very unlikely that they were taken to the third heaven and beheld the very face of God. That surely had to wait for Christ and his ascension with all the members of his Body, the Church, to take his seat at the Father's Right. But there is no other way to the Father except through Christ. Thus, it is more likely that Moses, Elijah and Enoch were taken to some heavenly realm, instead of Sheol (the usual abode of the dead that was shadowy and generally described in unpleasant terms), but not into the third heaven, into the very presence of the Father.

Q58: Matthew 25:31-46 describe that the Lord will judge fiercely those who did not give food to the hungry, drink to the thirsty etc. But what

about those who take advantage of the charity of others and are either lazy, or break immigration laws and so forth. – *Albert Dee, Fairfield, CT*

A: They, like any of us, will have to answer to God for what they did or failed to do. But our summons to what is just and charitable does not cease because some take advantage or are not sinless in their need. It is a general norm to care for the poor and required of us. There may be individual cases where we discover that we are not helping an individual, but only facilitating their sin and we can adapt the general norm to the specific case.

At a larger level too, the obligation to care for the poor can have undesirable effects such as creating welfare dependence etc. But the solution to this must seek to fix the problem, not wholly cast aside our general obligation to care for others.

We fix what we can, but some things just have to be left to God and to the Day of Judgment. Meanwhile, we err on the side of care.

Q59: I was reading an article that says the Magi didn't actually visit Jesus in Bethlehem as our Nativity sets depict. Is this true or just more modern skepticism? -*Brian MacArthur, Pittsburgh, PA*

A: While there is a lot of modern skepticism and a tendency to be hypercritical of even small biblical differences, the article you refer to is probably making a valid point.

The Biblical references to the visit of the Magi are vague as to time frame. Further, the text that describes their visit says: *and going into the house they saw the child with Mary his mother* (Mt 2:11). So the text speaks of them finding Jesus in a house (*oikia*), not a cave apart from an Inn or other proper dwelling. So there would seem to be some undetermined period of time from Christmas night when the shepherds found Christ, and when the Magi found him.

Some scholars think this could be as long as two years later since Herod called for the death of boys two years and younger. However, it does not seem likely that Joseph and Mary would stay two years in Bethlehem, since the went there originally to register for a census. So it may have been much sooner after Jesus birth that the Magi came. But the location does seem to have been different than the actual place of birth.

Nativity sets and many stories and songs of the Nativity weave together many details from Matthew and Luke and, as such, tend to simplify what is more complex. Clearly the Scriptures must be a more fundamental source for us than carols or other cultural traditions.

Q60: In Genesis 23:23 Rebecca is pregnant with twins, Esau and Jacob and they struggle within her womb. She is distressed and asks the Lord why. *And the LORD said to her, "Two nations are in your womb, and two peoples, born of you, shall be divided; the one shall be stronger than the other, the elder shall serve the younger.* **My questions: What are the two nations, and does this text mean that God cursed Esau from the beginning?** – *Frank Donall, Fort Wayne, IN*

A: The two nations are Israel and Edom. Jacob was the Patriarch of the twelve tribes of Israel. His name was changed to Israel by God and his twelve sons headed the twelve tribes of what would become the nation, the people of Israel. Esau became the patriarch of what would become the Edomites and the nation of Edom, who were known for their reddish and hairy skin which Esau had.

In many ways the story of Jacob and Esau is a dark tale, full of treachery. Jacob acted manipulatively and deceitfully against his brother and Father, Isaac to obtain the birthright. Rebecca participated in this. Esau, though a physically strong man and a good hunter, was somewhat weak-willed, going so far as to "sell his birthright" to Isaac for a bowl of soup (for he was very hungry). Jacob was something of a "Mamma's boy" and stayed close to home, but he was shrewd and conniving and secured his Father's blessing by deception, with his mother's help. Esau, realizing he had been tricked sought his brother's life and Rebecca arranged for Jacob to flee to the north and live with her brother, Laban. And while there is a touching reconciliation between Jacob and Esau later, the nations and peoples they founded had tense relations down through the centuries.

To say that God "cursed" Esau from the beginning may be too strong. God is Lord of history and he mysteriously permits many human struggles to unfold on their own, but uses them for his designs. The ancient Jews were more prone to attribute the flow of history to God's direct will more than his permissive will. They were more comfortable in emphasizing that God was the primary cause of all that happens since he holds everything in existence. God the Holy Spirit also spoke to them in this way. We moderns tend to emphasize secondary causality, which looks to cause of things in the created order and the decision of human beings.

Both insights are important. God is sovereign, but man is also freedom and there is a mysterious interaction between both truths. Jacob, though quite sinful at times, was someone God chose to work with and establish as the Patriarch of his Chosen People. Esau's descendants were less favored in this sense (cf Rom 9:13). But in Christ, all are now called to be God's people.

Q61: The Bible says, in Luke that Jesus was presented in the Temple after forty days. But Matthew says they fled to Egypt. How can these incidents happen at the same time? - *Francis Talbot, St Joseph, MO*

A: There is no indication that they *did* happen at the same time. Matthew is unclear as to the timing of the visit of the Magi.

In the popular imagination many think of the Magi visiting the same night as the Shepherds, but this is unlikely. Matthew says the Magi found Jesus and Mary in a house" not in a stable or cave. Hence some time has elapsed since the birth. It could be days, months or even up to two years (since Herod ordered the death of boys two years and under).

Hence, it is likely that the Holy Family stayed in Bethlehem after the birth of Jesus, eventually found lodging, and after forty days made the short journey to Jerusalem to present Jesus in the Temple. Returning the Bethlehem, the Magi visited sometime afterward and the flight to Egypt took place shortly after that.

Q62: I am 87 and have prayed the Lord's Prayer all my life. I was surprised to notice in certain forms among non-Catholics they say "forgive us our debts," where we say "forgive us our trespasses?" What does it mean to have debts forgiven and for us to forgive our debtors?
- *Carmine Alfano, Smithtown, NY*

A: There is no essential difference at work. Rather "debts" is an older English translation that has fallen away in favor of "trespasses." Both are references sin.

The Greek word in question is *opheilēmata* which most literally refers to having debts. But debts are not understood as financial here. Rather we have incurred a debt of sin. St Jerome who translated the most widely used Latin translation (the Vulgate) used the Latin word *debitoribus* which most naturally came into English as "debts." Later because of the tendency of "debt" to refer more exclusively to financial matters the term "trespasses" became a more common translation in English. However, "trespasses" has its problems too since it tends in current English to mean that I am illegally on someone else's property.

Currently there are those who want to simply say, "forgive us our sins as we forgive those who sin against us." But this loses some of what the original Greek, and likely the Lord, conveyed. For what is said here is not merely that we sinned (in some abstract sense) but that we have incurred and enormous debt, and that we have strayed into places we have no business being. Indeed our debt is huge. The Lord in summoning us to forgive one another as we have been forgiven speaks of a man who owed ten thousand talents (an almost unimaginable amount). But that man is us.

So sin is not an abstraction, it is a very heavy debt of sin we cannot pay on our own. This is what the Greek word *opheilēmata* (debts) is conveying.

Q63: Psalm 149 in the Morning Prayer of the Church speaks of the faithful as wielding a sharp two-edged sword and dealing our vengeance to the nations. I have trouble interpreting this and wonder what it means for us. – *Wally Smith, Alexandria, LA*

There are, in fact, many warlike images in the Scriptures in reference to the spiritual life, especially the Old Testament. Part of this is historical, since ancient times featured a lot of warfare and skirmishes. Part of it too is a more vigorous stance that ancient Israel took against intermixing with or being influenced by the nations around them. The Lord and his prophets warned that such interaction would cause them to lose the purity of their faith. The vigorous spiritual opposition to the gods and practices of the nations sometimes took voice in a kind of militaristic language.

Even today we have some notion of spiritual warfare or battle. We do not mean such phrases literally in the sense of guns and tanks. The ancient Jews however sometimes did mean these expressions literally and looked for God to help them vanquish their foes militarily. At other times these expression are meant more spiritually.
The psalm you reference is a curious combination of praise and vengeance. Is the psalm a kind of war dance? Are the references literal or figurative? It is not clear. For us today who read it the psalm it should be seen as psalm of praise that is meant to drive out the enemies of our joy and faith and vanquish them by the "sword" of God's Holy Word (cf Heb 4:12).

Q64: I was surprised to hear on a radio show an advocate for the gay community say that the story of Sodom and Gomorrah is not about

homosexuality at all; that the sin for which God destroyed that city was greed and a lack of hospitality. What do you think of this?
— *Christina Jensen, Chicago, IL*

A: It is a strange but unfortunately common notion among the advocates you describe and others. If the assertion that the destruction of Sodom and Gomorrah has nothing to do with homosexual acts then the Holy Spirit, writing in the Book of Jude was never told. There it is written: *Sodom and Gomorrah and the surrounding towns gave themselves up to sexual immorality and practiced unnatural vice. They serve as an example of those who suffer the punishment of eternal fire* (Jude 1:7). So clearly the destruction of those towns is not merely about greed or a lack of hospitality.

This does not mean that homosexual practices were the only sin of those ancient towns. And thus Ezekiel adds: *Now this was the sin of your sister Sodom: She and her daughters were arrogant, overfed and unconcerned; they did not help the poor and needy. They were haughty and did detestable things before me. Therefore I did away with them as you have seen* (Ez 16:49-50).

And therefore it is proper to see that there were many sins in those ancient towns but among them were fornication and homosexual acts. Any straight-forward, non-ideological reading of the story in Genesis 19 will show that homosexual acts are not only mentioned, they are central to the story. At the moment of critical tension, the townsmen, young and old, stand outside Lot's door and demand: *Where are the men who came to you tonight? Bring them out to us so that we can have sex with them.* (Gen 19:5) So the text is not unclear. It is rather straight-forward. And while we ought not deny the fact of other sins which scripture also declares, neither should homosexual acts as a central aspect of the story be denied.

The Catechism of the Catholic Church, while reminding that persons with same-sex attraction are to be accepted with respect, compassion, and sensitivity also cites Genesis 19 among other texts in the assessment of homosexual acts: Basing itself on Sacred Scripture, which presents homosexual acts as acts of grave depravity, [Cf. Gen 19:1-29; Rom 12:4-27; 1 Cor 6:10; 1 Tim 1:10.], tradition has always declared that "homosexual acts are intrinsically disordered....Under no circumstances can they be approved (# 2357)

3. LITURGY AND SACRAMENTS

Q65: It is a very common practice for parishes to refuse baptism during Lent, and I am wondering what recourse parents can take. Is there anywhere in the Church's teaching that supports this practice? Is there anything that explicitly condemns it? – *name withheld*

A: Parents have the right and obligation under law to have their infants baptized shortly after they are born. Canon Law states this clearly: *Parents are obliged to see that their infants are baptized within the first few weeks. As soon as possible after the birth, indeed even before it, they are to approach the parish priest to ask for the sacrament for their child, and to be themselves duly prepared for it. If the infant is in danger of death, it is to be baptized without any delay(Can. 867 §1,§2).*

Further, since there is certainly no requirement, or even a provision in the law for pastors to deny, or for parents to refrain from, the baptism of infants during the entire season of Lent, there is no basis to introduce or maintain such a practice in a parish.

If the birth occurs very late in the Lenten season, one might envision a pastor suggesting that the baptism be delayed until Easter. In this regard, Holy Week is not usually a fit time to celebrate a baptism (except in danger of death), though even here, it is not strictly forbidden on Monday – Thursday of Holy Week.

Hence, I would say you are on good ground to appeal such a pastoral stance if your pastor is unmoved by your request for reconsideration.

I suppose if a dialogue with the pastor is not fruitful, the Bishop, the Dean, or the priest personnel director could be consulted and asked to direct the Pastor in this regard.

Q66: My best friend (since Kindergarten) is renewing her marriage vows. I stood up for her when she was married in the Church 10 years ago and she's asked me to do the same this time around--except that she has since left the Catholic Church and this ceremony is taking place in a Methodist church. Am I permitted to witness the renewal of her vows?
- *name withheld*

A: There are cases when a Catholic ought not be present at a wedding, or wedding related ceremony. For example, when a Catholic is marrying outside the Church without permission, or, when one of the parties is unqualified to enter the marriage (e.g. when one or both have been married before and there are no annulments). In such cases, Catholics, even family members, ought not attend such ceremonies.

However in the case you describe, there are no canonical issues involved.

In the first place, this is not actually a wedding, or the celebration of a sacrament *per se*, just a renewal of vows for an anniversary. Secondly, even if this were an actual marriage, and presuming both were free to marry, it would seem, from what you sadly state, she has left the Catholic Church by formal act. Thus she is not obliged to follow all the Catholic norms for weddings, such as having her marriage witnessed by a Catholic priest or deacon.

Thus, we are left with a prudential judgment on your part. Usually in such cases we ought to do what will best keep the relationship strong, and the lines of communication open. This will likely help a possible return to the Church. To unnecessarily defer from attending might cause hurt or alienation and make your friend's return to the Church even less likely.

Your attendance at this renewal of vows, even standing for her as one of the "wedding party" does not, of itself, affirm her decision to leave the

Church. Rather, it would seem, it is an affirmation of ten years of marriage, which is certainly something worth celebrating.

Q67: On this most recent Good Friday, at my parish, Communion was offered, at the evening service, under both forms (i.e. the Host *and* Precious Blood). I am new to the parish, and this surprised me. When I asked the pastor, he said it was a long tradition at the parish to save the precious blood from the night before and receive it on Good Friday. He told me, of all days, Good Friday, when Christ shed his blood, was the most fitting day to receive the Precious Blood. Is this practice allowed?
- *name withheld*

A: No, it is completely irregular to have done this.

Not only is the practice itself wrong, but the sacramental theology to justify it is erroneous. The doctrine of the Church teaches that under either species alone, the whole and complete Christ, and the true sacrament is received. To suggest, therefore, as it seems the Pastor does, that the Precious Blood is somehow not received, or less perfectly received, when only the Sacred Host is consumed, is a flawed notion.

Further, since no Mass is celebrated on Good Friday, the practice you describe requires that the precious blood be reserved overnight. But the norms currently in force forbid the reservation of the Precious Blood after the celebration of Mass, stating: *The consecrated wine, on the contrary, should be consumed immediately after communion and may not licitly be reserved.* (*Inaestimabile donum*, n. 14; GIRM 163, 182, 247, 249; *Redemptionis Sacramentum*, n.,107).

Canon Law (# 925) does state that, in the case of necessity, it is permitted to give Communion under the species of wine alone to a sick person. In this case, the Precious Blood may be reserved briefly in a properly sealed vessel in the tabernacle after Mass. However, it should not be considered an ordinary occurrence.

Q68: If a priest who has had five years to discern his vocation can be laicized, why does a couple, who may court only six months to a year need a Church annulment, especially if it was due to abuse or alcoholism and the like. Doesn't a person who wishes to remarry

deserve happiness without having to go through a long emotional process? – *Jeannine*

A: Your question seems to imply that laicization is a simple process. It is not, and often takes investigation, the preparing of a petition, and sometimes the gathering of testimony. This may take years to complete. Annulments, while not easy, can often be accomplished in six months to a year, depending on the diocese and complexity of the case. But the fact is, neither are easy.

That said, there is an important difference. Laicization does not generally seek to prove an ordination never took place or was invalid. It presumes the man was validly ordained and only releases him of his ecclesial obligations to live all the disciplines of priestly life such as perpetual celibacy, and the duties of the saying the Liturgy of the Hours, and celebrating Mass, etc.

Annulment on the other hand, is the recognition by the Church, based on evidence given, that a valid Catholic Marriage never occurred, since something essential was lacking. This of course requires proof that must be presented and then considered. And that, like the process of laicization, takes some time.

Both processes ultimately involve matters of great sadness and have significant pastoral implications. For while recognizing human struggles, the Church must also seek to uphold the gravity of vows that are made. Showing compassion to the individuals who seek annulments or laicization must be balanced with the common good, the reality of sacraments, and what Scripture teaches. The happiness of certain individuals cannot be the Church's only concern. Hence, the pastoral process involved must necessarily be thorough and careful.

Q69: Since the Pulpit is no longer used to inform Catholics what the Church teaches (the sermons I hear only reflect the Gospel of that day), how are Catholics to know Church teaching? - *name withheld*

A: It is true that many Catholics today are poorly formed in the faith. Yet there are many reasons for this, not just silent pulpits. Neither is it necessarily fair to describe pulpits as silent. I know my own isn't, and I know many brother priests who carefully teach the faith from their own pulpits. This is certainly an ongoing process. I would say it takes at least five years in a parish before I can say, with St. Paul, that I have proclaimed "the whole counsel of God" (Acts 20:27).

All that said, it is problematic to place exclusive focus on the pulpit. For there are many ways that the Catholic faith must be taught. This is especially the case since most Catholics Masses have sermons lasting little more than twelve minutes. Thus, other things must be added beyond the sermon in order to teach the faith.

At the heart of handing on the faith, is the family. And thus, catechesis must focus on renewing and equipping the family to better teach the faith. In my own parish, while the children are in Sunday school classes, I, as pastor, teach the parents what their children are learning. I also model for them how to teach. For example, we read Bible stories together, and then show them how to teach using those stories. We also learn how to use the Catechism to find answers.

Beyond the parish, there are many wonderful resources for Catholics to learn of their faith. There are also many publications, blogs, websites, and various forms of Catholic media, including movies and lecture series.

Hence, beyond the pulpit, many other things are both needed, and offered. Indeed we are very blessed today with many resources that help to teach the faith.

Q70: Our new assistant pastor sometimes uses his iPad on the altar instead of the Book. This seems strange to me. Is it allowed? – *Jeff*

A: You are not alone in thinking it strange. It is one of those new things on the scene that seem odd in the context of an ancient liturgy. To most I have discussed this with, the iPad is not ready for prime time, in its current form, for liturgical use.

Indeed, the Bishops of New Zealand recently clarified for the priest that while the iPad may have many good uses, for the Liturgy, priest should stick with the liturgical books. New Zealand's bishops are praising the usefulness of the iPad and other such electronic devices, but clarifying that for the liturgy, it's important to stick to the book. They wrote on April 30th of this year: *All faiths have sacred books which are reserved for those rituals and activities which are at the heart of the faith. The Catholic Church is no different, and the Roman Missal is one of our sacred books, and its physical form is an indicator of its special role in our worship.* Based on this, they go on to say that electronic devices may not be used by the priest at the liturgy, in place of the sacred books.

One can envision a time in the future when sacred books may take on electronic form, just as current printed books replaced ancient handwritten scrolls, and paper replaced parchment and lambskins. But now is not that time.

Q71: I am a Veteran and currently debating with my pastor who refuses to allow the American Flag to be displayed in the front of the Church. He has it back in the vestibule. Are there rules about this? – *Joseph, PA*

A: There are no specific rules about flags in either the liturgical books or the Code of Canon Law.

However, some time ago the Bishops' Committee on the Liturgy encouraged pastors not to place the flag within the sanctuary itself, which is for the altar, the ambo, the presidential chair and the tabernacle. They recommended an area be found outside the sanctuary, or in the vestibule of the church. But these are recommendations only and it remains for the diocesan bishop to determine regulations in this matter.

So, your pastor is on fairly good ground. Patriotism remains an important virtue for Christians. But how that patriotism is expressed in the location of the flag can admit of some local differences, and should conform well to liturgical norms as well as pastoral solicitude.

Q72: I attend a parish named Immaculate Conception. We recently built a new church which has an altar and a crucifix that hangs well above it. There is also a lovely state of our Lady holding the child Jesus off to the right. Recently our pastor also installed a large painting of Mary on the back wall behind the altar and I was upset since I think the altar area should remain wholly dedicated to Christ and not give the impression we are directing worship to Mary. I am so upset that I may leave this parish. – *Susan*

A: Your concerns are not without merit. While there are no rules absolutely forbidding images of the saints in the sanctuary, current norms and customs speak of the sanctuary area of the Church as emphasizing the altar, the ambo (pulpit), and the chair. There should also be, on or near the altar, a crucifix. Further, the tabernacle, in most parish settings, is usually in a prominent place, either within or very near the sanctuary (*cf* Built of Stones, #s 54,57,74-80).

That said, while images of Mary and the Saints in the central axis of the sanctuary are not common in modern Church design, it is not absolutely forbidden either. There may be some merit to have the patron of the parish

Church, in your case Mary, prominently displayed (as many older churches do) somewhere near the front, presuming it does not overly dominate the sanctuary.

Perhaps, since you mention the Crucifix being high above the altar, there may be some merit in placing a small crucifix on the altar. But only if the high crucifix is well out of sight since more than one crucifix in the sanctuary is discouraged (*cf* Built of Living Stones #91).

It is regrettable that this has caused you such grief as to consider leaving the parish. Perhaps a spiritual way to accept what you consider less than ideal, is to remember that we *do* gather with the saints at Mass. Scripture says *We are surrounded by a great cloud of witnesses* (Heb 12:1). There may also be benefit in recalling the description of the early Church at prayer: *They all joined together constantly in prayer, along with the women and Mary the mother of Jesus* (*cf* Acts 1:14).

As you rightly express, we pray *with* the saints, and they with us, we do *not* worship them.

Q73: When I learned the second precept of the Church, as a child it was "To go to Confession once a year if you have mortal sin." The current Catechism states on the 2nd precept: "To go to confession at least once a year" (#2042). Have the Bishops, changed the 2nd precept on their authority? - *Ed Smetana*

A: The catechism, while less than exact in the quote you supply does footnote Canon 989 for greater precision, which says: *All the faithful who have reached the age of discretion are bound faithfully to confess their grave sins at least once a year.*

The Catechism states elsewhere: *According to the Church's command, "after having attained the age of discretion, each of the faithful is bound by an obligation faithfully to confess serious sins at least once a year." Anyone who is aware of having committed a mortal sin must not receive Holy Communion, even if he experiences deep contrition, without having first received sacramental absolution, unless he has a grave reason for receiving Communion and there is no possibility of going to confession.* (#1457).

Thus, there is no change in the precept, though one may admit the catechism could have been more precise in the text you cite.

That said, it may be of some pastoral advantage to remember that there is a tendency today to minimize the possibility and frequency of mortal sin. It is not hard to understand that most of the adult faithful out to be getting to confession more than once a year anyway. It is quite likely that most adults, even if not guilty of sins against life and sexual purity, are often guilty of rather serious sins against charity. It is quite possible to cause serious harm, and emotional or spiritual distress to people by harsh things we say. Further, lies can cause more than minimal harm, reputations can be tainted, people misled, and error flourish. Sins of omission through greed, neglect or laziness can also cause grave harm. Missing Mass is a mortal sin, and being significantly neglectful in handing on or defending the faith can also become quite serious.

More could be said here, but one ought not to causally dismiss that they should likely get to confession even more than once a year. Further the Church also encourages the faithful to confess frequently even if they are not aware of mortal sin since the Sacrament of Confession not only confers the grace of absolution, but also the grace to avoid sin in the future.

Q74: If I'm aware of a sin, either mortal or venial, may I receive the Eucharist at mass? Or would I have to go to confession first? - *Rachael*

A: As the quote from the Catechism above notes, only mortal sins would exclude one from receiving Communion. If one is aware of mortal sin(s), one should refrain from going forward to receive if they have not first gone to sacramental confession.

As the Catechism notes, there are rare exceptions to this rule. Canonists define "grave reason to receive communion" in different ways, but most all concur that the reason must be more serious than ordinary embarrassment at not going forward. Most restrict it to danger of death. Even in such cases the communicant is required to make an act of contrition that includes the intent to confess the sin later, if a priest can reasonably be found.

There are some who struggle with habitual mortal sin, e.g. Masturbation, and in such cases they should work closely with a confessor so as be able to stay faithful to communion.

Q75: I was taught there were seven sacraments (including Marriage) that give grace, and also that there were things called sacramentals that do not give the grace the way that the sacraments do. Why then in my Church bulletin do I read in my Church bulletin about classes being offered to prepare people for "sacramental marriage."
- *Rosemary Easley, Baltimore, MD*

A: Well, in your bulletin "sacramental" is being used as an adjective, not a noun. Hence it is not wrong to speak of sacramental marriage. But, your bulletin could be clearer by saying "Sacrament of Marriage (or Matrimony)." That said, your distinction between the nouns, "sacrament" and "sacramental" is sound. Sacramentals include things like blessings, blessed objects, holy water, medals etc. They bear a resemblance to the sacraments. But sacraments, as "efficacious signs," absolutely confer the grace they announce, presuming the recipient is properly open to receive them. Sacramentals are signs that prepare us to receive grace, and dispose us to cooperate with it, but are much more dependent on our disposition to be fruitful. More at the Catechism of the Catholic Church (#1667*ff*)

Q76: Are women permitted to have their feet washed on Holy Thursday? Someone told me that Cardinal Sean O'Malley claims to have a letter from Rome permitting the practice. – *Rev. John Petrocelli*

A: "Permitting" might be a strong word. The Archdiocese of Boston issued a statement (in the April 1, 2005 Archdiocesan paper, "The Pilot") that read in part: "At the time of the ad limina visit to Rome, the archbishop sought clarification on the liturgical requirements of the rite of foot washing from the Congregation for Divine Worship, which has the responsibility for administering the liturgical law of the Church. The Congregation affirmed the liturgical requirement that only the feet of men be washed at the Holy Thursday ritual, which recalls Christ's service to the apostles who would become the first priests of the Church. The Congregation did, however, provide for the archbishop to make a pastoral decision concerning his practice of the rite if such a decision would be helpful to the faithful of the archdiocese."

And while Cardinal O'Malley did not comment publicly on the response from Rome, his practice since has been to include women in the Holy Thursday foot washing. The statement from Rome stops short of "permitting," and issued no official indults. In the end it left the matter to the pastoral judgment of the Cardinal, and, presumably, all Ordinaries, while reiterating the norm of men only.

Sadly, the Holy Thursday foot washing has become a kind of countersign, emphasizing power and rivalry, instead of service and unity. What should bespeak charity has often issued in conflict. Though the norm has never been unclear, it must be admitted that the practice of including women today in the ritual is widespread. While priests today are generally more obedient to liturgical law, many have inherited the practice and, for similar pastoral reasons, have accepted it, choosing not to further inflame an already tense matter, which occurs only once a year and is optional.

Q77: When God's name is mentioned in the prayers of Mass, the plural "have" (instead of has) is used. Why? - *Beverly*

A: The grammatical answer is that the word "God" in these prayers is in the vocative case, rather than being the subject of the verb "have." The actual subject of the verb in these prayers is either "who" or "you" as in, "O God, who...." or "O God, you..."

Your question implies that the verb "have" is only a plural verb. It is not. It can also be the first and second person singular (e.g. I have, you have). Thus, the sentence "O God, you have every perfection" requires the second person singular form of the verb. The form "has" would not work.

The difficulty to our ears is that the formal address "O God who...." is rare in English today. Normally "who" is a third person singular as in "Who has it?" But we can also use "who" in the second person singular if we supply a vocative, as in, "It is you, who have the answer." And this is what we do in the prayers. We supply the vocative "O God." Thus the verb must be "have."

Q78: There is a long-standing practice in our diocese, where the members of the charismatic movement anoint one another, and especially the sick with something called "St. Joseph's Oil." Some others call this the "Oil of Gladness." Does the Church permit this practice of laypeople anointing the sick with oil? - *name withheld*

A: It is not permitted. In a letter dated September 1, 2008, the Congregation for Divine Worship and the Discipline of the Sacraments issued the following directive: *"This Dicastery observes that Canon 1003.1 expressly forbids anyone, other than a priest, to administer the Sacrament of the Anointing of the Sick. Furthermore..., no other person than a priest may act as ordinary or extraordinary minister of the Sacrament of Anointing since such constitutes simulation of the sacrament. This Congregation also observes that there are only three blessed oils used in the Roman Ritual namely, the Oil of Catechumens, the Oil of the Sick, and the Sacred Chrism. The use of any other oil or any other "anointing" than those found in the approved liturgical books must be considered proscribed and subject to ecclesiastical penalties (cf. canons 1379 and 1384)"* (Prot. 824/08/L).

The letter goes on to direct that the bishops of South Africa who requested the ruling should restore proper sacramental discipline where it is lacking, and give catechesis.

Hence, it would seem that such anointings, as you describe in charismatic prayer services, should cease. Even if well intentioned, such anointings cause confusion and are difficult to distinguish between the very similar looking Sacrament of the Anointing of the Sick.

One might certainly pray for the sick, and even lay hands on them. But anointing them with oil is going too far, for the reasons stated.

It would therefore be proper for pastors to end such practices that might be occurring in their parish. Clearly, such a move would be accompanied by a charitable catechesis and the presumption of goodwill.

Q79: Why can we not receive the Eucharist by intinction? At one time it was permitted. Why has it been stopped, especially in this age of communicable diseases? - *Donald Pellegrino, Ocala, FL*

A: Communion by intinction (where the host is dipped in the precious blood by the priest or minster and then given to the communicant) is still permitted. Hence, it would seem that the decision to end the practice is a decision rooted in your own parish.

Though permitted, intinction is not a very widespread practice in most parishes in America. There are likely several reasons for this.

First, the practice introduces a complexity into the distribution of Communion. For example, when intinction is used, Communion cannot be received in the hand, which is an option some prefer. Thus it would seem that only some stations could have intinction. This then creates further complexities about who lines up where, and how various options are explained to the faithful at each Mass.

Further, the practice requires either special equipment, (i.e. a paten with a small cup for the precious blood) or someone standing nearby with a chalice of precious blood. The norms also require the use of chin paten when intinction is used. None of these complexities are impossible to overcome, and intinction can be, and still is practiced, in some places, but the complexities to help to explain the rarity of the practice.

As for wanting to receive the Precious Blood in a way other than a shared cup, please note that in fact you *do* receive the precious blood. For in the Host alone, even in the small fragment, there is contained the whole Christ: Body, Blood Soul and Divinity.

The use of the common cup(s) has reference to the fact that Christ shared his precious blood from a common cup. The concern for communicable disease is understandable, but not a definitive concern for most healthy people. The option always remains to refrain from partaking under that sign, and the Precious Blood is still received in the host alone.

Q80: throughout the prayers of the liturgy, e.g. the Kyrie, we often speak of and to "the Lord." Are we referring here to Jesus, or the Father?
- *Helen Streeter, Englewood, FL*

A: In the Kyrie we are referring to Jesus. This is made fairly clear in the verses, e.g., "You are the Son of God and the Son of Mary, Kyrie Eleison."

However, more frequently "Lord" refers to the Father. Most of the prayers of the mass, and especially the Eucharistic prayer, are directed to the Father, through Christ. There are certain exceptions to this, in the opening and closing prayers, but in those cases, that we are referring to Jesus, rather than the Father is made clear from the wording and context of the prayer.

Generally then the Mass is understood as a prayer of Christ the High Priest, directed to his Father, and it is in Christ's own prayer that we join.

Thus, with certain clear exceptions, "Lord" almost always refers to the Father.

Q81: When Holy Communion is distributed why is "The Body of Christ" said? Why not say, "The Body and Blood of Christ." Or better yet, "This is Jesus." - *name withheld, AL*

A: We use the word "body" for several reasons. First of all, Jesus himself used the word "body" (*soma* in Greek) when giving the Eucharist for the first time: "Take and east this is my Body (*soma*)." Hence we, in conformity to Christ, use this way of speaking of the Eucharist.

Secondly, both the English word "body" and the Greek word "*soma*" can refer strictly to the physical dimension of a person, or more broadly to the whole person. In English, I can say, "My arm is part of my body." Here I am referring to my physical dimension. However, I might also say, "I am somebody," which refers no only to my physicality but to my whole self. We can also do this in the plural such as when we speak of the "body of believers," or the body-politic." Here we do not refer to a physical body, but rather to the sum total, or the majority of some group.

Hence, we do not exclude any dimension of Christ by referring to his "Body," as if we were only referring to his flesh. Rather "Body" here refers to the whole Christ. Surely it pertains to a living human body (and Jesus is quite alive) to have not only flesh, but also blood and soul together. We also receive with his body, his divine nature since it is untied to him hypostatically.

And while we do speak of what is in the Chalice more specifically as the Blood of Christ, this is only to distinguish its species (i.e. what we perceive) from the host. But once again, Jesus is alive and glorified and his body, blood, soul and divinity are together. Hence, even in the smallest drop of Precious Blood, the whole Christ is received.

Q82: Our CCD students never received a penance at recent confessions. The priest involved did not deny this, but offered little explanation. Is the giving of a penance by the priest required, and is the performance of it necessary for the sacrament to be valid? – *name withheld*

A: The priest is required to impose a penance, or satisfaction on the penitent. It should be a helpful, prudent, just and suitable based on the kind and number of sins, and on the character and the condition of the penitent. The priest is only excused from imposing a penance when there is some physical or moral inability on the part of the penitent to perform it, e.g. if the penitent is near death, or too weak.

The penitent has a serious obligation to accept and fulfill the reasonable penance imposed by the confessor. If a penitent considers a penance unreasonable they are free to ask for another penance from the same or a different confessor.

The giving and fulfilling of the penance does not *per se* affect the validity of the absolution that is given, unless perchance the penitent approaches confession with such a determined will to refuse any penance that it affects the necessary contrition he must bring.

More often, the failure to give or fulfill a penance is due to forgetfulness, and in such cases the validity of the absolution is not affected. If however, the giving of or the fulfilling of a penance is intentionally neglected, while the validity of the absolution may not be affected, one does incur sin. The gravity of that sin is weightier if the material of the confession was grave, or serious.

Q83: Since the Eucharist is the Body of Christ, when we eat it, are its elements still existing as our Savior, or are they digested and become part of our own body? Or, do we become part of Jesus body? And, would those receiving the Eucharist, become part of each other's bodies in Christ? – *Vernon Edwards, Nelsonville, OH*

A: In John 6, the Lord Jesus teaches a kind of mutual indwelling, for He says, "Whoever eats my Flesh and drinks my Blood remains in me, and I in him" (Jn 6:56). Thus, while this process is mysterious and not easily reduced to mere human language, the mutual indwelling is very real, such that we are in Christ, and He is in us.

At one level, the Eucharist, the Body, Blood Soul and Divinity of Christ, is food. As Jesus says, "For my flesh is true food, and my blood is true drink" (John 6:55). As human beings, the food we receive, in this case the Holy Eucharist, is wonderfully assimilated into us, and becomes the very stuff of which we are made. That is, our food becomes the very building blocks of the cells in our body. And thus the very food of Jesus' own Body Blood Soul and Divinity, becomes part of our very substance. In this sense, St. Augustine says, "Christian, become what you are" (*cf* Sermon 272).

But, as all the Fathers of the Church note, unlike every other food we receive, the fruit of Christ is both living, and greater than we are. All other foods we received, are dead. But since Christ is alive, it is not merely that we take Him into ourselves, but even more, that he takes us into Him, making us a member of His own Body. And this assimilation of us into him is far greater than our assimilation of him and to us. Thus, we most properly speak of becoming a member of his body, for that is the greater effect of Holy Communion. But it is not untrue that he also becomes one with us, as the quote from John 6:58, above, teaches.

Ultimately, our oneness with each other is in Christ. And thus, while avoiding overly physicalist notions, we can say that we have communion in and with one another, in Christ, for we all members of the one Body, and when we receive Christ, we receive the whole Christ, which includes all his members. This is why faith and orthodoxy is also essential for Communion.

For one to be truly a member of the Body of Christ, requires that one live in union with all the members, and with its head. Ultimately the Church is *Unus Christus, amans seipsum* (On Christ, loving himself – St Augustine, *Homilies on 1 John*, 10, 3)

Thus, properly understood, and with necessary distinctions, your insights are correct.

Q84: The Catechism of the Catholic Church makes a rather heavy distinction between the "We believe" of the Nicene Creed, and the "I believe" of the Apostles Creed (cf # 167). In effect, it teaches that the Nicene Creed emphasizes the communal nature of faith, and the Apostles Creed emphasizes the faith professed personally by each believer. If the original Nicene Creed had "We believe," and the Catechism teaches on this so clearly, why then did the new English translation of the Mass render it, "I believe?" This seems to be erroneous both in the light of the Greek text, of the Creed and also the teaching of the Catechism. – *Deacon Lawrence Gallagher, Titusville, NJ*

A: The new English translation of the Creed to "I believe" is to bring the text in conformity with the authorized Latin text which has "Credo," namely, "I believe" for the opening word of the Creed.

You are correct in noting that the text of the Creed coming forth from the Council of Nicaea used the Greek word Πιστεύομεν (pisteuomen) a first-person plural meaning "we believe." It was worded in this way because it came forth as a statement of all the bishops, speaking as a body, or college of bishops. Thus they rightfully said "we believe."

However in the years that followed, when the Creed was brought into the liturgy, the form was switched to the first person singular Πιστεύω (pisteuo) "I believe." This change was made because the Creed was now said by the individual believer, in the context of the liturgy.

This liturgical adaptation of the text is quite ancient and has been respected by the Church ever since. As the Greek liturgy moved to Latin in the West, the first person singular, "Credo," (I believe) was thus used.

Your frustration related to harmonizing the new translation with the Catechism is understandable. However, it is possible to expect too much of liturgical texts, which have a particular context and are, of their nature more brief, when it comes to expressing the faith. The Catechism however is able to develop richer aspects of the teachings of the faith, and to explore historical and/or biblical roots. Thus, rather than to see the Catechism and the Mass in competition or conflict, one can see them as complementary, in this case, the Catechism helping to further articulate with the liturgy announces.

Q85: At several recent family funerals a number of my family members who are not Catholic insisted on receiving Communion despite my explaining they should not and the priest inviting only practicing Catholics to come forward. How can I better explain our practice of limiting Communion and are there dangers with them receiving?
— *Thomas O'Neil*

A: The Catholic practice of reserving communion fellow Catholics is fundamentally rooted in two things. First there is a norm of Scripture: *A man ought to examine himself before he eats of the bread and drinks of the cup. For anyone who eats and drinks without recognizing the Body of the Lord eats and drinks judgment on himself* (1 Cor 11:28-29).

For St. Paul, the issue is not only sin, (which might exclude some Catholics as well), but also, the need to "recognize the Body." Yet a great majority of Protestants do not believe Holy Communion to be the Body of Christ, but only a symbol. Hence they cannot truly say the "amen" that is required to the acclamation, "The Body of Christ." Thus, out of respect for both them and the Sacrament, we do not ask them to assent in faith to something which they regretfully do not believe.

A second reason for not sharing Communion is rooted in the fuller meaning of the Sacrament. In receiving Holy Communion, we do not merely speak of a personal communion of the believer with Jesus, but also of Communion with one another in the Church. But sadly, there are many things that divide Catholics and non-Catholics. In coming forward, one attests union with Jesus Christ, but also union with his Church, and all she teaches. Since this is also what Communion means, it is inappropriate for those who do not share this communion with us to come forward and signify what is not fully true, nor should we ask them to pronounce the "Amen" that affirms this community.

Thus, there is no rudeness intended by this practice of ours. Rather, there is a respectful, but regretful acceptance that others do not share our beliefs in certain significant matters.

As to dangers, note that St. Paul warns of incurring condemnation if we receive Communion either in serious sin or without discerning the Body.

When we consider the meaning of our "Amen" at Communion, it is also sinful to solemnly affirm what may not in fact be believed.

Q86: Why do we celebrate the visit of the Magi on a day different from Christmas? Also someone told me there we more than three wise men who visited. – *Gene Smith, OR*

A: There are details of the Christmas story in the modern imagination that come to us sources other than Scripture, details which may or may not be accurate.

So, it is true we do not know the exact number of the Magi who came. Many presume the number three, since three gifts are mentioned, gold frankincense and myrrh. But there may have been two Magi, four or more, we just don't know for sure.

Likewise, the modern imagination tends to bring them the Magi the crèche the very night of Jesus' Birth. Yet Scripture implies that their visit took place, likely, at a later time. This is because the text speaks of them finding Mary and the child in a house (Matt 2:11), not at the crèche.

Thus, liturgically we distinguish the two events and emphasize as well in Epiphany the "manifestation" (which is what "Epiphany means) of Christ to the Gentiles and the call of the nations to faith and worship of Christ.

Q87: I regularly attend daily mass, and I must admit I get a bit confused at Christmas time. The very day after Christmas we are celebrating the feast of St. Stephen the Martyr and later in the week we celebrate the feast of St. John the Apostle. Why do we jump around so much at Christmas? It feels like we lose the focus on Jesus birth.
-James, St. Louis, MO

A: Yes, and to add to your reflection, we also seem to move forward and backward in time during the Christmas cycle. The Feast of the Holy Family, celebrated on the Sunday between Christmas and New Years features a Gospel of Jesus at 12 years of age. And then at Epiphany, celebrated more than a week later, Jesus is back to being an infant. Further, we observe the feast of the Holy Innocents on December 28, a terrible slaughter that took place after the visit of the Magi, and then we move backward in time to celebrate the feast of the Epiphany on the Sunday near January.

Some of these anomalies are explained by the fact that the liturgical year did not develop evenly over the centuries. The feasts of St. Stephen Martyr, and St. John the Apostle, are very ancient feasts on the Church's calendar. The celebration of Christmas, and at the feasts related to Christmas, developed in later centuries.

It surprises many of us moderns that the ancient Church did not focus a great deal on the birth of Christ. We are very sentimental about Christmas and the baby Jesus. But the early church focused primarily on the Paschal mystery of Jesus' passion death and resurrection.

In later centuries the Christmas feast became more elevated. But the focus was still more theological than sentimental. Thus, It did not seem so alarming that the very day after Christmas, we were back to celebrating other saints such as St. Stephen, and St. John.

Later, as a celebration of Christ's incarnation deepened, theologically and culturally, there was developed the octave of Christmas. But the Church did not feel free simply to move aside the feast of St. Stephen and St. John, which were very ancient.

As for the chronological whiplash of moving back and forth in time, within the Christmas feasts, we should recall that in the celebration of the Sacred Liturgy we access eternity, rather than merely chronological time. For God, all times and events are equally present, and we meet him there, rather than simply on our schedule.

Q88: I think that the reception of Holy Communion is probably the most precious time a person can have to commune with the Lord. Why, then are we forced to sing hymns the whole time communion is being distributed making it impossible for us to converse with the Lord?
– *David Tomko, Butler, PA*

A: The norms of the Roman Missal state that, *While the Priest is receiving the Sacrament, the Communion Chant is begun, its purpose being to express the spiritual union of the communicants by means of the unity of their voices, to show gladness of heart, and to bring out more clearly the "communitarian" character of the procession to receive the Eucharist. The singing is prolonged for as long as the Sacrament is being administered to the faithful....* (GIRM # 86). The instructions also state: *When the distribution of Communion is over, if appropriate, the Priest and faithful pray quietly for some time. If desired, a Psalm or other canticle of praise or a hymn may also be sung by the whole congregation.* (# 88).

Note then the emphasis on the "communitarian" nature of this moment. And while private prayer is not wholly excluded, neither is it extolled as the main point or purpose to be pursued at the time of receiving Holy Communion.

The Sacred Liturgy is fundamentally a public and corporate act of worship of the whole Body of Christ together. It is not essentially a private devotion. The norms *do* permit a time after communion for silent prayer, if this seems appropriate. The length of such time and the use of this option will vary depending on the needs the congregation and other factors.

Your concerns are understandable, but they need to be balanced with what the Church teaches us the Liturgy most fundamentally is. Consider that in the first Mass, at the Last Supper, the Apostles did not go off and have private conversations with Jesus. Rather, they experienced him corporately, and the Scripture says, that after partaking of the Sacrament, they "sang a hymn" (Mt 26:30). If we extend the first Mass to the foot of the Cross, there too, those that made it that far, stayed together and supported the Lord and each other.

Private prayer and Eucharistic devotion are to be encouraged, but, there is a context where this is best. Public prayer is also good and to be encouraged. It too has a context that should be respected for what it is.

Q89: At our parish when the psalm is sung, the text used routinely varies from my new and authorized prayer book. Is it acceptable for the musicians to change the words as they do? – *Jim Schafbuch, via email*

A: No, if that is what they are doing. The proper responsorial Psalm, from the day should be said or sung, however there are exceptions. Liturgical norms state the following:

[T]he responsorial Psalm, ... should, as a rule, be taken from the Lectionary. It is preferable that the responsorial Psalm be sung ... In order, however, that the people may be able to sing the Psalm response more readily... Psalms... chosen for the various seasons of the year... may be used in place of the text corresponding to the reading whenever the Psalm is sung. If the Psalm cannot be sung, then it should be recited.... There may [alternately] be sung either the Responsorial Gradual from the Graduale Romanum, or ... Graduale Simplex...or an antiphon and Psalm from another collection ... providing that they have been approved by the Conference of Bishops or the

Diocesan Bishop. Songs or hymns may not be used in place of the Responsorial Psalm (GIRM # 61)

As can be seen, an exception can be made for reasons stated to using the psalm for the day. In some parishes, the ability of the musicians and or the people to learn and use different responses each week varies a good bit. Thus pastoral provision permits the use of certain seasonal psalms and refrains. But, substituting hymns in place of the responsorial Psalm is not permitted and only texts approved by the Bishops are to be used.

Thus it is possible to see how the words of the psalm that are sung may differ from what is in your prayer book, but only if the variant text is approved by the Bishops.

For musicians, parishes or pastors to make unauthorized changes to the texts of the psalm is strictly prohibited. Most commonly the forbidden changes involves altering the text to be "inclusive." But theologically, the "Man who walks not in the counsel of the wicked" etc., is often a reference to Christ, and altering the text loses the Messianic reference. Hence bad and unauthorized changes yield bad theology. It is rightly prohibited.

Q90: Our new pastor says the altar in our Church is too far away from the pews, so for daily mass he uses a table outside the sanctuary. Is this proper? - *name withheld, OR*

A: Generally, the norms of the Church indicate that the altar should be fixed, that is, immovable, made of stone, and located in the sanctuary of the Church, that is, in an area of the church distinguished from where the people gather and are seated. ("Built of Living Stones" 54, 57)

At first glance, it would seem that your pastor is operating outside these norms and that the appropriate place for him to celebrate Mass is at the main altar of the church.

Sometimes however, in older, or larger churches, the pastoral challenge you described is present. In such cases the use of a smaller altar, closer to the people, (as is some done larger basilicas), is employed.

The movable altar, should be truly noble, not a simple folding table, and dedicated to no other purpose other than the celebration of the sacred liturgy. While this is not ideal, in some instances it may be pastorally allowable, especially if recourse to a chapel for daily Mass is not possible.

Q91: Who can give blessings? There are lay people in my parish giving blessings and this does not seem right.
-*Sr. Mary Gemma Younger, Versailles, KY*

A: Context and content are important in answering a question like this. In the liturgical setting only a priest (and sometimes the deacon) should be conferring blessings since they are present and available for such. Thus, the practiced observed in some places of lay people who are distributing communion also giving blessings is inappropriate. The priest should be sought for this, apart from the communion line.

However, in other settings lay people can give certain blessings in certain ways. For example, a parent can bless a child, an elder can bless a youngster, etc. In doing this, however, they ought to avoid priestly gestures such as making the sign of the cross over others. Perhaps tracing the cross on the forehead is enough, or simply laying a hand on the head, or no gesture at all, are better.

In settings where lay people are praying for one another, say in a prayer for healing or deliverance, similar rules should be followed, avoiding overt priestly gestures, and being content to lay hands, or make no gesture at all.

In the rare instances where lay people lead formal liturgical gatherings, such as the Liturgy of the Hours, they must not only avoid gestures, but also follow prescribed texts which merely ask God's blessing on the assembled believers, but do not imply they are bestowing such blessings.

Finally there are certain specific prayers and blessings that can only be given by a priest. The norms are too specific to be given here in a general answer. But most blessings of objects and sacramentals are reserved to clergy, and the laity ought to be content to offer simple prayers, asking blessings for one another only in appropriate contexts.

Q92: We hear of priests leaving the priesthood and then subsequently getting married. Is Sacramental Marriage possible for a man who has received Holy Orders? I thought "once a priest always a priest"?
- *Kathy Cain, Yampa, CO*

A: Your insight "once a priest, always a priest" is a correct one. Thus, a man who, "leaves the priesthood," is not leaving the priesthood, *per se*, but is setting aside the practice and discipline of the priestly ministry.

For a priest to validly and licitly marry in the Church, he must first be "laicized." That is, while his priestly character remains, he is permitted and then required to live as a layman in the Church. And so, except in very rare "danger of death" situations, he cannot hear confessions, or give anointing of the sick, and in nowise celebrate the Sacred Liturgy or exercise other offices related to the priestly ministry.

Further, when laicized, he is usually dismissed from the discipline of celibacy and free to marry. Note that celibacy is a discipline. And while a common and expected discipline of most priests, it is not utterly intrinsic to the priesthood. There *are* married priests, most of them in the Eastern Rites of the Catholic Church. But even in the Western (Roman) Rite there are some married priests. Most of these have come over from Anglican or Lutheran ministry and were then ordained Catholic priests.

Thus, when a man leaves the active priesthood, and is laicized, he can also have the discipline of celibacy relaxed for him by the Church, such that he can marry.

It is certainly lamentable that some men do leave the priesthood, a ministry they agreed to accept for life. And yet the Church, as the loving mother, does make some pastoral provision for men who regrettably have need of leaving the active priestly ministry for grave reasons. These provisions are in place so as not to utterly lose them to the practice of the faith, and to hold them as close to Christ and the Church as possible.

Q93: At a recent funeral of a friend her ashes were brought into the Church for the Mass. I thought this was not allowed?
— *Madeline Kerek, Huntington, IN*

A: The practice you describe is allowed. In 1997 the American bishops received permission from the Congregation for Divine Worship for the celebration of funeral rites in the presence of cremated remains.

There are some adaptions to the rites, however. The priest may greet the remains at the door and sprinkle them with holy water, but the covering of the remains with the cloth (the Pall) is omitted. The Easter candle may be placed near the cremated remains, but there was no mention of the priest incensing the remains. Otherwise, the funeral masses celebrated his laid down in the Roman Missal and the funeral ritual.

Prayers, which do not make reference to honoring the burying of the body of the deceased, should be chosen, instead of those, which have these references (cf Funeral Ritual #428). The prayers of final commendation at the end of the funeral mass are largely followed in the normal way. It is uncertain at this point whether the remains are to be incensed or not. It would seem this is permitted, but not required. The deacon or priest concludes the funeral Mass with an alternate dismissal listed in the rite, which makes no reference to the body.

The forbiddance of cremation by the church in the past was due to the fact that many made use of it as a denial of the resurrection of the body. This is seldom the case today, but such an attitude must be ruled out before cremation is permitted. But note, "*Although cremation is permitted by the church, it does not enjoy the same value is Burial of the body. The Church clearly prefers and urges at the body of the deceased be present for the funeral rites, since the presence of the human body better expresses the values which the Church affirms in those rites.* (# 413)

Q94: Since the Church says that having children is intrinsic to sex and marriage, should we just strip the sterile and older people of their right to marriage? -*name withheld, WI*

A: The *Catechism* says that sex must be ordered *per se* to the procreation of human life (# 2366). "Per se" does not mean every act can be fertile but only that "by itself" (i.e. *per se*) the act is not intentionally hindered from its natural ends. This is what contraception, homosexual acts, and certain heterosexual practices, that do not complete or naturally render the marital act, do. But it is clear to any biology novice that not every sexual act results in conception.

Consider by analogy, that I call a friend, and this might result in speaking with her, or perhaps being sent to a voice mail. Whatever the final result, my reason and purpose for calling was to try to reach my friend. One would likely consider me a madman if, in dialing the numbers, I had no intent of reaching my friend, and was angry if she did pick up the phone and begin to speak. Whatever the final result, the calling of my friend is *per se* related to speaking with her.

And this is what it means that marriage, and sexual activity, must be "per se" related to the procreation of children, even if the results of that activity do not always attained the full purpose of that action.

Older and/or sterile people do not intentionally exclude one of the two fundamental reasons for marriage and sexual activity.

Q95: Why is Easter a floating holy day? Why can't the Church celebrate Easter on the same Sunday each year? The Bishops have moved other Holy Days, for convenience, why not Easter?
- *Bill Bartkus, San Diego, CA*

A: The date of Easter varies each year because it is linked to the cycle of the Moon, relative to the cycle of the Sun. In order to set the date of Easter one must first look for the vernal (spring) equinox, which is March 20. The word "equinox" refers to that time when the length of day and night are equal. It is also the date we set for the official beginning of spring.

Having the set our sights on March 20, we next look for the first full moon following March 20. Some years, the first full moon occurs quickly, within days of the equinox. Other years it occurs weeks later. This year, the first full moon after the equinox occurs on March 27 so Easter is early.

For the Jewish people, this first full moon after the equinox also signaled Passover. And since it was at the Passover feast that our Lord Jesus suffered and died and rose we Christians always fix Easter to coincide with Passover.
So then, Easter, (which is always on a Sunday since Christ rose on the first day of the week), is celebrated on the Sunday, following the full moon, after the vernal equinox.

Historically there were great debates within the Church in the East and the West about setting the date of Easter. The system described above was finally settled upon. But today, but we still find that the exact date for Easter varies a bit in the western and eastern parts of the Church since many of the Eastern rites still use the more ancient Julian calendar, rather than the Gregorian calendar used by the church in the West.

Your wish for a fixed Day for Easter, as is the case with Christmas and other feasts, is understandable. But as you can see, the relationship of the Moon relative to the sun doesn't fit perfectly into our modern systems of timekeeping and to fix the date as you suggest would probably open old debates that caused great harm in the early Church.

Q96: Is there a difference in meaning between the words Hallelujah and Alleluia. And if not, why are they spelled differently?
— *Donella Matthews, New York, NY*

A: No, both words are the same. Hallelujah is a Hebrew word, (הַיְוּלְלָה Hallal (Praise) + Yah (The LORD). Hence "Hallelujah" means, "Praise the Lord!" But the exact way that the Hebrew letters are transliterated into English and other languages has varied a bit over time. Perhaps most influential is the fact that the Greek New Testament rendered the Hebrew word Hallelujah as ἀλληλούϊα (allelouia). And since Greek is generally more influential in English spellings than Hebrew, many English translations render the word as Alleluia.

However, not an insubstantial number of English translators have preferred over the centuries, especially when translating the Old Testament Hebrew, to render the term Hallelujah. Some translators will use Hallelujah for the Old Testament and Alleluia for the New Testament.

Music has also influenced the decision over which spelling to use since some of the famous compositions from the Baroque period such as Messiah used the spelling Hallelujah that was more common in earlier English translations of the Bible.
At the end of the day, it is the same word, just with different spellings.

Q97: I recently saw the picture of Pope Frances seated near the back of the chapel instead of up front in the special chair for the Celebrant. I am moved by this humility, and wonder why must the priest sits up front during Mass. - *name withheld, San Diego, CA*

A: To clarify, Pope Francis was seated in the back of the chapel *prior* to the sacred liturgy. Once the liturgy began he vested and moved forward to the celebrant's chair.

The celebrant of the mass sits up front in virtue of the fact that he acts *in persona Christi*. Hence, the celebrant's chair, and he, being seated in a prominent, visible place in the sanctuary, is not honoring of "Fr. Joe Smith" the man, but, rather, of Jesus Christ who acts in and through the priest, who is configured to Jesus by holy orders.

In this sense, through the Sacrament of Holy Orders, the priest in the liturgy is a kind of sacrament of the presence of Christ. It is Christ who is honored, and has a prominent seat. Jesus Christ is the true celebrant and high priest of every liturgy.

Q98: I have asked my local bishop to have all the parishes restore the St. Michael Prayer after all Masses. We need to call on St. Michael. I

have not heard from the Bishop and wonder what I can do to see this practice restored. – *Diane Siereveld, Hamilton, OH*

A: Your desire to pray this prayer is understandable, and good. The prayer can in fact be said. However, perhaps a little history and context is appropriate to understand why it fell away in the early 1970s.

Historically, the liturgical movement beginning in the 1940s and continuing through the Second Vatican Council., sought to reemphasize the Eucharistic liturgy, by distinguishing it from some of the devotions that had grown up around it. The hope was to emphasize participation in the Mass as the greatest devotion.

Among the devotions that attached themselves were a number of prayers said following the dismissal from Mass. Thus, although the priest turned and said *Ite Missa est* (Go the mass is ended), this was not exactly so. First there was a blessing, then a recitation of the last Gospel, and then after most masses, prayers, which included the prayer to Saint Michael. In many parishes Benediction of the Blessed Sacrament was also done.

Liturgist of the time sensed that lesser devotions following the greatest devotion somehow implied an inadequacy in the prayer of holy Mass.

Whether or not you agree with all these points, it was the thinking at the time, which led to the elimination of many, if not all, devotions immediately following the Mass.

That said, you and fellow parishioners, are not forbidden from praying certain prayers and devotions following mass, even with the priest. It is best however, to allow those who need to depart, e.g. for work, to leave prior to the beginning of devotions. Otherwise, people feel trapped, and the instruction that they may go, is lost or reduced in meaning.

Please also be aware, while that the St. Michael Prayer is an important prayer, many others also insist on other devotions for similar reasons. Thus some pastors are reticent in fostering such public devotions, since requests tend to multiply. So pastoral discretion in needed, and solutions will vary from parish to parish.

Q99: A friend wants a grandmother and aunt, to be the godparents for her daughter. But the pastor says this is not possible, one must be male, the other female. I know other pastors permit this practice. What is correct? – *Sharon Malay, Fredericksburg, VA*

A: The first pastor is correct. The code of Canon Law says regarding sponsors for baptism, *One sponsor, male or female, is sufficient; but there may be two, one of each sex.* (Canon 873).

Catechesis is necessary today regarding the role of sponsors. Too frequently, the role is seen as merely ceremonial, and is often misconstrued as a way of bestowing honors on certain adults.

The role of a sponsor in infant baptism, is to ensure the Catholic formation of the child, if the parents are unable to do so. In this regard, only one sponsor is needed. However, if two are chosen, they are usually called "godparents," and ought to be in the model of parents: male and female. Otherwise, one suffices.

Q100: In our hymnal there are many lines in the hymns which concern me. One line says "I myself am the bread of life...you and I are the bread of life." Another says "we become for each other the bread, the cup."
-name withheld, via email

A: Such lines ought to cause concern. For, interpreted in a rather literalistic way, they seem to declare equivalence between the sacrament of the Holy Eucharist, and of our communion with one another.

It is true, the concepts are related, but they are not equivalent or substitutable. One in fact causes the other. That is to say, our communion with Christ in Holy Communion effects our communion with one another. And I suspect that is what these hymns are trying to get at. But they do so in a clumsy sort of way, as if the two were simply and merely the same. They are not.

For Christ is not simply reducible or equivalent to the sum total of his members, but he, as God, is greater than and is the cause of the communion we enjoy with one another.

That said, we must accept the limits of what art and poetry do. Hymns are a form of poetry, and cannot always have the doctrinal precision that we might expect of a theological treatise. Context is important, and hymn use a poetic genre.

Nevertheless, some of the older Eucharistic hymns were able to speak politically, and yet not sacrifice doctrinal precision. Perhaps we could hope for more than we often find in many modern compositions.

Q101: Why is there no dress code in the Church? There is immodesty and a lot of overly casual dressing for the miracle that takes place.
– *Lois Doelz, via email*

A: There is an understandable concern today about the way many people dress for Mass. There are double issues of modesty and also of people attending in clothes that seem far too casual for the holiness of the Mass and of God's house. The problem begins as a cultural one. The fact is Americans seldom dress up any more for anything. Even many work places that once featured uniforms and/or suits and dresses, have become very casual. Modesty too is a cultural problem that includes clothes that are often too tight or revealing.

Now culture is very influential for most, often, sadly, more influential than faith. Deep faith would seem to inspire a devotion, and sense of the sacred for the Holy Liturgy and for God's house. But due to poor formation in many, the influence of culture prevails and most think little of how they dress when going to Holy Mass. Frankly most do not intend any irreverence, but simply dress without a lot of thought.

Thus a problem in issuing a dress code is that there is a range of acceptable views on clothing. In fact the word "modesty" comes from the word "mode" referring to the middle of some range of views. And frankly, standards vary across time and cultures and especially regarding age. I have often found that many younger people are surprised to hear that what they wear might be considered irreverent and express a little irritation. Older folks (such as me) remember different times when standards were different.

That said, a general norm for men might be: trousers, not jeans, a button down shirt, or at least a T-Shirt with a collar, no crazy slogans. For women, a skirt and blouse or dress at knee level or lower. Women should avoid low cut blouses. Sleeveless blouses are debatable. But in saying this I know I am going to get a lot of mail with very different opinions.

Hence, perhaps the best we can do is to gently remind all people of sacredness of the Holy Mass and seek to grow their faith in how special the Mass is. As for modesty, more significant moral issues are involved, but so are greater sensitivities. It is a very delicate matter for a priest to speak in great detail about women's fashions. Frankly we wish older women would take the lead here, and speak to younger women. Priests and men can speak to younger men, but here too, laymen ought to lead in this manner.

Q102: Is it permitted for the cantor to add tropes or phrases such as "King of Kings" to the Lamb of God? Also should it be sung during the sign of peace? - *Bill Manners, Philadelphia, PA*

A: No. The USCCB clarified this in September 2102 that is it is no longer permissible to alter the text of the Lamb of God. The number of times it is sung may be lengthened however to cover the action.

The Agnus Dei is meant to be sung during the breaking of the host. The sign of peace, which should be brief, ends and then the Agnus Dei is sung. It remains problematic that the sign of peace is often difficult to end since many treat it as a kind of meet and greet rather than a quick sing of charity to those immediately nearby. Catechesis is necessary to keep the sign of peace brief.

Q103: At the Mass, when the priest offers the bread and wine we say, "Blessed be God forever." But how is it possible for us to bless God? He does not need our blessings and blesses us.
- *name withheld, Milwaukee, WI*

A: Linguistically the response you cite translates the Latin *Benedictus Deus in saecula*. The *benedictus* in Latin, literally means to speak well or favorably about someone or something (*bene* = well + *dictus* = say or speak). Hence what we mean by "blessed" and the phrase "Blessed be God forever" is that "It is well that God should be forever praised." We are not claiming to confer some sort of grace or favor upon God, as is often the meaning of the word "blessing" in English.

Theologically though we can distinguish between God's intrinsic glory and his external glory. As you point out, there is not one thing we can add or take from God's intrinsic glory. God is glorious and blessed all by Himself and has no need of our praise.

However, we can help to spread God's external glory by our praise and acknowledgment of him before others, as well as by reflecting his glory through lives of holiness, generosity and conformity to the truth.

In this sense we can also understand the phrase "Blessed be God forever" to mean, "May God's external glory and blessedness be extended and experienced in all places and times. May God be blessed (praised) everywhere, and unto the age of ages."

Q104: At our parish the priest says a shortened creed. Some Sundays he omits it altogether. When I talk to him about it he gets angry. Should I go to the bishop? - *name withheld, via email*

A: The creed is to be said each Sunday. It is possible that the shortened version you mention is the Apostles Creed, which is a permitted option.

Complete omission of the Creed is wrong, and if your request that the priest follow the requirement continues to be ignored, you should inform the diocesan bishop and ask for a written reply from his office as to how your concerns will be addressed.

Many have died for what the Creed announces. It is no mere ritual recitation.

Q105: Our new priest does not wash his hands at offertory in daily mass. He says without a server it is hard and the rite no longer has practical use. Is this right? - *Bill Eitenauer, Plains, NY*

A: The priest celebrant should wash his hands, even if there is no server. Though it is a bit awkward to pour water over one's hands from a cruet, finger bowls can perhaps be used for the purpose.

Father's explanation that there is no practical necessity for him to wash his hands does not hold. It is true that the hand washing in ancient times had more practical purposes due to the reception of many and varied gifts during the offertory procession. Handling these things often soiled the priest's hands. But liturgical rites don't have a merely practical point. The washing of the priest's hands has an important spiritual dimension as well, indicating his desire to be free of sin before offering the Holy Sacrifice, and handling the Body and Blood of Christ. Omitting this rite is not permitted.

Q106: When I was young I was taught to conclude my confession by saying, "For these and all the sins of my past life, I ask pardon and absolution." This is a strange expression and almost seems to imply a kind of reincarnation, as if I've had other lives in the past, does it not?

— John R., via email

A: No, it does not. This is a mode of speaking, an expression, and should not be understood in a strictly literal manner. There are all sorts of expressions and manners of speaking which, if read in a literalist manner, make little sense, but everyone knows what they mean euphemistically.

For example, a mother may say to her child, "Put on your shoes and socks." Literally, this would be difficult and clumsy, since it seems to say that I should put on my shoes, and then my socks on top of the shoes. But of course, it means no such thing. And while it is more true to say one ought to put on his socks and shoes, everybody knows what it means. Another example is the expression "coming and going." But of course one cannot really come, until they first go. So the expression more accurately should be "going and coming." But despite poor word order, everybody knows what "coming and going" means and adjusts.

And thus, when we ask forgiveness for the sins of our "past life," it is clear we are referring merely the sins we have committed in the past. If this saying this is bothersome to you, then you may amend it, for it is not a formal or prescribed way of ending the confession, but it is simply a common sentence many use to tell the priest they are done mentioning their sins.

Theologically, one is not required to ask forgiveness for sins of the past which have already been forgiven in the sacrament. And thus, another way a penitent can end his confession is to say something like "For these, and other sins I cannot recall, I ask for pardon and absolution."

Q107: I was delighted to see three million people at Mass on the beach in Rio with the Holy Father. However, this stands in contrast to the Church's stricter rules that a marriage must be celebrated inside a church building. I wonder what to tell my nieces who are upset they cannot have weddings outside. – *Karen Nelson, Tampa, FL*

A: All the sacraments, as a general rule, should be celebrated in a sacred space. Therefore, a dedicated parish church, or oratory is almost always the proper place for the celebration of any sacrament.

But, as is almost always the case with general norms, there are exceptions. For example, in danger of death, baptisms are sometimes celebrated in the hospital. On account of urgency, or as the result of a pastoral moment, confessions are sometimes celebrated in settings other than the church.

In the example you cite, no Church building exists to accommodate the three million who assembled in Rio last August. The use of the beach was actually a backup plan that had to be implemented when the large open field that had been designated was rendered soggy by pouring rains.
Hence, for urgent pastoral reasons, many general norms can be adapted where necessary.

Regarding weddings, certain permissions can be obtained for weddings to be celebrated outside of the sacred space. However, the reasons ought to be serious, not just because it would be more convenient or pleasing to someone in the wedding party.

While permissions are sometimes granted, most dioceses resist granting these permissions too easily. Of all the Sacraments, the celebration of Holy Matrimony tends to be most influenced by secular trends. And many of these trends take the focus off Christ, and the actual Sacrament that is being conferred. The emphasis too easily falls on dresses, flowers, food, and other social aspects. Moving weddings to beaches, backyards, reception halls and other such places, shifts the focus even further away from the Sacrament itself. It also tends to open the doors even further to certain passing trends, many of which are questionable, even frivolous or scandalous.

Hence, the celebration of the Sacraments ought generally to take place in the parish church. For serious pastoral reasons, such as stated above, exceptions can be made. But weddings seldom present pastoral conundrums significant enough to warrant the movement of the Sacrament outside the church and, more problematically, shift the focus even further from where it should be.

Q108: The new Gloria prayer says, "On earth peace to people of good will." The Old Gloria said, "and peace to his people on earth. Are we only praying for non-evildoers? What is the emphasis of this change?
— *Kevin Hansen, Brookings, SD*

A: The phrase you cite from the Gloria, (itself a quote from Luke 2:14), is not about who or what we are praying for. Rather, it is about *how* God's peace comes to rest upon us, and upon this world.

God's peace is not just a human wish that we can have for others; it is the result of being in conformity to His will and about being reconciled to Him. There can be no true peace where there is a refusal to live according to the vision of his kingdom.

The biblical concept of peace, (*shalom*), does not simply mean an absence of conflict, it means that there is present in the relationship everything that ought to be there, e.g. justice, love, reciprocity, and truth.

Hence, God's peace can only rest on those who are of "good will". The Greek word from Luke's Gospel translated here as "good will," is *eudokia*, a word which describes one who manifests a desire, and delight, who is disposed and open to the Kingdom of God.

Hence, the new translation is both more accurate in terms of the biblical text, and also more theologically accurate. Peace does not just drop out of heaven, on all people. But rather, it results for those who, by God's grace, are open and disposed what he is offering. Peace is the result that accrues to those who, by their good will, and openness accept what God offers.

Q109: At the local nursing home, a religious Sister, who is very traditional and wears the full habit, conducts a communion service. During communion the non-Catholics are also brought forward and she traces the cross on their forehead and says God bless you. Is this allowed? – *Pat Reagan, Davenport, IA*

A: The conferral of a blessing, even with the sign of the cross, is not forbidden to the non-ordained in all circumstances. For example, parents should be encouraged to bless their children, even trace the cross on their forehead. In some settings and cultures, elders often bless youngsters. Laypeople even bless themselves whenever they make the sign of the cross.

However, in the liturgical setting you describe, some parameters should be observed. The moment of the distribution of Holy Communion, at a Mass, or communion service, is not really the moment for people to seek other sorts of blessings. In a Mass, the priest will surely give the general blessing at the end of the liturgy with the sign of the cross over the whole congregation. Hence, all those present will in fact receive a blessing.

There are however pastoral concerns of how best to deal with a practice that has become widespread, and is not done in bad faith. Frankly, most pastors overlook the practice and when requested confer blessings in the communion line. Even if they do dissuade their parishioners from the practice, many visitors still often come forward requesting blessings. Thus, the matter may better be resolved at the diocesan or national level.

While the situation you describe is wrong, Sister is probably trying to make the best of a difficult situation wherein people expect such blessings, even if they are not Catholic. Finding a teachable moment to gently instruct the faithful is not always easy given the presence of many visitors.

Nevertheless, the goal to move toward is to teach that the distribution of Holy Communion is not really the time to seek other blessings. An additional confusion is created when, though priests and deacons are present at masses, laypeople at other communion stations are often giving out what appear to be priestly blessings. Finding a gentle way to clear up the confusion becomes increasingly important.

Q110: Why was the acclamation "Christ has died, Christ is risen, Christ will come again" eliminated from the new Roman Missal. It went from being the most popular of the memorial acclamations to becoming non-existent. - *Jason Jackson, Bell Harbor, ME*

A: The acclamation you cite, was a loose translation of the first acclamation *Mortem tuam annuntiamus Domine....* Which is now rendered more faithfully as, *"We proclaim your death, o lord, and profess your resurrection, until you come again."*
There were some requests to retain the "Christ has died" version since it was so familiar, but those requests were not heeded.

The essential problem with that rendering of the acclamation was that it addressed Christ in the third person, speaking about him, as if he were not present. All the memorial acclamations speak directly to Christ in the grammatical second person "You" for he is present on the altar, after the consecration, e.g. *"We proclaim YOUR death, O Lord ... Save us savior of the world, for by YOUR death ...* etc. Hence the acclamations speak directly to Jesus, not about him.

The old familiar acclamation Christ has died...could not withstand this critique and was dropped. Of itself it is a valid acclamation, and can be used in songs, or in other settings, but it is not suited to the moment just following the consecration when the faithful are invited to speak TO Christ in the grammatical second person "you," for He is present.

Q111: Do you know of a document that gives norms of what Extraordinary Eucharistic Ministers can and can't do? Also, are they able to expose and repose the Blessed Sacrament for adoration?

-name withheld, via email

A: Yes there are norms. The most authoritative norms come from the United States Conference of Catholic Bishops, which takes the universal norms of the Church and applies them to the American setting. The title of the document is "Extraordinary ministers of Holy Communion at Mass."

The general nature of your question, and the brevity of this column makes it impossible to speak of every aspect of this ministry in the Church. However, some of the more common questions and concerns that are addressed in this document are as follows.

Extraordinary Ministers of Holy Communion should be theologically and spiritually trained for this ministry. They should exhibit the greatest reverence for the most Holy Eucharist by their demeanor, their attire, and the manner in which they handle the consecrated species. They should only be used if ordinary ministers of Holy Communion (bishops, priests, deacons) are not present. They should not approach the altar, until after the celebrant has himself received communion. If patens or ciboria are brought from the tabernacle, this should be done by the priest or deacon. They must receive communion before distributing it to others. They should not take patens or chalices from the altar themselves, they should receive them from the priest or deacon.

In distributing Holy Communion they must follow the wording, "the Body of Christ" or "The Blood of Christ." No words or names should be added.

Only a priest, Deacon, or instituted acolyte may purify the vessels after Communion. If there is an extra amount of the precious blood that remains, extraordinary ministers may assist in consuming it.

In the absence of a priest or deacon, an Extraordinary Minister may expose and repose the Blessed Sacrament. But his may only be simply. They do not confer blessings, wear the cope, or veil. Neither do they incense or say prayers. They simply place the Blessed Sacrament out for adoration or return it to the tabernacle.

Q112: Our priest uses large quantities of incense at Mass, creating difficulties even in being able to see with so much cloud. Also people with respiratory issues are struggling. When we speak to us he is dismissive and goes on about history and liturgy. Any thoughts?
- John McElroy, Grand Haven, MI

A: As with most things, moderation is proper when it comes to the use of incense. It would seem, as you describe, too much incense is being burned at one time. And while certain factors such as the size of the church, the height of the ceiling and the ventilation may affect how much can be used, the goal in the modern use of incense is not to overwhelm, or make it difficult to see.

Your pastor's reference to history may indicate that he has something of the Old Testament concept in mind. When the High Priest went into the Holy of Holies of the ancient Temple, ample amounts of incense were used, lest he catch sight of God, and be struck dead.

But given Jesus' ministry to us of sanctifying grace, this sort of concern is not a preoccupation today. Indeed, we are instructed in the liturgy to "Behold the Lamb of God". So, the use of incense to create a kind of impenetrable cloud, is something of a misapplication of an Old Testament concept, and also an excess to be avoided.

However, also to be avoided is the complete rejection of the use of incense in the liturgy which is increasingly demanded by some in parishes.

The use of incense is permitted, even encouraged by the Church for feasts of greater solemnity. It is a beautiful image of prayer and worship ascending to God, as Psalm 141:2 says, *Let my prayer rise like incense, the lifting of my hands as an evening offering.* And so incense symbolizes our prayers and praises going up to God, and it's fragrant aroma is a sign of his blessings to descending gently upon us.

Incense is not to be equated with cigarette smoke, it is not a known carcinogen, it is not a pollutant when used moderately. In fact, incense, like holy water, is often blessed by the priest, and therefore brings blessings.

That said, there are some who suffer from various forms of respiratory distress who may suffer with excessive incense, at least physically. One compromise in these sorts of situations, is to follow the older norms of the Traditional Latin Mass. According to those norms, incense was not carried in the aisle, or the opening and closing processions, but was only imposed and used in the sanctuary area around the altar. As such, at least in larger churches its effect on the whole congregation can be moderated.

Q113: I know women cannot be priests because Jesus chose only men to be apostles. A priest recently said another reason is because of the nuptial meaning of the body. What does this mean?

- Alfred Corigan, Loma Linda, CA

A: To speak of the nuptial meaning of the body, means that the very design of our body orients us toward a marital relationship. The man is meant for the woman, the woman for the man. And in this complementary relationship which we call marriage, there is the fruitfulness of children. In effect, our body says to us, "You were made for another who will complement and complete you, making your love fruitful."

This is also an image for the spiritual life, wherein God speaks of his relationship to his people in marital, imagery. Israel was frequently described as God's bride. In the New Testament, Jesus is the Groom and his Church, is his bride. The Church, and her members are called to relate to the Lord, to be completed by him and complemented by him such that their love bears fruit.

The sacrament of Holy Matrimony, is also a sign of God's relationship to his people, he the groom, we the bride. Even celibates, manifest the nuptial meaning of the human person. As a priest, I am not a bachelor. I have a bride, the Church. Religious sisters also manifest a marital relationship, where Jesus is the Groom, they his bride.

To speak, therefore, of the nuptial meaning of the body, is to insist that the sexual distinctions of male and female are not merely arbitrary physical aspects. Rather, they bespeak deeper, spiritual realities that we must learn to appreciate, and respect. Men and women are different, and manifest different aspects of God's relationship. Women, manifest the glory of the Church as bride. Men manifest the glory of Christ as groom.

In terms of the priesthood, this is important, because Christ in his humanity, is not simply male, he is groom, and the sacred liturgy is a wedding feast; Christ the groom, intimately with his bride the Church.

Thus, your pastor, is invoking rich theological teaching, which helps to explain one reason *why* Christ chose only men for the priesthood.

Q114: I belong to a rather traditional parish. We had successfully evaded the use of the advent wreath, until our new pastor put one out this past Advent. I don't like the advent wreath for two reasons. First, it is a modern innovation, not proper to the Roman Rite. Secondly, it had its origins in the Lutheran Church. Are not advent wreaths really an illicit intrusion into the Roman Catholic liturgy? *-name withheld, via email*

A: I don't suppose it's an unwarranted intrusion, any more than poinsettias are during Christmas, or any other extraneous decoration. Things like decorations, are not intrinsic to the liturgy, and are not really referenced in liturgical books.

Perhaps there is some violation of liturgical norms in some parishes where a kind of para-liturgical service is conducted for the lighting of the advent candle. I have observed where the families are invited to come up to light the candle while some verse of Scripture is read etc. These sorts of things might be considered an intrusion. But if the advent wreath is simply there, and the candles lit before Mass, there seems to be little harm in it.

As for Lutheran roots, most historical researchers would probably confirm this. Catholic parishes have adapted the advent wreath by the use of purple, rather than red candles.

You are certainly free to like or dislike the tradition of the advent wreath. Most Catholics I speak with find it meaningful. But some caution is in order regarding your rejection of something simply because it is either modern, or comes from outside Catholic sources.

In the first place, your concern is somewhat at odds with the Catholic instinct, which down to the centuries has often taken up things from the secular world, or other religious traditions, even non-Christian ones. It is part of the genius of Catholicism to take up whatever is good, true or beautiful in the cultures where she interacts, and give them a distinctively Catholic meaning and flavor.

I would also caution you based on the words of Jesus, who counsels a kind of prudential wisdom about things like these he says: *Every scribe, trained for the kingdom of heaven is like a master of a house, who brings out of his treasure what is new and what is old.* (Matt 13:52)

Therefore, categorically excluding something because it is modern, or outside explicit Catholic origins is not the instinct either of the Church or the Scriptures.

Q115: I read in a certain spiritual work that at the Last Supper the Holy Eucharist returned to being bread only when received by the traitor Judas Iscariot. Is this true? - *WB Flores, Pleican, LA*

A: No, when the bread and wine are consecrated and become the Body, Blood, Soul and Divinity of Jesus Christ, this effects a permanent and substantial change, such that the Body and Blood of Christ will not go back to being something else. Further, there's no reason, biblically or theologically, to hold that the case of Judas would be any different.

Q116: I was taught to abstain from food or drink at least one hour before receiving Holy Communion. Lately I've been seeing people at Mass drinking bottled water before Communion. This includes a Deacon sitting with the priest at the altar. I don't understand this. Has there been a change in the rules for fasting, etc.? – *Joe Sikora, via email*

A: Drinking water does not break the fast before communion. The current rule, in place since 1964 says, "*A person who is to receive the Most Holy Eucharist is to abstain for at least one hour before holy communion from any food and drink, except for only water and medicine.* (see Canon 919).

It is a bit odd for a liturgical minister to be drinking bottled water in the Sanctuary. Perhaps the deacon has a health problem. But, precluding that, one would think it was usually possible to go without water for an hour or two. Water bottles are a kind of modern fad. We used to manage quite well without them.

Q117: Our parish posted the availability of "gluten free hosts." Is this not another diminishment of the true presence? How could the Body of Christ make anyone sick? – *Susana Gilardi, Poolesville, MD*

A: So called "gluten free hosts" are not utterly free of all gluten. There are still some trace amounts. The US Bishops Conference allows the use of very low gluten hosts and urges additional caution by listing three reputable suppliers of them on the USCCB website.

As for the Blessed Sacrament making some one sick, it is not the Sacrament that does so, but the "accidents." While your acknowledgement of the True Presence is laudable, it is important to remember that Catholic teaching states that though the bread is transubstantiated, the "accidents" remain.

The "accidents" are the physical attributes of the bread and wine - that is, what can be seen, touched, tasted, or measured. These remain, though the substance of bread and wine change to become the Body, Blood, Soul and Divinity of the Jesus. Hence it does not follow that one could not be affected by gluten in a consecrated Host, or by alcohol in the consecrated Blood, for these attributes remain to our senses.

Q118: Our archdiocese has decided that all receiving communion should remain standing until all have completed receiving. The rationale is a sign of unity. However, this does not seem very worshipful, and though we are permitted to be seated after the celebrant is seated, very little time is given for prayer. I've chosen not to remain standing, but to observe the traditional practice of returning to my pew, and kneeling in prayer. And I being disobedient? *-name withheld, Lakewood, WA*

A: The instructions in the Missal are silent regarding the posture of the faithful during the Communion Rite. Though after the Rite they may sit or kneel during the silence (# 43). A Bishop does have some authority to establish norms that do not violate universal norms. Other things being equal, it would seem the faithful should give due consideration, and strive to follow these norms.

However, the norm you have articulated does present a few practical issues. Most notably, it would seem that the elderly, and others with issues of physical stamina, might find it difficult to stand for so long. Also, as you point out, it does make prayer difficult at a time that is often very precious to people for a quiet moment with the Lord. Given the rather hurried nature of most American liturgies, it seems unlikely that significant time will be reserved after all are seated quiet prayer.

Given that the local bishop does have the authority to request certain norms to be observed, I might encourage you to strive to listen to what he's teaching. Perhaps there is an issue in the local church is trying to address. While prayer certainly pleases the Lord, obedience pleases him even more. Scripture says, *Sacrifice or offering you wished not, but ears open to obedience you gave me"* (Ps 40:4)

In terms of answering your question in an absolutely legal sense, while not a canonist, I suspect that this norm should be interpreted in the same way that the norm for receiving communion standing in this country is interpreted. While the norm requests, for the sake of unity, the faithful receive Communion standing, an exception is to be made for those who strongly prefer to receive kneeling. (GIRM #160) So it seems allowance needs to be made for the faithful we strongly prefer kneeling in silent prayer.

As in all things, balance is required in understanding the nature of Holy Mass. Mass is essentially the communal act of Christ with all his people, it is not essentially a private devotion. However, times of silent prayer and reflection are often mentioned the general norms. But frankly, with the rather hurried masses, of modern times, periods of silent reflection are often nonexistent. In this sense, your concerns are understandable

I surely encourage you to stay in communion with your bishop, and to continue to raise your concerns.

Q119: This past Sunday our priest had us sing a Protestant version of the Our Father. The congregation really enjoyed it but I wonder if it is approved for use in the Catholic Mass.
— *Carolyn Pohlen, Hutchinson, MN*

A: Presumably, you refer to the well-known musical version of the Our Father by Albert Hay Malotte, which has the soaring doxology at the end: "For thine is the Kingdom and the power and glory for ever and ever. Amen"

Liturgically, this presents two problems. One is the translation of the doxology, which though the difference is minor, is at variance with the approved Catholic translation.

The second problem is that the musical arrangement does not reasonably allow the celebrant to proclaim or sing what is known as the "embolism," the prayer that begins "Deliver, Lord we pray from every evil, graciously grant peace in our days...." This is because the musical arrangement of the Malotte Our Father is reaching a climax and moves right into the doxology. To stop the song at that moment and have the celebrant recite the embolism is clumsy at best, and does dishonor to the musical setting as well. It is almost like stopping the National Anthem at its musical climax "For the land of the free...!" and inserting a verbal interjection. It just doesn't work well.

Hence, when the Malott Our Father is proposed for use in the Catholic Mass it is usually sung straight through. But this is improper liturgically. Thus, beautiful though it is, the Malotte Our Father cannot reasonably be used during the Mass. It would seem that it can however be used in other liturgical settings with minor adaptions, since in those liturgies the embolism is not required.

Q120: If a permanent deacon gets divorced and remarried, would he still be a permanent deacon? - *Allen Eberle Hague, ND*

A: No, a man in the situation you describe could not continue to function as a permanent deacon. However, some distinctions are necessary so as to clarify the answer.

While celibacy is not required of a married man who becomes a permanent deacon, celibacy *does* apply to some permanent deacons. And this can happen in a couple of different ways. First of all, if an unmarried man becomes a permanent deacon, he is required to promise celibacy at his ordination, and to remain celibate for the rest of his life. Secondly, if the spouse of a permanent deacon dies he is expected to live celibately from that point forward. He is not to date, or seek a new spouse.

In the unfortunate situation you describe of a deacon who is divorced, he also would be expected to live celibately from that point forward. This would be truly even if his marriage received a declaration of nullity from the Church.

In the thankfully rare situation where permanent deacons become divorced, the local bishop usually permits such a deacon to continue ministering as a deacon. But the bishop also needs to ensure that the deacon did all he could to reasonably save his marriage, and did not casually cast aside his marital vows, which would be a scandal. Presuming this can be assured and that scandal can be avoided, the bishop can permit a divorced permanent deacon to continue ministering. But, as already stated, he must live celibately from that point forward.

What if the Deacon where to refuse to follow Church law, either by flagrantly divorcing and remarrying, or by remarrying after the death of a spouse? In such cases, he would be suspended from practicing his ministry as a deacon, and likely be laicized. Since ordination confers a character he would still "be" a deacon, but could not, in any way, perform the ministry of the diaconate.

Q121: Where does the word "Lent" come from? In my native Spanish we just call the season, "cuaresma" which seems more descriptive.
— *Anna Gonzalez, via email.*

A: You are right. The Latin title for this period is Quadragesima and is best translated, "fortieth day (before Easter)" or more loosely "the forty days." Most of the Romance Languages keep this root in their words for the season (e.g. *cuaresma, quaresma, carême, quaresima*) and these are as you say, more descriptive and less abstract.

The word "Lent" seems to come from Germanic roots wherein the words *lenz* and *lente* refer to the spring season when the days "lengthen." Thus the word "Lent" describes less the liturgical time frame and more the seasonal one. So, as the days lengthen our thoughts move to Easter and, beginning forty days before, we spend time spiritually preparing for that greatest feast of the Church's Year.

The notion of forty days of course reminds us of the forty days Christ spent in the desert fasting and praying in preparation for his public ministry. We are encouraged to go into the desert with him spiritually and thus also be strengthened through the spiritual exercises of resisting temptation, praying and fasting.

"Giving up something" for Lent is not merely for its own sake, but rather to make room for other things. Thus, if we forgo some lawful pleasure, we can perhaps be freer to pray; and whatever money we may save by simplifying, can be given to the poor.

Q122: With premarital sex and cohabitation so common, what is a priest to do when preparing these couples for Matrimony? It seems most clergy just look the other way. Is that right? -*name withheld, Boston, MA*

A: As you rightly point out, fornication, (premarital sex), is a very serious sin, which has sadly received widespread acceptance in our culture. The related sin and trend of cohabitation makes matters even worse because of its public nature and capacity to give scandal. Scripture in many places describes the sin of fornication as a mortal sin, declaring that it excludes one from the kingdom of heaven; (for example Ephesians 5:5; one Corinthians 6:9; Galatians 5:21, among others).

God consistently condemns fornication because of the harm it does the human person, the sacrament of holy matrimony, and children. Children conceived of fornication are at high risk for abortion since 85 % of abortions are performed on single women. If they survive this risk, they are still likely to be raised in irregular situations that are not best for them. This in turn leads to many other social ills.

Consequently fornicators not only sin against God's gifts of marriage and sexuality, but also sin against justice by engaging in behaviors that harm society and children.

What then is a priest to do when he prepares couples for marriage who are often cohabiting? Of course there are many prudential factors involved. At least the couple is trying to set things right. Having them seek separate domiciles is best but not always feasible. But surely every priest ought to teach such couples of the seriousness of their sin and insist they live chastely and sleep in separate rooms. While he cannot enforce this, he ought to instill in them a holy reverence for God who sees all things.

In order to avoid scandal that is easily given by cohabiters who cannot separate many priest make some mention at the wedding of the fact that he instructed the couple to live chastely and was glad that they were willing to give heed to the holy instruction of God. He can be discrete but clear, and even use a little humor. But simply ignoring the issue altogether when a couple has publicly cohabited offends against the common good by giving the impression that such behavior is good or no big deal. Silent pulpits are a sadly common source of scandal

Q123: Why does the priest put water in the wine at Mass?
— *name withheld*

A: The practice of mixing water and wine was common in the ancient world. Wines were usually heavier than most modern vintages and to dilute them a bit made them more palatable and less inebriating. People also drank more wine since water in the ancient world could not be purified easily as is done today. Thus the wine used at Mass was mixed with water before the consecration in the usual manner of all wine.

Mystically it came to represent our inclusion into Christ's Body by our baptism. The priest says: "By the mystery of the water and wine, may we come to share in the divinity of Christ who humbled himself to share in our humanity".

Though the practical reason to mix water and wine no longer is needed, it still remains a powerful symbol and so its practice remains.

Q124: I recently received an annulment from the Church and had my current marriage validated by the priest. And yet, in Matthew 19 Jesus says to divorce and marry another is to commit adultery. What am I to do? -*name withheld, Angus, TX*

A: Trust the Church in this to which Christ gave the power to bind and loose.

In the Passage you reference, Jesus says, "What God has joined together let no one separate." (Matt 19:6). But not every exchange of marriage vows is *ipso facto* a work of God. Vows must be properly exchanged by people of requisite maturity etc. The annulment process seeks to investigate if God had in fact joined the couple or not, based on evidence supplied. If not, a person is free to marry, for they were not truly married the first time.

Q125: In my parish at daily Mass the Alleluia and verse before the Gospel is omitted. Is this permitted? -*Roseanna Miller, Bayonne, NJ*

A: Yes. The General Instruction of the Liturgy (# 63) indicates that the Gospel acclamation, if not sung, may be omitted. And while this does not seem to forbid reciting it, the acclamation is generally envisioned as a sung text. Hence if no one can reasonably lead the singing, it is permitted to omit it. Another possibility is to sing the "Alleluia" without the verse. Generally most congregations are able to sing a well known melody of Alleluia without a cantor. But here too, situations vary and the celebrant remains free to omit the Gospel Acclamation.

Q126: Can Catholics, confess their sins directly to God, as do Non-Catholics, to have their sins also forgiven - even though it is not as efficacious as the Sacrament? - *A. F. Koselke, via email*

A: When he comes to venial sins, Catholics are able to confess their sins directly to God. Mortal sins however require the sacrament. While it suffices to confess venial sins privately to God, Catholics are still encouraged to get to confession with some frequency, even if they are not aware of mortal sins. There are many salutary reasons for this. On the one hand, it instills a reflective discipline regarding sin. Being accountable, to another person is also helpful. Alone we are often too easy or too hard on ourselves. Ideally, most priest have training and experience that can help them to guide people in their moral reflection. Also, when we sin, we usually harm not only ourselves, but also the community. And the priest represents not only God, but also the community of the church.

Also, as you point out, the celebration of the sacraments are always more efficacious. The sacrament of confession, grants absolution, and the grace to avoid sin in the future, along with sanctifying grace.

Q127: In my new parish, the prayers of the faithful go on for a long time, including the reading of long lists of the names of the sick, and selections from the prayer request book in the vestibule. Is this proper?
— *name withheld*

A: The prayer the faithful is general in nature and should thus avoid overly specific prayer requests. For example, we pray for all the sick, not just some of the sick mentioned by name. *The intentions announced should be sober, be composed freely but prudently, and be succinct, and they should express the prayer of the entire community.* (GIRM 71)

When intentions become too specific they stray from the needs of the whole community and become too individualistic.

Q128: With all the talk about annulments and the Synod lately, I have heard of something called the Pauline Privilege. Someone the radio was saying how this is just another example of how the Church plays loose with Jesus teaching anyway, and should further loosen her rules.
— *Ed Jensen, Tampa, FL*

A: The Pauline Privilege is the dissolution of a natural (not sacramental) marriage which was contracted between two non-Christians, one of whom has since become a Christian. It is called the Pauline Privilege because it is based upon St. Paul's words in 1 Corinthians. *If any brother has a wife who is an unbeliever, and she consents to live with him, he should not divorce her. If any woman has a husband who is an unbeliever, and he consents to live with her, she should not divorce him...But if the unbelieving partner desires to separate, let it be so; in such a case, the brother or sister is not bound. For God has called us to peace."* (1 Cor 7:12-14)

Such marriages began with neither party as a Christian or a Catholic. But at a later time, one partner converts and is baptized.
The Pauline Privilege is not really an annulment because it dissolves a real but natural marriage, whereas an annulment is a declaration that there never was a valid marriage to begin with. But it is possible to see at least some "natural marriages" as meeting Jesus' own exception to forbidden divorce

and remarriage. For Jesus only forbade the dissolution of "what God has joined together."

But note, as St. Paul says, if the non-believing party agrees to live with the believer in peace, then they should remain married. Only if the non-believing party does not agree to live in peace (e.g. by abusing the Christian religion, tempting the Christian to infidelity, or preventing the children from being raised in Christian faith) can the believing party be released from the bond of the non-sacramental marriage and be free to remarry.

It is hard to argue that the Church "playing loose" with Jesus' teaching when the Pauline Privilege is drawn right from the same inspired Scripture, and from the writings of one of the Apostles whom Jesus commissioned to teach and given in his Name. In hearing St. Paul we hear Jesus (see Luke 10:16).

Q129: Where is the Sacrament of Confirmation in the Bible. Growing up in as a Protestant we had no reference to this and did not practice Confirmation. – *Mary Tempi, Newark, NJ*

A: On Pentecost Sunday the apostles and disciples experienced a powerful outpouring the Holy Spirit that they continued to share with later converts by the laying on of hands. The Scriptures describe this as distinct from Baptism.

Thus, Phillip (a deacon) went to Samaria and baptized many there. Hearing of the conversions and baptisms Peter and John came north and laid hands on them and they received the Holy Spirit (Acts 8:14-17). This was done as the text says, *because the Holy Spirit had not yet come on any of them; they had simply been baptized in the name of the Lord Jesus.* (Acts 8:16) This shows some separation in the celebration of these sacraments and a reserving of Confirmation to bishops.

However, later in Acts we see St. Paul (who was a bishop) first baptizing a group, and them imposing hands on them so they would receive the Holy Spirit (Acts 19:5-6). This shows the sacraments, though distinct, being celebrated together.

Q130: Our young priest faces the altar rather than the people for Mass. Is this allowed? – *name withheld, SC*

A: Technically yes, and there are good liturgical and theological roots for the practice. Pastorally however, as your puzzlement shows, a lot of teaching is necessary to explain the practice. Further, one might also argue that an individual priest ought not make a large change like this at a Sunday Mass without consulting his bishop.

Careful teaching and organic change is the better way to reintroduce the ancient, and many would say, correct stance for the Eucharistic Prayer. This can help avoid misunderstandings and backlash, as well as local and regional divisions that become a countersign of the charity and unity that should pervade the Sacred Liturgy.

Q131: Are there theological reasons that only the priest or deacon can purify the sacred vessels at Mass? – *Chris Cunningham, Arlington, VA*

A: I am not aware of theological reasons for this norm. More likely, it is a prudential pastoral stance, which exists to encourage the priest to be more vigilant that vessels are properly purified.

Over the past decades there have been problems associated with the proper purification of vessels, which led to small fragments of the host, and drops of the precious blood being found about. There were also problems associated with the precious blood being poured down sinks etc. Priests are expected to be guardians of the sacred Eucharist. The requirement that the priest now personally attend to purifications seems more a disciplinary norm than a strictly theological matter.

Q132: Although the Church insists on the biblical teaching of marriage, in the current marriage debates many of our critics like to point out that the Bible reports polygamy is a widespread practice that is not condemned by God or the prophets and thus even the Bible sets aside What we call God's plan for marriage. How should I answer this?
- *Mary Carter, Washington, DC*

A: That something is reported in the Scripture should not necessarily be seen as approval. Murder, incest and theft are reported but this should not be seen to condone what God elsewhere condemns.

It is clear that many of the patriarchs, including those highly favored and praised by God, did practice polygamy. David, and Moses were among them, along with Jacob and others. How widespread the practice of polygamy was in ancient Israel is unclear, but it seems unlikely that most Jewish men would have had enough money to support more than one wife.

It is notable, and mysterious that there are not strong denunciations of polygamy from God and his prophets. However, though reporting the fact of polygamy rather neutrally, the Scriptures also do not neglect to report the many problems that emerge from polygamy. The problems occurred not so much among the wives, but between the different sons of the different wives. At stake were inheritance rights and other significant blessings that accrued to the favored sons.

The Memorable story of Joseph, and the way his brothers conspired first to kill him, and then later to sell him into slavery, emerges from the jealousies of different brothers by Jacobs different wives, and the perception that Jacob favored Joseph.

King David's house was also wracked by many internecine conflicts related especially to a rivalry between Absalom and Solomon. Horrifying bloodshed also occurred in the household of Gideon. And while the Bible does in fact record the polygamy, it also teaches that it brings with it many awful problems.

By the time of Jesus, the practice seems to have all but disappeared. Jesus also makes it clear that whatever provisions Moses and the patriarchs may have allowed in the reign of sin, in the reign the Kingdom of God, God's original plan was going to be observed. That plan was announced in Genesis 2 and clearly states that God's vision for marriage is one man for one woman in a stable, lifelong relationship bearing the fruit of the children.

This has been, and remains the Church's constant teaching.

Q133: in my last confession, the priest used words of absolution that were not what I'm used to hearing. I can't remember what they were, but they weren't even close, and I did not hear the word "absolve." Was the sacrament valid? - *name withheld, Minneapolis, MN*

A: It is doubtful. Matter (in this case the imposition of hands) and form (in this case proper words of absolution) make the Sacrament. It is not possible to affirm that a sacrament took place when one or both of these is significantly violated. It is of course hard to imagine God holding you responsible for the sinful or inept actions of a priest, since you approached the sacrament in good faith. Hence you need not fear the judgment of God, regarding any serious sins you might have confessed in the botched confession.

However, it is advisable for you to consult another priest in the sacrament of confession and review with him any serious sins since the last good (valid) confession you had. You might also seek his advice on reporting the incident to local church authorities. I am sorry this happened.

Q134: Does the Church have a position on saying Mass in a private home? A retired priest lives near our parish and says Mass in his home. A few people who do not seem to like our liturgies attend it, and this causes tension. *—name withheld*

A: There is not a juridical problem here, given the situation you describe. However, "home-masses" ought not be conducted without the approval of the territorial pastor. These days many dioceses have limited the celebration of home masses, which used to be very popular. Masses are best celebrated in a church or oratory, at the dedicated altar. Home masses should only be celebrated for serious pastoral needs (See *Redemptionis Sacramentum* # 108)

However, the norm can allow for a retired priest to celebrate in his home (especially if he has mobility issues) and a few of the faithful can attend.

So, if the local pastor and diocesan norms permit, what you describe is allowable as a pastoral provision for a retired priest.
As for the tensions you describe, it is unfortunate, but allow the two priests to work that out. Pastors sometimes choose to leave certain things unresolved, since resolving them might cause more problems.

Q135: Please explain the difference of a priest who is suspended and one who is defrocked. - *Barry Quinn, Philadelphia, PA*

A: The term "defrocked" is not a term used in the Church's Canon Law and even its secular use varies. Church law speaks of priests who might be suspended, and those who are laicized.
A priest who is suspended has his faculties to publicly preach and celebrate the sacraments removed. In certain cases he may be permitted to say Mass privately and may still retain some obligations to say the Divine Office. He still lives celibately. If the troubles that led to his suspension can be resolved, he can be restored to public ministry.

A priest who is laicized however is legally regarded as a layman. He cannot say Mass at all, even privately, he is no longer obliged say the Divine Office, and may get married. Some priests are punitively laicized because they committed serious sins as a priest. Other priests are laicized at their own request because they sadly are no longer willing to live the life to which they were ordained.

Q136: As a youth, the American flag was displayed in the church, and at each church I attended thereafter. But now, the flag has disappeared when a new pastor arrived. It is stored in a closet and only displayed when the Knights of Columbus holds a function in the social hall. . I was told the Vatican had suggested the national flag not be displayed. Is this so? - *Nicola Tranchitella, Clarksville, MD*

A: There is no specific policy in the norms regarding the display of flags in the church. According the USCCB website: Neither the Code of Canon law, nor the liturgical books of the Roman rite comment on this practice. As a result, the question of whether and how to display the American flag in a Catholic Church is left up to the judgment of the diocesan bishop, [or] the discretion of the pastor.

Sensibilities about this matter very from place to place, and person to person. There had developed a fairly widespread tradition of displaying the American and Papal flags in the church, even within the sanctuary. In more recent decades, some preferred to move the flags outside the sanctuary, and even outside the nave and into the vestibule. Some churches do not have flags at all.

These differences reflect any number of things to include: custom, space, liturgical preferences, and even political notions. Each pastor needs to prudently weigh a number of factors in deciding the best place for flags.

In my own parish, the American and Papal flags are within the sanctuary of the church to either side of the high altar. None of this causes any debates or concerns among the faithful in my parish.

While some in the wider Church object of the display of the American flag within the sanctuary, theologically it can be justified by considering that patriotism is related to the Fourth Commandment that we should honor our father and mother. To a certain degree, our country nourishes and provides for us like a parent and it is here that we are born. A properly balanced patriotism and love of one's country, which avoids triumphalism, is a virtue. The presence of one's national flag, can point to this virtue, well as remind us of our duty to pray for our country and its leaders.

However, certain pastors and communities might prudently decide the sanctuary is not the best place for flags. Nevertheless, one would hope that a suitable and significance place on the parish grounds for the display of flags could be found. I would encourage you to stay in conversation with your pastor about this a reach a charitable solution that respects his concerns and yours as well.

Q137: In John 3:5 Jesus says that no one can enter the Kingdom of God except by water and the Holy Spirit. So it seems that unbaptized children, Muslims, Jews et al. cannot go to heaven. I am personally worried about my five un-baptized grandchildren.
– *John Rebar, West Seattle, WA*
A: The Church teaches the necessity of baptism for salvation in concordance with the Holy Scriptures. Thus, a person who willfully refuses to do so, knowing the requirements for faith in Jesus and the reception a Baptism, cannot be saved.

However, not everyone does fully know or understand necessity of baptism and faith in Jesus. Some as you note are young children who cannot reasonably know, and whose parents have failed in their duties. Others may be raised in largely non-Catholic settings, or even in settings that are hostile to the Christian faith. God does not absolutely require of people what they cannot have reasonably known. Thus we presume that since God is just, he can and does deal with these sorts of situations in ways known to him, and that people will be judged on what they could have reasonably known. Though we cannot know absolutely of the fate of unbaptized children (since God has not revealed it), or of adults, we can be confident that God, who wants to save all, will deal with them justly and reasonably.

Jesus' clear teaching however on the necessity of Baptism must not be lightly cast aside either, simply based on reasonable speculation by us. You as a Grandfather should firmly admonish your own children of the need to have their children baptized at once, and warn them that their own salvation may be at stake if they fail to do so. Mere encouragement, if it is not enough, may need to give way to insistence and vigorous warning. You may do well to consult with your parish priest and other family members to turn this rather unfortunate state of affairs into an evangelical and teaching moment.

Q138: I was told that we can't sing the song "Yahweh, The Faithful One" anymore. I haven't heard anything from the church magisterium about this issue. - *Craig Kappel, Dickenson, ND*

A: In 2008 the Bishop's Conference did send word that the Tetragrammaton YHWH should not be said or spoken aloud in Catholic Liturgy. In Jewish times, it was held to be unpronounceable and hence was replaced by an alternate name: 'Adonai' (Lord). Similarly, Greek translations of the Bible have used the word "Kyrios" and Latin, "Dominus"; both of which also mean Lord. This request to avoid the speaking this particular form of the divine Name is a way of remaining faithful to the Church's tradition, stretching back even into Jewish times.

The original Roman directive was given in "Liturgiam Authenticam," the 2001 document on liturgical translations.

Hence it seems clear that songs and Biblical translations that use "Yahweh" should be adapted so that this form of the Holy and Divine Name is not said or sung aloud.

Q139: A friend told me he was insulted that, in confession, priest asked him how many times he had committed a certain sin. How specific does one have to be when confessing sexual sins. And does one have to mention how many times a certain sin is committed? — *Armel Audet, via email*

A: Serious or mortal sins need to be confessed in kind and number. Sexual sins are considered, objectively speaking, to be serious sins and thus it is important to say how many times a certain sin was committed since one's last confession. This helps the priest gauge whether a mortal sin is a frequent problem, or rare.

Likewise mortal sins need to be specified to some degree: missing Mass, telling a serious lie, committing a certain sexual sin, being violently angry, and so forth. Since sexual sins come in various types it is also important to distinguish what sort of sexual sin is meant: entertaining lustful thoughts, looking at pornography, looking with lust, masturbation, inappropriate touching, fornication, contraceptive sex, adultery, homosexual acts, etc. Simply to say, "I sinned against the 6th commandment" or "I was impure" is not usually enough.

Thus sins of this sort should be confessed in kind and number. If the number is not exactly known, some estimate is fine.

In a way it is like going to the doctor and saying, "I have had serious headaches." The next thing the doctor needs to know is how frequently, and to some degree the nature of the headache: throbbing or dull, is one's eyesight affected, does it hurt more in the back or front of the head etc. Then the doctor can help more, and know if it is a serious matter or not.

It should also be said that, regarding sexual sins, one should avoid giving too much information. The list above should usually be sufficient for the priest to understand. Too much information can unsettle the priest and cause temptation. If a priest is confused, or needs some clarity he can discretely ask, but should himself avoid asking in ways that humiliate or in any way seem to pry. The goal is to have the necessary information, no more and no less.

Q140: A couple of questions about the altar. I noticed in one parish in our area that the altar had six candles, at another parish there are only two. Is there a proper number? Also one group in another parish places flowers ringing the whole altar. But in our pastor will not let us do this and says flowers cannot be placed on the altar.
– *Agatha Morris, Newark, NJ*

A: As for the number of candles, there are different options and traditions. The General instruction in the Roman Missal says, *The altar is to be covered with at least one white cloth. In addition, on or next to the altar are to be placed candlesticks with lighted candles: at least two in any celebration, or even four or six, especially for a Sunday Mass or a Holyday of Obligation, or if the Diocesan Bishop celebrates, then seven candlesticks with lighted candles.* (GIRM 117). Since many altars today face the people, fewer candles have been preferred. However in recent years, following the lead of Pope Benedict, some have taken to placing six candles and a cross on the altar again as was common before 1970.

As for flowers, your pastor is right. The Instructions in the Missal state: *Floral decoration should always show moderation and be arranged around the altar rather than on the altar table.* (GIRM # 305).

Q141: I was visiting a parish out of my area and was surprised to see that the altar was bare until the offertory when, along with bread and wine, altar cloths and candles were brought in procession. The altar was then clothed and candles placed and lit, along with the bread and wine. Is something new? - *Janet Murphy, via email*

A: No, it is an innovation not allowed except in the rare circumstance of an altar being consecrated, or on Good Friday when the altar remains bare until the distribution of Holy Communion. But in no case are altar cloths brought in the offertory procession.

The General instructions of the Roman Missal direct and presume that the altar is prepared before the Mass begins. It says, under the heading "Things to be prepared:" The altar is to be covered with at least one white cloth. In addition, on or next to the altar are to be placed candlesticks with lighted candles: at least two in any celebration, or even four or six, especially for a Sunday Mass or a Holyday of Obligation, or if the Diocesan Bishop celebrates, then seven candlesticks with lighted candles.... (GIRM # 117)

Thus the instruction direct that the Altar should be prepared in this way, prior to Mass.

Q142: A Friend of mine in another diocese of the U.S. told me that her pastor said January 1st is not a Holy Day of obligation. Is this correct?
— *name withheld, Des Moines, IA*

A: No, January 1 the Solemnity of Mary Mother of God is a holy day of obligation, UNLESS it occurs on a Saturday or a Monday. When that is the case obligation to attend Mass does not bind.

The Statement of the American Bishop on Holy Days of Obligation goes as follows: In addition to Sunday, the days to be observed as holy days of obligation in the Latin Rite dioceses of the United States of America, in conformity with canon 1246, are as follows: January 1, the solemnity of Mary, Mother of God, Thursday of the Sixth Week of Easter, the solemnity of the Ascension; August 15, the solemnity of the Assumption of the Blessed Virgin Mary; November 1, the solemnity of All Saints; December 8, the solemnity of the Immaculate Conception; December 25, the solemnity of the Nativity of Our Lord Jesus Christ
Whenever January 1, the solemnity of Mary, Mother of God, or August 15, the solemnity of the Assumption, or November 1, the solemnity of All Saints, falls on a Saturday or on a Monday, the precept to attend Mass is abrogated.

Also in some diocese Ascension is moved to Sunday, so that results in one Less Holy Day of obligation.

To many, this system seems confusing where days bind in some years and not others. It was a kind of compromise the Bishops made between two viewpoints. On view said that Holy Days were important and should be observed. The other view emphasized a pastoral solicitude wherein Catholics ought not be required to come to Mass two days in a row.

Thus the Holy Days that fell in a given year on Monday or Saturday did not bind, otherwise they did. However December 8th (because it is the patronal Feast of the U.S) always binds, as does Christmas and Ascension (where it is celebrated on Thursday).

As you can see, even experienced priests and parish staffs struggle to remember all this. The old system, though more demanding, was easy to understand and remember. As you might suspect, attendance at holy days has plummeted in recent years. This is due as much to confusion as to a perception that most holy days are only relatively important (when they don't inconvenience too much), not intrinsically important.

One may wish for a simpler rule in the future, but it seems unlikely we will ever have "high holy days" in the Church like we once did.

Q143: It seems to me that, at Mass, priority should be given for the congregation to hear the priest and be involved with him in the preparation of the gifts and the prayers he says as he mixes the water and wine etc. But it appears that more emphasis is given to singing at these times. - *William Dignan, Hanover, PA*

A: Liturgical norms of the Church seek to balance a number of things, such as the experience of Mass as a personal encounter with Christ and yet as a communal act of worship, or, actions that pertain to the priest, and what pertains to other liturgical ministers and the faithful who are gathered.
It is clear that you prefer less singing and being directly engaged with the actions on the altar.

However, in the prayers of the preparation of the gifts, the norms implicitly presume and favor that some sort of singing is going on. The celebrant is instructed to say these prayers inaudibly, if singing is going on, and that otherwise he "may" (not must) say them aloud.
Other prayers at that time are always to be said inaudibly by the priest, such as when he mixes the water and wine, and bows to say the prayer that begins "With a spirit of humility..." The prayer that the Lord wash away his iniquity as he washes his hands is also to be said inaudibly even if there is no music.

All of this is the way of demonstrating that during the preparation of the gifts, the direct engagement of the faithful in the action is not the only or primary point. Hence, congregational singing, or the taking up a collection etc. are not distractions. The priest is performing these actions as a priest along with the deacon and other ministers, on behalf of the faithful.

As for hearing and seeing everything the priest is doing, this has value but is not the only value. Prior to 1970 the priest who was turned toward the altar whispered almost the entire Eucharistic prayer. (In the Eastern Churches, today, the Priest often goes behind an iconostasis) Though today this is seldom the case in the Ordinary Form of the Roman Rite, Mass, the principle still applies that the priest at the altar has gone up before God and is speaking to Him and acting on behalf of the faithful in the person of Christ.

Q144: Our pastor uses a single crucifix for the Veneration of the Cross on Good Friday. He explains that this is the Church norm (which I don't doubt). However with the large crowd, it took 50 minutes this past Good Friday to complete the adoration. Other parishes I know use multiple crosses when there are large numbers. Your thoughts please.
– *John Downs, Fairfax Station, VA*

As you have noted, the norms do specify that only one cross should be used for adoration at the Good Friday Service. The norm states: *Only one cross should be used for adoration. If, because a the large number of people, it is not possible for all to approach individually, the Priest, after some of the clergy and faithful have adored, takes the Cross and, standing in the middle before the altar, invites the people to adore…and holds the cross elevated higher for a brief time, for the faithful to adore in silence.* (Missale Romanum # 19)

The adoration of only one Cross, though time consuming, makes sense. Only one cross is solemnly brought into the Church and unveiled. It is the real focus of the Good Friday service.

Thus, a pastor and congregation have a decision to make when large numbers are present. Either they are going to extend time for adoration and make it a time of meditation while all adore, or the adoration will be shortened in the way the missal describes. Adoration is accomplished in other ways than a kiss.

Further, The full singing of the reproaches and other chants, and meditating on them, is one way the Church seeks to draw us into prayer rather than merely waiting for the adoration to be done.

The 50 minutes you describe is surely long and probably required abbreviation. In less extreme cases, we ought not be in a hurry during the triduum services which are, of their nature, extended and meant to provoke deeper meditation on the sacred mysteries.

Q145: Many years ago in my youth I recall that Passion Sunday and Palm Sunday were different Sundays. Is this so, and why then is the Passion read on Palm Sunday? – *Leo Renne, Jackson, MI*

A: Yes, prior to 1970 the Fifth Sunday of Lent was called "Passion Sunday" and Statues and Crosses were traditional veiled beginning that Sunday until Easter. The reason for this title was that the Church was setting her sights on the Passion. The following Sunday was called Palm Sunday and opened Holy Week. After 1970 the two Sundays were combined on Palm Sunday and the Fifth Sunday of Lent became Passion (or Palm) Sunday.

The Reading of the Passion on Palm Sunday however is a very old tradition since it was accepted that many would not or could not attend on Good Friday. Give the importance of the passion being heard in its entirety by the faithful the Church assigned the reading of it on Palm Sunday, the Sunday closest to Easter.

Q146: The Nicene Creed says "he suffered death and was buried and rose AGAIN on the third day." Why the word "again"? Did he rise more than once? – *name withheld, South Burlington, VT*

A: Christ rose from the dead only once. The Latin text of the Creed says merely, *resurrexit tertia die* (he rose on the third day).

The use of the word "again" is merely an English mode of speech. While not strictly required, we tend in English to use "again" to indicate a restoration of a previous state. Thus, I might say, "Joe went to the store and came back again." I clearly don't mean he came back more than once. In a general sense "again" is emphasizing his return, that he is here NOW, that his status of being away is no longer the case. But more basically, it's just the way we talk. The translation of the Creed is simply using this common mode of speaking.

4. MORAL ISSUES

Q147: It has come to my attention that my 22-year-old son, who does not live with us, views a lot of Internet pornography. What can I say to him to dissuade him? — *name withheld*

A: Biblically, pornography is sinful, and unfit for a Christian. Jesus, for example, forbids a man to look with lust on a woman (Matt 5:28-30), which of course is the precise purpose of pornography. Other passages forbid sexual immorality as well (1 Cor 6:9, 18ff; Eph 5:3ff; Col 3:5ff), etc. As these passages make clear, such sins are mortal and un-repented of, and exclude one from the Kingdom of Heaven.

Psychologically, pornography is unhealthy because it is unreal. It is rooted in fantasy. The photos and movies are photographically enhanced, the models are often surgically altered, etc.

In a way, pornography is cowardly, and appeals those who cannot, or will not, take the risk to live in the real world and make the commitment to live and interact with a real spouse and all that entails.

In real life sex is not had with a body, it is had with a real person, who may not measure up to the fantasies and exotic wishes of pornography addicts. Real people have limits, preferences, moods, and do not simply disappear when sexual pleasure is had. Thus, pornography turns one inward, instills unrealistic notions, and often destroys interest in normal marital life.

Addiction to Internet pornography is growing dramatically, and many are locked into terrible and descending cycles. It is a grave evil and takes terrible personal and family tolls. Many need significant help to break free. Often, a 12-step program under the strict care of a sponsor can help some.

I pray your son will consider the grave spiritual, moral, and psychological ruin that can come from indulging this vice.

Q148: I am an Extraordinary Minister of Holy Communion and was called to the house of a man with a brain tumor who, it was said, would likely die soon. He was unconscious in the room and was being given no food or fluids and according to the wife had been in this condition for days. In effect he was being starved to death. What should I have done?
- *name withheld*

A: Church teaching on this matter is clear. Nutrition and hydration, even by artificial means (e.g. a feeding tube), cannot simply be terminated because doctors have determined that a person will never recover consciousness. The Congregation for the Doctrine of the Faith issued the latest statement back in 2007, and emphasized that administering food and water to a patient in an persistently unconscious state is morally obligatory "to the extent to which, and for as long as, it is shown to accomplish its proper finality, which is the hydration and nourishment of the patient." "In this way suffering and death by starvation and dehydration are prevented,"

Exceptions may occur when patients are unable to assimilate food and water or in the "rare" cases when nutrition and hydration become excessively burdensome for the patient because the fluids swamp the body.

Nutrition and hydration are not extraordinary care since they are not excessively expensive and do not necessarily require hospitalization. Giving them is not a treatment that cures the patient, but is, ordinary care aimed at the preservation of life.

A priest should certainly handle these sorts of cases. The priest for his part, in encountering cases like this should ascertain the facts and be sure it is not a rare case where the food or fluids, because they cannot be digested offer no help, and only intensify suffering. Precluding such rare cases, he should then instruct and admonish the family to see that caretakers provide food and water (usually via a tube).

Unfortunately, if the family or caretaker with medical power of attorney refuses, there are very few legal remedies in most jurisdictions. Judges have usually ruled that food and water through a tube is not required care for those who are unconscious.

Many do die prematurely on account of this flawed understanding of ordinary and necessary medical care. It is another tragic example of the world's rejection of Church's teachings on life.

Q149: St. Thomas Aquinas wrote that life does not begin until the second trimester. How should we answer this, especially in regard to abortion? - *Thomas, Dincher, Williamsport, PA*

A: The wording of your question is slightly inaccurate. St. Thomas did not deny that life in the womb was, in fact, life. The teaching of Aquinas to which you refer is that an unborn baby receives a soul 40 or 80 days after conception, depending on gender. (Note this is much earlier than the second trimester). Aquinas held this opinion based on Aristotle, who said a child has a soul when it first has a human "form"--that is, when the child looks human. The difference in gender was based on the point at which genitals could be observed on miscarried children, earlier for boys, later for girls.
While many link this position of Aquinas to the abortion debate, the date of ensoulment is not essential to the Church's position on the sinfulness of abortion. The Church roots her teaching in Scripture (e.g. Ex 21:22-23; Ps 51:5; Ps. 139:13-16; Job 10:11; Is 44:24; Jer 1:5), Tradition and Natural Law.

St. Thomas never wrote directly on abortion. There are only a couple of indirect references in the Summa (IIa, IIae, q.64, a 8; q.68, a 11). But surely St. Thomas was well aware of the Scriptures above, as well as the ancient teaching of Tradition forbidding abortion at any stage. Beginning with the Didache written around 110 AD which said "Thou shalt not murder a child by abortion" (2:2), and continuing with Barnabas, Clement, Tertullian, Hippolytus, Basil, Chrysostom, Ambrose, Jerome and many other Fathers, and also authoritative Councils, the Church had consistently condemned abortion in no uncertain terms. Hence we ought not presume Aquinas, who never spoke on abortion directly, ever intended by engaging in a discussion of ensoulment, to contest the immorality of abortion at any stage.

Regarding his teaching on ensoulment, theologians do not hold such an opinion today and most regard Thomas' positions as rooted in a primitive understanding of embryology. Clearly natural science today demonstrates the existence of a genetically unique individual at conception.

Finally, even if one wanted unreasonably to hold that Aquinas supported early abortions, St. Thomas, venerable and respect though he is, is not infallible and is not the magisterium. While his teachings are influential, they have not been universally adopted by the magisterium. One obvious example is that St. Thomas was not supportive of the, then unofficial, belief in the Immaculate Conception of Mary.

Q150: I don't understand how mere humans are supposed to *forgive everyone everything* but we are taught that God/Jesus *only* forgives us *if we are repentant*. How are we supposed to be more forgiving than He is? - *Nancy*

A: I am not sure where you learned that the Lord Jesus only forgives if we are repentant. This is quite contrary to what he did at the Cross. With the exception of John, Mother Mary and several other women, we collectively mocked him, scorned him and thought nothing of his sufferings. Yet, in our most unrepentant moment he said, "Father forgive them."

Scripture also says, *But God demonstrates his own love for us in this: While we were still sinners, Christ died for us....when we were God's enemies, we were reconciled to him through the death of his Son....* (Rom 5:7,9-10).
Perhaps you have in mind the judgment we will face. And many do think of our Last Judgment as God withholding forgiveness. However, the Lord makes it clear *As surely as I live, declares the Sovereign LORD, I take no pleasure in the death of the wicked, but rather that they turn from their ways and live.* (Ez 33:11). It also says *God wants all to be saved...* (1 Tim 2:4).

Thus our Last Judgment, is not about God's desire to condemn, or his refusal to forgive. Rather, the judgment in question is more about our final answer to the invitation of God to receive his offered mercy and accept the values of his kingdom. There are some who mysteriously reject the Kingdom and its values, who refuse the offered mercy of God or their need for it. Without pleasure, God accepts the final and lasting choice of some to dwell apart from him.

For us, forgiveness should not be seen so much as an imposed obligation, but as a gift to seek and receive from God. Forgiveness does not always mean we can go on in close relationships with people who may cause us great harm. It does not always mean that there should be no consequences for sin. Rather, forgiveness is letting go of the need to change the past. It is a gift from God that helps us to put down the weight of anger, resentment and the desire for revenge that can consume and destroy us. Forgiveness is for us, not against us.

Q151: The church condemns artificial birth control because it violates God's will in our life cycle. Should not the same logic condemn mechanical interventions and organ transplants extending life is contrary to God's will in that cycle? -*Bill Bandle, Manchester, MO*

When an artificial device such as a knee replacement is used, or in the case of an organ transplant, we are seeking to repair something which is no longer working properly. However, in the case of contraception we are seeking to render dysfunctional, something which is functioning properly, and is a normal aspect of a healthy body. This is a rather big difference and renders your example more of a contrast than a comparison.

Further, it is too simplistic to say that the Church condemns artificial birth control merely because it violates God's will in our lifecycle. It is more proper to say that the Church condemns artificial contraception because it violates our obligation of safeguarding both the unitive and the procreative dimensions of the conjugal act. In other words, contraception violates the intrinsic meaning of human sexuality.

The replacement of a knee or a kidney however, does not violate the essential meaning and purpose of the body. Rather, it helps to enhance the body's overall function which has been diminished somehow, either by injury or disease.

There are of course limits to bodily interventions that we might make. There should be good reasons to replace organs or body parts, and our interventions should enhance the proper, God-given functioning of the body, not alter its intrinsic meaning. There are increasingly strange practices today involving exotic piercings, and extreme "body art," some of which come close to mutilation and which may hinder the proper functioning of the body. So called "sex change operations" would also be excluded since they seek to fundamentally alter what God has given.

However, other things being equal, it is not inappropriate to make proper medical interventions to ensure proper and healthy functioning of the body.

Q152: In my younger days the priest would remind us that missing Mass on Sundays or Holy Days was a mortal sin. I don't hear this anymore. Is it still a teaching of the Church? *—Bill Messaros, Luzerne, PA*

A: Yes, the Catechism of the Catholic Church says, *The faithful are obliged to participate in the Eucharist on days of obligation, unless excused for a serious reason (for example, illness, the care of infants) or dispensed by their own pastor. Those who deliberately fail in this obligation commit a grave sin* (# 2181)

The Lord Jesus also warns, *If you do not eat the flesh of the Son of Man and drink his Blood, you have no life in you* (Jn 6:53) Thus, to miss Mass and stay away from Holy Communion is a form of spiritual starvation. Further, we fail to give God the praise, worship and thanksgiving He is due.

It is a sad fact that this precept and moral teaching is underemphasized today. Priests, catechists and parents must be clearer in teaching and witnessing to this requirement rooted in the Third Commandment. They must also teach why.

There is a modern tendency, not wrong itself, to emphasize "positive" reasons to do things rather than simply quoting laws. But the gravity of the offense against God's Law should not go unstated. Further, obedience to God's law is of itself good, and brings with it many benefits and blessings such as the instruction in God's Word at Mass and the astonishing blessing of being fed on the Lord's Body and Blood.

Q153: You said in a previous answer that the Church condemns artificial contraception because it violates our need to safeguard the intrinsic meaning of the conjugal act, namely, both the unitive and procreative dimensions. But then why allow women over 50, for whom there can be no procreative dimension, to be married? Jesus hates legalism.
— anonymous, PA

A: In speaking of the intrinsic purposes and meaning of human sexuality, the Church looks to what God himself has set forth, and upholds that.

In our younger years, is clear that God has joined together for the married couple, the desire for sexual union, and procreation. His design is both beautiful and reasonable, since the pleasure of the marriage act and the unity it helps foster, assists the couple in becoming closer. This very unity in turn helps to them to be the effective parents that the marriage act is also designed to bring about through procreation. And so both purposes are beautifully and reasonably linked.

God has also set forth that, as couples age, their fertility decreases and, after age 50, for the woman, childbearing becomes rare, if ever. This makes sense given the kind of stamina needed to carry and raise children. Nevertheless, the couple's ongoing unity remains important for the sake of their children, as well as grandchildren and the marital act can continue to assist that.

The key point, in speaking of the "intrinsic meaning" of human sexuality, is that the Church reveres what God has set forth. God's own design is the key element of what we mean by intrinsic meaning. This is also why the Church permits, for serious reason, the use of Natural Family Planning which respects and makes use of the fact that, by God's own design, a couple's fertility runs in a recognizable cycle.

As for your note about legalism, it would seem to be exactly 180° out of phase. You are correct in asserting that Jesus resisted legalism. But the legalism Jesus rejected was legalism which sought to set aside God's law, and what God has clearly established.

In terms of human sexuality, the Church exhorts the faithful to wholeheartedly except what God has set forth, and not to engage in legalism and minimalism, as a way to set aside what God has established (e.g. Mk 7:13).

With this in mind, it would seem that those who seek to justify contraception are more connected with the kind of legalism which Jesus scorned.

Q154: I am very careful to attend Mass each Sunday. However, next year I will make a nature trek in Nepal for 16 days and will be unable to attend Mass. Can I go even though I will miss at least two Sunday Masses? - *V. Silva, India*

A: While Mass attendance is required of a Catholic each Sunday unless there is a serious reason to miss (*cf.* Catechism 2181), when attendance is unreasonably difficult or impossible, one can be excused. Hence, things like inclement weather, significant health issues, and travel, especially in remote locations, will often excuse one.

There are legitimate values in the journey you wish to make that may, in fact, help you to appreciate the glory of what God has created. Hence, it would be hard to argue that the trip would not be of sufficient value to permit a limited absence from Mass, if this cannot be reasonably avoided.

Catholics are however, obliged to secure permission from their proper pastor (*cf* Canon Law, 1245) and thus you ought not fail to discuss the matter with him.

Q155: A recently published book that claims to dispels "myths and maybes" of the Catholic Church, says that "grave" sin is not "mortal" sin. Thus the author says that missing Mass is a grave sin, but it is not a mortal sin. Is this so? – *Thomas Simpson, Gilbert, AZ*

A: No, grave and mortal mean the same thing in Catholic moral teaching. Hence, missing Mass without a serious reason is a mortal sin (*cf* Catechism No. 2181).

It is true today many moral textbooks, and Church documents use the word "grave" more often than "mortal." There are likely pastoral reasons behind this. For it was a growing tendency for many poorly catechized people to think "mortal" sin referred only to killing someone. So, there came the tendency to use the word "grave," meaning "weighty or very serious sin" to refer to mortal sin. But, as you point out, this has led to other pastoral problems, wherein people do not often understand that grave mortal mean the same thing.

Pope John Paul II found it necessary In 1984 to clarify that grave and mortal mean the same thing. He wrote: *In the Church's doctrine and pastoral action, grave sin is in practice identified with mortal sin....There is no middle way between life and death.* (Reconciliation and Penance # 17)

Q156: I think homosexual people are born homosexual. What is the Roman Catholic Church's theological or scientific position?
- *Charles O'Neill, via email*

A: The Catechism states regarding Homosexual orientation: *Its psychological genesis remains largely unexplained* (# 2357). Hence the Church has no official doctrine that would either affirm or deny your assertion.

The moral requirements for a person of same-sex attraction do not vary based on the origin of the orientation. Rather, *"Basing itself on Sacred Scripture, which presents homosexual acts as acts of grave depravity, tradition has always declared* that *"homosexual acts are intrinsically disordered. They are contrary to the natural law. They close the sexual act to the gift of life. They do not proceed from a genuine affective and sexual complementarity. Under no circumstances can they be approved."* (Catechism # 2357).

It is not unlike a diabetic, who may be so for genetic reasons, or by acquiring the condition, (perhaps by overeating). The bottom line is the same; they must carefully regulate their diet. Thus, whatever the origin of homosexuality, the requirement is clear, one must embrace the life of celibacy that God enables.

Q157: In the Nicene Creed the phrase "rose again" appears related to Christ's resurrection. Does this imply that there is more than one resurrection or is this some quirk in the translation?- *name withheld, Normal, IL*

A: Yes, it is more of a quirk in the translation and of how we speak in English. There is only one resurrection.

The English word "resurrection" comes from the similar word in Latin, "resurrexit" which can be translated "he arose" but more literally means "He stood up again," for *re*=again and *surrexit*=he stood up. The Greek text of the Creed also uses this construction: ἀναστάντα (anastanta) means to stand up again, *ana*=again, *stanta*= to stand.

Thus when we render these concepts into English we use the word "again" to capture more the sense of the Latin and Greek texts, which speak of the resurrection in very physical terms. While in English we could simply say "He arose" or "He rose from the dead" but, in a sense this is abstract and doesn't quite capture the Latin and Greek which emphasize the physical fact that Christ who was freely struck down in death is now standing up once again.

It is true that in English "again" can mean that someone has done something more than once, as in "He did it again," implying that this is at least the second time he has done something. But "again" can also mean simply to return to a former state. As in "He is back home again," meaning he who had left has now returned. It is this second sense of the word "again" that is meant when saying Jesus "rose again." In other words, Jesus who once stood among us fully alive, is now doing so again.

Q158:I have been offered a job with a large pharmaceutical company, which, among other things, supplies materials for stem cell research. Am I able to take such a job? - *name withheld, Portland, OR*

A: Part of the answer depends on an important distinction, which many lose, in the Church's teaching about stem cell research. The Church does not oppose all, or even most stem cell research. There are, for example, no moral issues with using stem cells harvested from adult humans, or from the umbilical cord after birth. It is only the use of stem cells acquired from human embryos, which the Church opposes, because it requires the killing of human life in order to obtain them.

Hence, the company in question is not committing sin *per se* in supplying material for stem cell research. Only those who wrongfully use stem cells acquired from human embryos commit wrongdoing.

However, let us suppose that it is clear to you that the company is certainly supplying some materials for the specific purpose of embryonic stem cell research. The morality of you accepting employment with this sort of a company would vary based on a number of factors.

Let us presume, as is usually the case, that pharmaceutical company is large and supplies a vast variety of pharmaceuticals for a wide array of medical purposes. In such a scenario taking employment with such a company would only involve you in remote material cooperation. And such associations, while not ideal, are morally permissible.

However, if the position in the company that you are taking would require you to promote embryonic stem cell research to advance the sales of specific products related to embryonic stem cell research, such work would be of a more direct material cooperation. In such a case, you ought not take the job which would involve you directly advancing and cooperating in a moral evil.

Q159: Is viewing pornography on the Internet a mortal sin? What is a good method to get away from what I know in my heart is wrong?
- *name withheld, via email*

A: Of its nature, the viewing of pornography is a mortal sin. As with any mortal sin, one's culpability (blame worthiness) is affected by how freely one consents to the act, and the degree to which one fully knows and understands the gravity of the evil involved.

Internet pornography presents a very serious temptation to many, and many pastoral challenges for the Church. The fact is, today, increasing numbers of people compulsively view this sinful material, and many are outright addicted to Internet pornography.

As any confessor, or pastor of souls will be able to attest, large numbers approaching the confessional and counseling and are quite "stuck" in Internet pornography. Many have seen their relationships and marriages greatly harmed, and some even end up with criminal charges related to the viewing of pornographic images of minors. Addiction to pornography is a slippery slope that leads to increasingly debased and degrading imagery. Pornography is indeed, a snare, which lures its victims with promises of momentary delights, only to leave them quickly hungry for more. This is due to the increasingly insatiable lust that it ignites.

One of the more effective remedies that has emerged recently is a system of accountability, wherein one's Internet activities are monitored and recorded, and a daily report is sent to someone of the pornography addict's choice. This "sponsor," of sorts, reviews the list and holds the addict accountable. Certainly too, filters can be of some help, to prevent tempting materials from appearing in the first place. These filters can be of great help to those who struggle more mildly with the problem. Sadly though, many true pornography addicts know their way around such filters.

Finally, this salutary reminder: absolutely nothing we do on the Internet is private. When we are on the Internet, we are out in public, and our browsing habits are not hard to discover, for those who might wish to know. What's done in the dark can be brought to the light.

Take Internet pornography seriously, it is a grave sin, which causes great harm, and is highly addictive to many people. The Scriptures say, Flee fornication (1Cor 6:18). And one does well to heed this prescription in a particular way related to Internet pornography. Flee pornography; it is a snare.

Q160: My Saturday was busy and I ended up folding laundry on Sunday. Is this a violation of the Third Commandment?
- *name withheld, via email*

A: As general rule, there is a precept that we *refrain from engaging in work or activities that hinder the worship owed to God, The joy proper to the Lord's day, the performance of the works of mercy, and the appropriate relaxation of mind and body.* (Catechism #2185).

That said, we also do well to avoid an excessive legalism against which Jesus himself taught what he said *The Sabbath was made for man, not man for the Sabbath.* (Mk 2:27)

Hence, while one might ordinarily seek to avoid folding laundry etc. on a Sunday, such activity is not intrinsically wrong. Perhaps one finds such an activity relaxing in the company of other family members. Perhaps too, since the activity could not reasonably be accomplished on Saturday, it is an act of charity that helps the family to be prepared for the week ahead.

Thus, we do well to seek a proper balance between maintaining the principles of joyful rest on Sunday, and avoiding excessive legalism.

Q161: Can Catholic actors accept roles that require of them nudity and enacting illicit sexual union on screen or stage?
- *Bill Bandle, Manchester, MO*

A: As general rule, no. To do this is to engage in scandal wherein one gives temptation to others, and contributes the lowering of moral standards. It is wrong to celebrate or encourage immoral activities.

There is, however, the fact that movies and drama do comment on life and the human condition, which includes violence, treachery, corruption and sexual sins and so forth. To treat of these matters in drama, (as even the Bible does), is not per se wrong. What *is* wrong is celebrate such sinfulness, or seek to justify and normalize it.

Even more erroneous is to unnecessarily display what should not be seen. For example, to include a murder in a movie does not require us to watch a person brutally killed and dismembered. Likewise, to report a sexual infidelity does require us to watch it pornographically portrayed. Subtlety and discretion are required to treat of topics like these.

So Catholics actors should not transgress when sin is either celebrated or inappropriately displayed.

Q162: Killing someone and missing Sunday Mass are both mortal sins, punishable by eternity in hell. This seems to make the two sins equivalent. But in my mind killing is far worse than missing mass. Are they really equivalent? -*James Becker, Woodstock, NY*

A: No, they are not equivalent. There are degrees to mortal sin just like there are degrees to venial sin. First-degree murder is more grave than missing Mass, or viewing pornography, or any other grave sin that we might imagine.

It is true that killing someone and missing Mass are in the same category of "mortal," (or grave) sin. But they are no more equivalent, than a rat is equivalent to or the same as a man, simply because they are in the same category "mammal."

Your description of both sins as being punishable by eternity in Hell also implies an equivalence by that fact. However, a distinction is necessary regarding the way you connect the notion of eternity to punishment. That one is in Hell eternally, is not due to punishment *per se*. Rather, the eternity of Hell (or heaven for that matter) exists because, at some point, our decision for or against God, and the laws and values of his Kingdom becomes a decision that is for us at death forever fixed. Thus, that Hell is eternal, is not by itself a gauge the punishment involved.

We need not presume that everyone experiences Hell in exactly the same way, any more than presume that everyone experiences heaven in exactly the same way. There may in fact be degrees of suffering in Hell, and degrees of glory in Heaven.

While there are mysteries involved here, it makes sense that there are some Saints who, on account of extraordinary virtue, have a greater capacity to appreciate God's glory in heaven. It also makes sense that for those in Hell who have rejected God, and his Kingdom, there would be degrees of suffering experienced, related to how deep their rejection of the light is. Scripture indicates we are judged according to what we have done (Revelation 20:11 -15). Thus, there is at least implied some relationship of reward or punishment rooted in what we have done or not done. Jesus also speaks of places of special honor in heaven, indicating levels of some sort in the afterlife (cf Matt 20:23).

Q163: My nephew and his fiancée, both Catholic, and despite being warned, are planning to be married outside the Church. Can I, and other family members attend the wedding? - *Art Osten, via email*

A: No, you ought not attend. Both of them are bound to have their marriage witnessed by a priest or deacon in the sacred setting of the Church. In celebrating the marriage outside the church without permission, they are entering into an invalid marriage. To attend, and to celebrate with them, signals support of this sinful action.

While these sorts of situations are awkward, you are not the source of the awkwardness, they are. A firm line is appropriate in such serious matters which underscores the sinfulness of the situation.

Your explanation to them of your incapacity to attend should be done charitably, leaving the door open for further discussions leading to convalidation in the near future, should they still go forward with their plans.

Finally, avoid harsh debates with other family members who may still go. While attendance at such weddings is strongly discouraged, Church Law does not absolutely forbid it given the human complexities involved in such situations. Some respect for prudential judgements that differ is appropriate.

Q164: I am a bit confused about the Catechism's treatment of acedia. What does the Catechism mean to teach by this sin? And how is it related to joy? - *Inigo Incer, via email*

A: The more common word for acedia is "sloth," one of the seven deadly sins. Unfortunately, most simply equate sloth with laziness. Although sloth can manifest as laziness, it manifests other aspects as well.

Fundamentally, sloth is a sorrow or sadness, an aversion, toward the good things that God is offering us. And thus the Catechism teaches, *Acedia or spiritual sloth, goes so far as to refuse the joy that comes from God, and to be repelled by divine goodness.* (# 2094).

The proper response to the good things that God offers us is joy. We should be joyful at the offer of a holy life, set free from sin and gloriously opened the love of God and others.

But the sinful drive of sloth influences many to respond to this offer with sadness and aversion. Perhaps it would involve too many changes, and many prefer to avoid change and fear it. Frankly, many like their sins, preferring to indulge their lower nature. Sloth therefore perceives God's gracious offer as a threat and moves to oppose it. We do this in obvious and subtle ways.

While sloth often manifests as a kind of boredom, aversion, or laziness toward spiritual things, one can also see it at work in the kind of frantic indulgence and workaholism common today. Indeed many indulge in an excessive activism in the world of politics, career, business, and other worldly pursuits. In no way are they lazy, but they often use frantic activism to avoid the spiritual contemplation of God or the things of God. The claim becomes, "I am too busy to pray, get to Church, or attend to moral and spiritual reflection, the reading of Scripture or the study of my faith. Such people are not lazy, *per se*, but they are averse to spiritual things and prefer worldly pursuits. And this too is sloth.

Thus, sloth is best understood as a sorrow or aversion to the good things that God offers. It is a deep and sinful drive rooted in a disordered preference for passing worldly things. We must ask for a joy for spiritual and eternal things and zeal to cultivate a deeper desire for God and the things of heaven, for our fallen flesh is strongly opposed to the desires of the spirit (*cf* Gal 5:17).

Q165: I have had a long association with the Shriners Hospitals and their work of providing largely free Medical care of the Poor. I want to remember them in my will but recently discovered that they are associated with Freemasonry. As a Catholic can I remember them in my will? - *name withheld, Philadelphia, PA*

A: Catholics are not permitted to join the Masons or to engage in specifically Masonic activity or ritual. However, what you describe would seem to fall merely under the category of remote, material cooperation. What you seek to support is the common humanitarian work of caring for the sick and the poor, an activity in keeping with Catholic vision as well. I am presuming your intention is not to support Freemasonry *per se*, and surely not its potentially anti-Catholic views. I say, "potentially," since not every Mason, or Masonic organization, especially in America, is specifically focused on being anti-Catholic, as was, and often still is, the case in Europe. Further, it seems you also have some personal history, tied to the particular hospitals in question, and are grateful for the care they have exhibited.

Presuming, that this is your intention, rather than to support Freemasonry directly, it is permissible for you to donate under the circumstances stated. It remains the case however that Catholics are not free to join the Masons or to directly support Freemasonry *per se*.

Q166: I would like to make a few comments regarding your frequent mentioning a mortal sin. It appears to me that a definition is in order, so as not to frighten people needlessly. For a sin to be mortal, three conditions must together be met: grave matter, full knowledge, and deliberate consent (*cf* Catechism 1857) I know good number of people who don't attend mass regularly or who look at pornography, but are not aware that they commit a sin. Actually, it might be pretty hard for the average person to commit grave sin, for who would purposely turn against God? -*Bernard Thyssen, Beverly Hill, FL*

A: We have discussed the three conditions for mortal sin, in previous columns. The nature of this column is to provide brief, answers. It is not always possible to give a full theological treatise in the approximately 300 words that are given to answer a question here.

While rightly referencing the Catechism and providing a helpful reminder about what is necessary for one to be fully culpable of mortal sin, there are aspects of your comment that bespeak troubling trends in modern thinking.

First, there is your notion that people don't seem to know any better. Scripture, Sacred Tradition, and the Catechism all speak of the conscience in every human person. The voice of God echoes in the depths of every human heart. While some suppress this voice, deep down it is still there. It is my pastoral experience that people generally *do* know what they are doing. When I speak to people who are missing Mass, or perhaps are cohabiting and fornicating, etc., they admit they know, deep down, what they are doing is wrong.

Secondly, your notion that mortal sin is rare also seems rooted in modern anthropology that minimizes human freedom and knowledge. While it is true, certain compulsions may marginalize or limit freedom, yet, we are freer than most like to admit. In summoning us to a moral life, and warning us of sin, the Lord in Scripture is not simply setting up a straw man. He speaking to us as moral agents, who generally act freely, making decisions for which we are responsible.

You may call all this "needless fear," but if so, the Lord never got the memo. Jesus often used vivid imagery, to stir fear within us of the consequences of sin. As with any pastoral appeal, fear must be balanced with other appeals as well. But the modern attempt to remove all fear from the preaching of the Church, has had poor results. Some degree of fear may be "needful" after all.

Q167: Our Sunday visitor recently quoted Pope John XXIII from an encyclical as stating that among the rights to belong to every person, Is the "freedom to form a family." Given the Church's stance on same-sex unions, and other non-biblical family structures, with which I am in full agreement, doesn't Pope John's statement give tacit license that anyone could adopt in order to "form a family." In other words, is not the expression "former family" too vague? – *Janet Cooper, San Diego, CA*

A: As with any quote, historical context is important. Pope John XXIII lived in an era when single-parent families, and cohabiting couples, were rare. And same-sex unions were inconceivable. Back in the late 1950s and early 60s, "family" meant a married father and a mother, and children. There was still a basic moral consensus, which could be presumed in using phrases such as "form a family."

Today, this is gone, and we must be much more specific. Thus, in reading Blessed John XXIII, we must adjust to the context in which he spoke, and cannot reasonably demand the precision that is necessary today. Neither would it be reasonable for our opponents on the marriage question to read into these remarks an approval for the current situation.

Q168: If a nation such as North Korea or Iran launches a nuclear weapon that causes major destruction, does the targeted nation have a right to respond in a way that virtually obliterates that nation. When it comes to nuclear war it seems hard to imagine a proportionate response. - *name withheld, Johnson City, TN*

A: The simple answer to your question would be no. The targeted nation could not simply retaliate in kind, and certainly not seek to obliterate the offending nation.

Some sort of military response might well be called for, even full-scale war. This would presume that the criteria for just war have been met. Namely, that the damage and threat was grave, lasting and certain (which would be the case in your scenario), that other means of ending the conflict has been tried or were not possible, that there is a reasonable hope of success in turning back the threat by military means, and the use of arms must not produce evils and disorders graver than the evil to be eliminated (*cf* Catechism # 2309).

Even once within a war, a nation must use means to distinguish between combatants and noncombatants. Hence, choosing to wipe out whole population centers, indiscriminately killing combatants and noncombatants, is not a moral option. Indiscriminate obliteration cannot be condoned under any circumstances. (*cf* Catechism # 2314).

It will be admitted, given the existence of large-scale nuclear devices, the most effective means to deter such attacks is complex and debatable. A short answer such as this cannot possibly explore all the points debated in the deterrence of nuclear threat. Simply here let it be noted that the Catechism expresses strong moral reservations regarding the modern "arms race" (*cf* Catechism # 2315).

Thus, to return to the main question, if a nation were lamentably to be attacked by a country in the way you describe, that nation is not thereby justified in indiscriminately retaliating by wiping out whole cities or in annihilating that country.

Q169: I have read that in some countries it is legal to sell blood and organs? What is the Catholic view of this practice?
- *Bernie Askew, Sacramento, CA*

A: Organs and blood should not be sold and no Christian can seriously propose such a thing. In the first place, it violates Scripture which says, *"You are not your own. You have been bought at a price! So, glorify God in your body"* (1 Cor 6:19-20). Hence, we are not owners of our bodies, merely stewards. We should not sell what does not belong to us.

To be a steward, means to use what belong to another in a way that accords with the will of the true owner. Hence, we are permitted in charity, to donate blood, and to donate certain organs, while we live, and other organs upon our death. These acts of charity conform to the will of the true owner of our body, God, who is love. Thus, Scripture encourages, *"The gift that you have received, give as a gift."* (Matt 10:8)

The second reason not to sell blood and organs is the harm that it does to the poor. If they can be sold, the number of those who simply donate them will decline. And the price of purchasing them will surely be high. This gives the poor less access to healing remedies.

Hence, the buying and selling of organs and blood is an offense against Catholic teaching. It violates both the principle of stewardship, and also of charity.

Q170: The Church teaches that we are born with Original Sin. But if the mother is baptized and thus freed from Original Sin how is it that her child is born with Original sin? – *Katey, McKinleyville, CA*

A: Human parents can supply to their children only the fallen human nature that came from Adam and Eve. They cannot supply what is divine and supernatural.

Even in terms of mere human nature, parents are only able to supply the basic elements. So, for example, the child receives from his parents a brain and an intellect, as basic elements that come with human nature. But parents cannot transfer at conception their knowledge of language, or mathematics, or history to the child. The child must acquire this for himself, with the help of others.

If this is the case with human nature, it is even more so with the supernatural life of grace. The mother may be baptized, and free of Original Sin, she cannot communicate this to her child, only God can. And thus she must bring her child to the Lord in baptism, who begins a saving work in which the child must grow.

Q171: While the Catechism technically permits the death penalty, it, and the bishops, foresee its use as rare if ever. If capital punishment is foresworn in all cases, a criminal often lives to commit another atrocity. Is society not left helpless? I write as one who has been robbed at gunpoint. – *Danny House, via email*

A: There are many complexities in discussing the death penalty, because there is some tension between the traditional doctrine regarding it, and the modern pastoral setting.

Unlike abortion, capital punishment is not an intrinsic moral evil for a couple of reasons. Firstly, in certain settings, the use of the death penalty has served the common good; ensuring that dangerous criminals are no longer able to cause harm. In punishing grave offenders, others can be deterred from capital crimes too. Secondly, Scripture does not forbid the practice. Even in the New Testament, St. Paul speaks to the State's right to punish grave offenders in this way, and even indicates that, in so doing, it acts as a minister of God's justice on the wrong-doer. (see Rom 13:4).

The Church cannot simply overrule scripture and declare intrinsically evil, what God permits in certain circumstances. However, that Scripture permits the death penalty in certain circumstances, does not mean that it is always wise or prudent promote such punishment.

In the modern pastoral setting, recent Popes, and the bishops of the world, have taught that recourse to the death penalty should be rare if ever. A significant part of this prudential judgment, is rooted in concern for what Bl. John Paul called the "culture of death."

The culture of death is a mindset wherein the death or nonexistence of human beings is increasingly proposed as a solution to problems. Abortion, euthanasia, and quick recourse warfare or other violent means, along with the antilife mentality of contraception, are widely promoted in our culture as a way to solve problems. The Church stands foursquare against such thinking.

And even though the death penalty has received reluctant approval in the past, the current pastoral setting seems to require that the Church stand consistently against yet another way wherein death is proposed as a solution to the regrettable problem of crime.

I regret the criminal assault you experienced. I too have been held up at gunpoint and was beaten. More needs to be done, to keep serious and threatening offenders off our streets. However, given the wider pastoral setting, it is the consensus of recent Pope and the world's bishops that standing against all facets of the culture of death is an important pastoral posture to maintain, even if our tradition does permit the death penalty is very rare circumstances.

Q172: In a recent issue of Our Sunday Visitor, there is an article entitled "Divorced Catholics." It states that some Bishops in Germany are allowing some divorced and remarried Catholics to receive Communion, citing a papal endorsement. What does this papal endorsement state?
- *Diane Reinke, Silver Spring, MD*

A: There is no papal endorsement. Church policy on Catholics who are divorced and remarried remains unchanged. As a general rule, divorced and remarried Catholics are not able to receive communion or absolution in confession. This is because they are living in an invalid marriage, where at least one of them has been married to someone else before.

In accord with what Jesus teaches in Matthew 19, Matthew 5, Mark 10, and other places, those who divorce and then remarry are in a state of adultery. And, since their marriage is ongoing, and regular conjugal relations are presumed, Catholics in this state are not usually able to make a firm act of contrition which includes the promise to avoid adulterous sex in the future. Hence they cannot receive absolution, neither can they be offered Holy Communion.

In relatively rare situations, some Catholics are able to live with their current spouse and a kind of "brother-sister" relationship where no sexual relations are part of the picture. Sometimes this is due to mutual agreement between the spouses, sometimes it is due to health related issues that preclude sexual activity and will not change in the future. In such rare cases, a Catholic is able to make an act of contrition, receive absolution and be restored to Holy Communion.

Regarding the German Bishops, it is been reported that some are either acting contrary to current Church law, or strongly requesting a change in the law.

Of itself, request to review current church policies is a legitimate matter to consider in any number of areas. As most priests know, many people today find themselves and very complicated situations. Many for example, have returned to the Church after many years away, and often do so with the irregular marriage situations. Some can be quickly and easily rectified. Others, because current or former spouses are uncooperative, create difficulties in people being restored to the full sacramental life of the Church.

Are there ways that we can more efficiently deal with these situations, and at the same time respect the Lord's clear teaching in Scripture? These are ongoing questions, and also questions that will surely be considered at the upcoming Synod on family life.

It is unlikely that there can be any major changes in Church policy in this regard. However, there can be great improvements in explaining our pastoral stance to Catholics who are often confused by what the Church teaches and why. The prayers of the faithful for the upcoming Synod will be very important, so the decisions that come forth are wise, prudent, and engender in that respect for Church teaching on marriage.

Q173: Is it morally permissible to divorce in order to be able to qualify for MEDICAID assistance to pay for nursing home costs? My wife has dementia and will soon need nursing home care which cost $120,000. My wife's savings would be wiped out in nine months, and then they come for my assets, which would be gone in three years.
- *name withheld, NJ*

A: You describe a difficult situation faced by many today. A brief column such as this cannot explore all the moral issues involved here, but the bottom line answer is, No you should not divorce.
The well-known axiom that the ends do not justify the means, applies here. And while the "end" of trying to save your money, (presumably to give it to your children), is a good and understandable end or goal, one cannot sin in order to obtain it.

What is the sin involved in what you ponder? Fundamentally it is either to divorce, which God hates (see Malachi 2:16) or it is to lie.

Regarding divorce, it is essential to recall the vow you made which is very pertinent in exactly the case described here. The vow said, "*I take you to be my wife, to have and to hold, from this day forward, for better, for worse, for richer, for poorer, in sickness and in health, until death do us part.:* Clearly sickness and poverty were anticipated as a possible scenario in the vows you both made.

But one might argue, "We are not *really* getting divorced, it is just a legal move regarding civil marriage. We will still consider each other as spouses." But in this case, a lie is being told to the State for the purpose of MEDICAID funds.

Either way, it seems that what is proposed is that one do evil (sin) that good may come of it. This is not a valid moral solution to an admittedly difficult and painful issue.

In recent years, Long Term Care Insurance has been a solution to some of this, but for an older person, this new device is seldom much help since, if they have it at all, the premiums were high and the payoff low.

I pray it might be of some consolation to recall that the goal in life is not to die with a lot of money in the bank. The goal is die in holiness. God has promised the Kingdom to those who are persecuted for the sake of righteousness, and who have done what is right, even at high personal cost.

Q174: You recently referenced Matthew Chapter 19 where Jesus forbids divorce. But you said nothing about an exception the Lord makes "for unchastity." Please explain what the Lord means here.
- *name withheld, Chicago, IL*

A: The particular verse you reference reads as follows: *And so I [Jesus] say to you, whoever divorces his wife (unless the marriage is unlawful) and marries another, commits adultery.* (Matthew 19:9)

The phrase, "unless the marriage is unlawful" is from the Catholic New American Bible, and is a rendering of the Greek, (*me epi porneia*) which most literally means, "except for illicit sexual union".

The Greek word in question is *porneia*. This word refers generally to any illicit sexual union. Depending on the context, it most often means premarital sex, but can also refer to incest, and more rarely to adultery and/or homosexual acts. I say "more rarely" because adultery and homosexual acts have their own proper Greek words and descriptions that are normally used (e.g. *Moichao* (adultery) and *paraphysin* etc., for homosexual acts).

Some, especially from the Protestant tradition, think *porneia*, as used here, means "adultery." Hence, they hold that divorce and remarriage is allowed if one (of both) of the spouses committed adultery. But this seems unlikely, since, if the Lord meant that, he could have used the more specific word for adultery (*moichao*) which he uses later in the very same sentence! It also seems a strange logic that one can avoid a second marriage being considered adulterous if the first marriage is rendered adulterous by one or both parties.

Catholic teaching and understanding regarding the word *porneia* holds it to mean in the context of this verse, "incestuous relationships."

This makes historical sense. The Jewish world had very clear understandings about permissible marital unions, forbidding marriage where the bloodlines ran too close, e.g. siblings, first cousins etc. But as the Gospel went forth into the Greek and pagan world, there were differing and unacceptable notions about who could marry who.

Because of these many strange marital practices, the so-called Matthean exception, seeks to clarify the Lord's teaching. Thus, the phrase "except for unlawful marriage" (sometimes also rendered "except for unchastity") clarifies that those who are in marriages that are illicit, due to incestuous and other invalidating factors, should not stay in them. Rather, these are not marriages at all and can and should be set aside in favor of proper marriage.

Q175: If I miss Mass for no good reason, may I receive Communion when I do go, even if I didn't get to confession?
- name withheld, Ballwin, MO

A: No, you ought to first go to confession. The Catechism, in conformity with ancient teaching about the necessity of attending Mass says, *"Those who deliberately fail in this obligation commit grave sin."* (#2181). Hence you ought to go to confession first. There are some reasons that one might miss Mass that are legitimate such as serious illness, the care of the sick, or some lack of capacity due to weather or distance. So also struggle with work schedules. But in this matter they should consult with their pastor or confessor and also seek solutions.

Q176: What is the Church's stance on artificial life support? May a Catholic be removed from it? - *Gene Bozek, Jefferson Hills, PA*

A: If, by artificial life support, you mean something such as a ventilator, the use of such machines is not required when they are no longer therapeutic, and the person is certainly dying. Neither is it required to revive a person who is approaching death each time their heart stops.

Allowing someone to die whom the Lord is certainly calling is morally very different from directly causing a person to die, which is what euthanasia advocates claim the right to do.

One exception to the non-required use of artificial means is that food and water, even if supplied by a tube, should still to be administered to those who are approaching death. Only in rare cases, where the major organs of the body have already shut down and can no longer process food or fluids, can this treatment be discontinued.

Q177: Can Catholics have Gay friends? If so, under what circumstances? – *Charles McKelvy, Harbert, MI*

A: Yes, though as you indicate, circumstances are important. In the first place, there are different kinds and degrees of friendships. Some friendships are close and personal, others are more peripheral. Some friendships are of a professional or business nature, whereas other friendships are more rooted in family and community ties. Some friendships involve very personal sharing, whereas other friendships involve only a general acquaintance.

Clearly it is more possible to overlook many things with people with whom we are only acquainted, or with whom we simply have professional relationships. In these situations our obligations to give and receive fraternal correction is less.

But in close friendships, more is expected and required. Generally, close friendships presume many shared values and similar respect for the truth. When such things are lacking in significant areas, close friendships are going to be strained.

Close friends also have greater obligations to instruct and admonish one another (e.g. James 5:19; Gal 6:1 etc). Hence it is not the proper nature of a close relationship to simply overlook significant matters. If I have a close friend and I know he is viewing pornography regularly, or living with a woman outside of marriage, I have an obligation as a Christian to seek to correct him. If I have a close friend who is destroying his life with alcohol or drugs, I have obligations to admonish him, and assist him to seek help.

All of these principles apply to someone with a homosexual orientation. If I have a close friend with this orientation and he or she is living celibately, this is fine and I should seek to offer encouragement in this regard. If however they are straying into elicit sexual union and/or advocating the so-called "gay lifestyle," same-sex unions, and so forth, I would have an obligation to instruct and admonish. It is difficult to see how a close relationship could continue if the individual were to utterly reject such correction about such a significant manner. The first concern for close friends ought to be each other's salvation, not merely their feelings.
Thus, while many prudential factors must be weighed in terms of how best to fraternally correct, close friendships must be rooted in the truth, and cannot really be called close friendships without reverence for the truth.

If a Christian were too weak to engage in this instruction then it would seem that the close friendship is really experienced as a friendship between equals, but a friendship wherein the other person has the upper hand. In this case one might consider the admonition of Scripture that *Bad company corrupts good morals* (1 Cor 15:33), and seek healthier friendships. For, once pressured to silence, many Christians give tacit approval, and the truth is no longer respected or proclaimed.

Q178: I am a transportation driver of an adult daycare center. My schedule is Monday to Friday. Do I have to work on Sunday if my supervisor asked me because they lack drivers or somebody called in sick? *– Ferdi Pac, via email*

A: Ideally, and to the degree that we are able, we ought to avoid working on Sunday. However, *Caritas suprema lex* (love is the highest law), and there will be times that charity may require us to assist others even on Sunday. This is especially the case in the situation you describe wherein you seem to be caring for the sick and/or disabled. In the observation of keeping the Lord's Day holy, exceptions are made for workers in critical jobs such as emergency care (fire and police), medical workers, and others who care for critical infrastructure and necessary tasks that need to go on even on Sunday.

Hence, what your supervisor asks of you is not necessarily sinful and if his request is reasonable, you ought to fulfill it.

However, if the problem becomes a recurring pattern, is not wrong for you to ask for other solutions to be sought so that your own religious sensibilities and requirements can also be met.

Q179: I'm a 50-year-old man, and was raised Catholic. But I have been married twice, divorced, and then lived with a woman. I now live alone and my Catholic friends tell me to return to the Catholic Church! Other than my job, I do lots of unpaid volunteer work. Is that good enough to go to heaven if I die suddenly, what should I do? *- name withheld, Atkinson, KA*

A: Your friends are right, return to the Catholic Church. What this means practically, is it you should go to confession, and resume receiving Holy Communion. In situations like yours, where one is been away from the Church for sometime and struggled to live some of the teachings (in this case, teachings on Holy Matrimony) you would do well to meet with your parish priest, or some other priest your friends can recommend. Simply going to confession one Saturday afternoon, and then resuming Sunday Mass with Holy Communion is technically permissible. However it is more fruitful spend some time discussing your life and struggles in the context of a longer confession, and/or counseling session with a priest.

In order to make a good confession, you must bring with you a purpose of amendment to live a chaste life, and follow the teachings of the Church Holy Matrimony. Perhaps the priest can discuss these with you, help you understand your struggles of the past, and assist you with the proper vision going forward. Dating and future marriage is not for you right now, until and unless annulments can be granted.

Praise God for your friends who encourage you. Regular prayer, the Word of God, Sacraments, and walking in fellowship with the Church are essential helps in finding our way through the desert of this world unto the promised land of Heaven.

As for your question about good works, we cannot purchase, as it were, forgiveness from God. Thus, good works cannot replace true repentance and returning to Christ, whose mercy is free. However, good works can reflect a repentant heart, and help to cleanse us from our sinful tendencies. So you are commended and encouraged to continue in the good works you have undertaken!

May God bless you and your journey back into the practice of the faith, and the reception of the sacraments.

Q180: I am confused with something said in the YOUCAT (the "Youth Catechism of the Catholic Church) which seems to forbid organ donation. The puzzling paragraphs read as follows: *The Fifth Commandment forbids also the use of violence against one's own body. Jesus expressly demands that we accept and love ourselves: "You shall love your neighbor as yourself" (Mt 22:39). Self-destructive acts against one's own body ("body piercings", cutting and so on) are in most cases psychological reactions to experiences of abandonment and a lack of love; hence they call first and foremost for our sincere and loving response. Within the context of organ donation, it must be made clear, however, that there is no human right to destroy one's own God-given body.* **(YOUCAT #s 386-387) Does this mean we can't be organ donors??**

— *Maureen Normann, Washington, DC*

A: The YOUCAT is a catechism aimed at youth, which was developed in conjunction with World Youth Day. While it is a valuable resource, it limits its answers to a very brief question and answer format. As such it does not always develop what it says briefly. The hope is to connect young people with the larger <u>Catechism of the Catholic Church</u> and the <u>Compendium</u>, published by the Bishops.

The passage quoted above is a bit murky. However, the YOUCAT later states more directly about Organ Donation: *Donating organs can lengthen or improve the quality of life, and therefore it is a genuine service to one's neighbor, provided no one is forced to do it* (# 391). The YOUCAT then points to paragraph 2296 of the Catechism which develops the matter further.

On the American scene organ donation is seen as altruistic, and an almost unqualified good; and surely it can be such. However, remember the Catechism (including YOUCAT) is written for a worldwide setting, where, in some places such as China, prisoners have been compelled to donate their organs. In other settings the buying and selling of organs is becoming a problem. Hence the Church wants to encourage organ donation, but balance it with the respect we should have for bodily integrity and the physical and emotional health of the organ donors. Increasingly the powerless and poor are being compelled to donate, or tempted to sell their organs.

The YOUCAT quote is likely aiming here in its analysis, and clarifies later the good of donation in the right circumstances.

Q181: My infant daughter is going to have her one-year check up and will be receiving vaccines related Measles/Mumps/Rubella and Chickenpox. I am concerned that some vaccines used today have been made using a process from cells of aborted babies. Can I have my daughter vaccinated? Do you have any further advice on what to do?
-Hannah Kim, via email

A: Generally the Church teaching is clear that Catholics cannot directly cooperate in evil. However, remote, material cooperation is permissible, and often impossible to avoid.

For example, few products we buy are wholly free from situations where injustice was involved in their production. Perhaps the products come from countries where unjust wages are paid, or child labor laws are poorly enforced, or working conditions are bad. And these injustices offend against human dignity, Church teaching and cause suffering. However, it is not reasonable or possible for us to stop all buying and participation in a worldwide economy. Thus while we cooperate materially in an economy that is based to some degree on injustice, nevertheless our cooperation remote, and we do not directly intend or cause the injustices in the chain of production and supply. Further, alternatives to purchasing many needed products are not always reasonably available.

As you describe it, your permitting of the necessary vaccines for your daughter might include vaccines developed using cells from aborted children. However, it seems clear that your involvement in the matter is quite remote, and you do not directly intend to cooperate in abortion or the evils that flow from it.

If you can reasonably find vaccines that are assuredly not part of any vaccine line even remotely connected with aborted children, you should do so, and request those vaccines. However, clearly identifying such vaccines is not always possible, and the vaccinations are important for your daughter. Thus do what you can reasonably do to request better alternatives, but if they cannot be found, realize that your cooperation in any evils associated with the vaccines is remote and unintended.

Q182: I am 93 years old and have told everyone that I don't want any medical interventions if I get sick. They say I sound suicidal. Thoughts? – *name withheld*

A: One ought not speak to broadly when it comes to such matters. Generally speaking, the Church teaches that we are not required to employ excessive and burdensome treatments that are not really therapeutic. However, what is, or is not, therapeutic may vary. For example, a breathing machine that is merely sustaining a person who will never recover is not therapeutic. However, a breathing machine is therapeutic for a young person who has been injured and is assisted by a breathing machine temporarily.

Even for an older person such as you, certain treatments may be therapeutic, or assisting in your comfort. Food and water even if it ministered by a tube, is helpful and therapeutic (except in the rarest of situations) and must be offered even to patients well into the dying process, according to Catholic teaching.

Rather than make a broad refusal of all treatments, you do well to speak with a local priest, especially one skilled in medical and bioethical issues, and your doctor, to set up some reasonable protocols. It also helps to have someone designated with a medical power of attorney to speak for you in the event that you are incapacitated.

Generally you are not required to employ extraordinary or excessively burdensome treatments. But particular circumstances are always going to be important and affect the determination of what is the moral and ethical thing to do, even at age 93.

Q183: A co-worker is a member of a very fundamentalist Protestant denomination and says the Catholic Church changed her teaching, which once forbade usury, and now permits it. He says the Bible forbids usury? Is this so? *—James Bulware, Birmingham, AL*

A: Usury must be defined. Perhaps the clearest definition of usury as understood by the Church was given by the Fifth Lateran Council in 1515: "For this is the proper interpretation of usury; when one seeks to acquire gain from the use of a thing which is not fruitful, with no labor, no expense, and no risk on the part of the lender." (DS 1442).
In the past, with more of a barter economy, those lending money were few, and often took advantage of others. This was rightly condemned as usury.

In current economic conditions money is used more widely can be fruitful in diverse ways. Thus, one incurs expense when lending it, since they could have used it in many other fruitful ways. Further, there is risk incurred when one lends.

But the wider use of money also means the lending market is rather competitive and interest rates are more commensurate with actual risk and opportunity costs. Reasonable reparation, in the form of interest for these costs and risks is not per se immoral. Thus, ordinary market interest rates do not usually merit the term "usury."

So usury is still condemned by the Church, but given changes in the marketplace, usury is no longer synonymous with the mere charging of interest, but only with excessive interest that does not reflect the actual costs to the lender.

Thus for the married, chastity means fidelity to one's spouse in body, mind and heart. Any sexual contact with anyone outside the marriage is adultery. Further the viewing of pornography is wholly excluded and fantasizing about someone other than the spouse, is a form of unchastity. The use of contraception is also annexed to unchastity since it willfully excludes openness to the procreative dimension of sex, which God intends as part of sexual intercourse.

For the unmarried, chastity means refraining from any form of genital sexual relations, to include inappropriate touching, immodest or inappropriate conversations, the viewing of pornography, masturbation, and sexually fantasizing.

Hence all three words are related and can be used interchangeably to some degree in their wide sense. But strictly they have more specific meanings.

Q184: On the cross Jesus said, "Father forgive them, they know not what they do." But if we don't know what we do, how can we ever sin or be blameworthy for it? – *Jerry Conlin, via email*

A: Jesus is speaking to a particular situation and we ought not generalize what he says here. The ignorance he likely refers to here is that they do not know or understand his true identity. Do they really know that they were killing their Lord and Messiah? Likely not.

While it is true that the Lord gave many proofs of his identity by fulfilling Scripture, and working miracles, along with the testimony of John the Baptist, and the Father's testimony in their heart, many of his accusers and condemners still did not understand or come to faith. Many considered Jesus a blasphemer and felt quite justified in their condemnation.

Now this of course does not mean that they are without any sin at all and as Jesus said earlier, "If you do not come to believe that I AM, you will die in your sins." (Jn 8:24). Hence, while those who kill him and conspired to have him killed may be acting in some ignorance at the moment of the crucifixion, the Lord is still calling them to receive saving faith and come out of their woeful ignorance. Many in fact, did come to faith later and repent (e.g. Acts 2:37), others seemingly did not.

Ignorance and its relationship to culpability speaks to what a person could reasonably know and understand given their history, the condition of their heart, and so forth. Vinceable ignorance is ignorance we could reasonably have overcome. Invincible ignorance is an ignorance a person could not have reasonably overcome at the time of the sin. And while the Church makes these distinctions, only God can know the true inner condition of a person and make this judgment. That is why the Church does not formally teach that specific people are in Hell. Only God can see into the heart of a person to make that judgment.

Q185: Several of my cousins, live together with others and are having sexual relations outside of marriage. They think that it is no problem for them to go to Holy Communion since, to their mind it is either not wrong at all or only a venial sin. Are there texts in the Bible or Catechism I can point them to? – *Doris O'Hare, via email*

A: The situation you describe objectively involves mortal sin which one must cease and receive absolution in confession before returning to Holy Communion. St. Paul instructs and warns, *So then, whoever eats the bread or drinks the cup of the Lord in an unworthy manner will be guilty of sinning against the body and blood of the Lord. Everyone ought to examine themselves before they eat of the bread and drink from the cup* (1 Cor 11:27-28).

In many places scripture teaches that fornication (sex before marriage) is a mortal sin. St Paul warns that fornicators will not inherit the kingdom of God (1 Cor 6:9; Eph 5:5; Heb 13:4 among others). Jesus too indicates that we should be more willing to put out our eye than to sin by lust and thus enter Hell (Mat 5:27-30).

The Catechism speaks of fornication as a grave offense
Fornication is carnal union between an unmarried man and an unmarried woman. It is gravely contrary to the dignity of persons and of human sexuality which is naturally ordered to the good of spouses and the generation and education of children. Moreover, it is a grave scandal when there is corruption of the young. (# 2353)

Thus, your cousins, if they are committing acts of fornication are committing the kind of serious (mortal) sin that requires confession, with a firm purpose of amendment prior to receiving Holy Communion.

Of itself, living together (though without having sexual relations) is imprudent (as a near occasion of sin) and might cause scandal. However, of itself and without illicit sexual union, it is not something that would necessarily require Confession.

Q186: My son and I own different large parcels of land adjacent to each other. His land, is in another jurisdiction and is exempt from sales tax; mine is not. We want to by a work vehicle that we will share. Is it wrong for me to give him the money and have him buy it entirely so we can avoid the tax? – *John S.*

A: Morally speaking there does not seem to be a problem here. Let me hasten to add that I am not a civil or tax lawyer and do not know all the ins and outs of what "Caesar" might demand.

But in moral terms it is not wrong to take advantage of opportunities and options presented by civil law. People look for tax shelters all the time. Presuming they are legal it not wrong to use them, even though paying just and certainly required taxes in annexed to the 4th and the 7th Commandments.

What you could *not* do in the situation you describe is lie to get the tax break. For example, suppose the duly authorized local state authorities stipulate that the vehicle is housed primarily or exclusively in the state, but you have no intention of doing this and will keep it entirely on your land outside the state. Even if you consider such questions intrusive, you could not lie to obtain the tax break. But neither do you need to wholly disclose that you will share or borrow the vehicle from you son unless the State reasonably requires such information.

Q187: In recently repented of having stolen a few things of moderate value, one from work, and the other from an acquaintance. I was surprised (and I guessed relieved) that the priest did not mention anything about making restitution. Is restitution required and does this matter affect my absolution? – *name withheld*

A: Yes, restitution is required in matters of theft. The Catechism teaches that in view of commutative justice the reparation of the injustice committed requires the return of the stolen things to their owner. (# 2412)

Ideally such restitution is made directly to the owner, and simple embarrassment does not excuse this.

However sometimes direct restitution is not possible. Perhaps the item is gone or used up. Perhaps the owner cannot be located or has died. Perhaps the actual owner is not known. Perhaps the one who stole is now depleted and cannot make the required restitution.

In such cases some form of indirect restitution is necessary. Perhaps one is able to make restitution in kind, for example, through money worth the value of the damage, or by extra work if something was taken from an employer. If the direct owner cannot be found, perhaps a contribution to the poor or some contribution of value to the wider community involving the spiritual or corporal works of mercy can be done.

Thus restitution seeks to repair for the damage caused by theft in two ways. First it restores to the owner, directly or indirectly, what was taken. Secondly it cancels and closes off the benefits that the one who stole received, which they have no just right to go on enjoying.

In terms of absolution, the priest does not grant absolution provisionally. Absolutions cannot be worded: "I absolve you from your sins provided that you do 'X'"

However, if a priest were to hear that someone stole an item of significance but was refusing to make any form of restitution, he might reasonably conclude that they did not have the necessary contrition. If this were the case he might find it necessary to withhold or delay absolution.

5. THE CHURCH

Q188: One of the common objections of my adult son raises about going to Church is that all the sin and hypocrisy in the Church is intolerable to him. Any advice on what to say about this? – *name withheld*

A: Well, of course, this is one of the objections that Jesus had to face from the Pharisees: *This man welcomes sinners and eats with them* (Luke 15:2). It's a remarkable thing, Jesus is found among sinners, even hypocrites. He is not found in the perfect places of our imagined "church." He is not simply found in the places or company considered desirable, he is found where he is found: among sinners. Indeed, one image for the Church is Christ, crucified between two thieves!

As for hypocrisy, we do well to wonder if any human being on this planet, save for the most heroic saint, is utterly free from this ubiquitous human problem. Surely your son cannot consider himself wholly free from it can he?

In terms of mission, the Church is a hospital for sinners, and that means sinners will be found there. But so will medicine of the sacraments, the wisdom of Scripture, healing, and encouragement, admonishment, too. And yes, sinners...even some in critical condition. We know our sin. That is why we have confessionals in every parish. Pray God, we always have room for one more sinner.

As for those who seek for Christ apart from the Church, i.e. apart from his Body: no can do. Christ is found with his body, the Church. He associates with sinners and holds them close. He incorporates them into his body through baptism and seeks them when they stray.

Tell your son that Jesus loves sinners and is not too proud to be in their company and call them his brethren. Join us!

Q189: I have been a Catholic all my 35 years. But I am becoming increasingly angry at how the Church abuses its power and, among many things, excludes gay people from getting married. Well, I pretty much know you won't agree, but I have to speak out. - *name withheld*

A: You exemplify an interesting phenomenon wherein the modern world, which is often disdainful of Church "power," then turns and expresses exaggerated notions of Church power.

In terms of divine moral law, the Church has no authority whatsoever to overturn the biblical teaching against homosexual acts, or to redefine the parameters of marriage as given by God in the Scriptures and Sacred Tradition. The Church is the servant of the Word of God (*cf* Catechism # 86), not an all-powerful entity that is able to tear pages from the Bible, cross out lines, or overrule it. The sinfulness of homosexual acts (and also illicit heterosexual acts, such as fornication and adultery) is consistently taught at every stage of biblical revelation to the last books.

Hence, I would urge you to reconsider that what you call an abuse of power, is actually, a humble recognition of the limits of her power by the Church.

Q190: Why don't the bishops excommunicate self-proclaimed Catholic politicians who not only dissent from Church teaching but actively work to undermine the Church's mission? – *Maurice*

A: When it comes to excommunication, or denying Holy Communion to someone, we are dealing not only with Church Law, but also with the prudential application of that Law. It would seem that most Bishops currently consider the application of these penalties, in public ways, to be imprudent and/or counter-productive.

In Scripture we see that Jesus himself gives various answers as to how to deal with sinners in the Church. On the one hand, he offers that for unrepentant sinners who will not even listen to the Church, they should be considered as a tax collector, or Gentile (i.e. excommunicated) – *cf* Matt 18:17. But elsewhere, Jesus tells a parable about field hands who urged the owner to tear out the weeds from the field, but the owner cautioned that to do so might also harm the wheat. He then said, let them grow together to the harvest – *cf* Matt. 13:30.

Hence, we see that a prudential judgment is necessary, and that many things must be weighed. Currently, many bishops have expressed concerns that to excommunicate, or apply other public penalties, would make "martyrs" of these public figures and further divide the Church, (for not all Catholics agree with the view implicit in your question).

What is clear is that the pastors of such politicians, and other wayward Catholics, should meet with them privately, to call them to repentance. And, if their repentance is lacking, they should privately be urged to stay away from Holy Communion and be mindful of their final judgment before God.

Q191: The Catholic Church teaches that Peter was given primacy amongst the apostles, yet Peter considered himself a "fellow elder" and thus, did not view himself as one superior to the other apostles. So aren't the local churches to be led by a plurality of elders?
- John C., Reformed Baptist

A: The text, which you cite is 1 Peter 5:1, wherein Peter exhorts the leaders of the Church to be zealous shepherds. But what you see as equivalency may simply be fraternity.

For example, when my Archbishop writes a letter to the priests, he begins, "My dear brother Priests..." Now the archbishop is a priest, and shares that in common, as a brother, with all the priests of this diocese. But his salutation is not a declaration that there is no difference, or that he does not also have authority over us as the Cardinal Archbishop.

In the letter you cite, Peter begins by writing of himself, *Peter, an apostle of Jesus Christ* (1 Peter 1:1). Hence your point that he thought of himself *merely* as a fellow elder does not seem supported.

Further, the Catholic Church's position on the primacy of Peter does not rise or fall based on one text. Our teaching is based on a number of foundational texts and also on Sacred Tradition.

Thus we see that Christ singles Peter out and calls him "the Rock," giving him the keys of the Kingdom of heaven, a sign of special authority (Matt 16:19). He also assigns Peter with the special role of uniting the other apostles, when the devil would sift (divide) them like wheat (Lk 22:31-32). Peter is also singled out by Jesus at the lakeside and told to "Tend my Sheep" (John 21).

In Acts we see Peter living the office Christ gave him. He is always listed first among the Apostles. He preaches the first sermon. He convenes the brethren and directs the replacement of Judas. He works the first miracle, pronounces sentence on Ananias and Sapphira, is led by the Spirit to baptize the first Gentiles, and presides over the Council of Jerusalem, bringing unity to its divided deliberations.

Relying not only on a wide biblical tradition, the Catholic Church also bases her understanding of Peter's office on the broad and consistent testimony of the Fathers of the Church and other witnesses to the practice of Christian antiquity. These sources attest that Peter and his successors were accorded special dignity. Their authority to rule over the whole Church in a unique and singular way is confirmed by these sources.

Q192: Are Catholics who reject the church's teachings on the Mass, the Trinity, the virgin birth of Christ, abortion, etc. no longer Catholics or are they one for life because of their baptism? - *John Clubine, Ontario*

A: Regarding baptism, the catechism affirms the following: *Baptism seals the Christian with the indelible spiritual mark (character) of his belonging to Christ. No sin can erase this mark, even if sin prevents Baptism from bearing the fruits of salvation. Given once for all, Baptism cannot be repeated.* (#1272).

That said, your question also seems to touch on the question of how deep one's communion is with Christ and his Church. And if one were to reject the teachings you mention they would, in effect, seriously harm, even sever their communion, their unity with the Church. At times the Church must ask those who intentionally dissent, to assess their own communion with the Church, and to no longer celebrate a communion that is seriously impaired by refraining from receiving Holy Communion. In rare cases the Church my see a need to formally declare an excommunication exists.

However, even in such cases, given the indelible mark that baptism confers, one can never utterly lose the status of belonging to Christ. By analogy, even if a son or daughter of yours were to wander far from you, live in total contradiction to what you believe, and even curse you to your face and act so badly that you had to erect legal protections for yourself, none of this would not change the fact that they are still your son or daughter.

Q193: Jesus embraced the sinner. The Church reconciles women after abortion and has prison outreach. Why won't the Church embrace homosexuals? - *name withheld, San Diego, CA*

A: For the record, the Church does have an outreach to homosexual persons known as "Courage." It emphasizes living the virtue of chastity by teaching that homosexuals live celibately. While many do except this outreach, it is also true many homosexuals reject this call to live celibately.

It is of course challenging for the Church to reach out to those homosexuals who insist that the only way we can "properly" minister to them is to accept wholeheartedly and uncritically what God teaches is sinful.

Jesus embraced sinners, but he also called them to repentance. Proper ministry, and love, is rooted in the truth of what God reveals. Scripture consistently and at every stage defines homosexual acts as gravely disordered and sinful. It also condemns fornication, adultery and incest.

Q194: Today, many politicians who call themselves Catholic are pro-choice when it comes to abortion. Are these politicians committing a sin by not forcefully condemning abortion? And why do the Catholic bishops not forcefully discipline them?
- name withheld, San Clemente, CA

A: To be supportive of the so-called "right" to abortion is indeed sinful and erroneous. Further, to vote to fund abortions is indeed a grave sin. The degree of culpability will be based on how directly the legislator votes for abortion. To go directly to fund abortions is clearly a grave evil. Sometimes however, abortion funding is tucked inside omnibus bills. And thus the culpability, of the politician involves a more indirect cooperation with evil.

Bishops and pastors, have a serious obligation to warn those who serve in public life against directly supporting, and especially funding, abortion. How this is best done, is a matter of tactics and prudence.

Consider for example that a man has some obligation to protect his family from home invasion. Theoretically, any number of alternatives might be possible for him. Perhaps he might booby-trap his property with lethal weapons that would instantly kill any trespasser. On the other hand, he might reasonably conclude that such a method would also endanger others whom might happen upon his property. Thus he might use lesser means, such as alarms, extra locks, and warning signs.

Which methods are employed, might vary from place to place. If a man lives in the country were civil wars raging, he might use more severe methods. On the other hand, if a man lives were civil law is generally in place, he may feel it is reasonable to use lesser methods.

It is the same with the bishops on how best to deal with dissenting and wayward Catholic politicians. In some cases, public disciplining and refusal of communion may make some sense. But in other settings, many bishops have concluded such measures might make martyrs out of such politicians. Perhaps the Bishop will prefer to privately warn a pro-choice politician that they will have to answer to God.

Many, who are quick to critique the bishops, ought to recall that matters such as these require careful prudence. Many who demand significantly punitive measures do not themselves take this approach in dealing with their own families. The Lord himself warns that, sometimes in our zeal to pull up weeds, we end up harming the wheat.

Reasonable people differ on how to handle matters of prudential judgment. Indeed, individual bishops vary in their approaches. This is the nature of such prudential judgments. Catholics do well to pray for priests and bishops, who have obligations to correct, but must do so in ways that do not cause more harm than good. Pray!

Q195: What do you think about women being ordained to the priesthood? I think if Christ wanted women in this role He would have ordained his mom. - *Allen Eberle, Hague, ND*

A: Your answer is not far from the point. People often give the Church exaggerated power, as though she can do anything she pleases. But, as the last three Popes have all stated, the Church has no authority whatsoever to confer priestly ordination on women. This is because Jesus, though he broke many conventions of his day, nevertheless called only men to be apostles. And in the call of the apostles is the origin of the priesthood.

The Church is can no more alter the matter and form of this sacrament than she can use beer and pretzels, for consecration, instead of bread and wine. There are just some limits we must observe.

Q196: By way of disclosure, I will say that I am a former Catholic who left out of annoyance at all the layers and structures we find the Church these days. The events surrounding the papal conclave makes me wonder if the apostles would recognize simple and humble Church they had, compared to the pompous and ceremonial church of today.
— *Jonathan Fischer, San Diego, CA*

A: Well, I am not so sure. It's kind of like asking if Orville and Wilbur Wright would recognize the simple wooden and cloth plane they flew, compared to the modern jetliner of today. To some extent they certainly would see the basic structure, but they would also marvel at all the magnificent developments that their simple idea at ushered in.

It would not be reasonable to assume that they would wag their finger and insisted we go back to planes made of cloth and wood and gasoline motors. It seems more reasonable that they would admire the developments that had ensued, all of which built on the basic ideas that they set forth.

I think it would be similar with the Apostles. It is clear that doctrine has developed over the years, as has liturgy and other necessary structures in the Church. But these things developed from the structures that were already there from the beginning. The seed of truth has become the mature tree. The hierarchal structure, established by Christ himself, has expanded to meet the needs of a now worldwide Church.

You are free to consider things you don't like as pompous, but others see such things as dignified and appropriate. God, and the things of God are rightly to be honored with some degree of ceremony and respect.

Q197: Does the Pope have the authority to overturn pronouncements of previous popes, for example, in matters of contraception and the ordination of women? – *Alice O'Hara, Isleboro, ME*

A: We must distinguish between different types of law and teaching. There are certain laws and precepts that are ceremonial and customary practices, or merely disciplinary rules. These can be changed, and are changed from time to time. For example, things such as the kinds and types of vestments and other regalia worn by the clergy and other merely ceremonial aspects of the liturgy can be changed. Disciplinary norms such as curial structures, canonical penalties, etc. can also be changed.

But in matters of defined doctrine by the Magisterium regarding faith and morals, rooted in Scripture and Apostolic Tradition, or from previous Popes and Councils, the Pope is bound to uphold them. There are some technical debates about *what* is definitively taught that are too technical to set forth in this short answer. But the two matters, which you cite, are certainly teachings to which the Pope is bound and may not overturn.

Q198: I have been asked recently if I am Christian or Catholic? What kind of question is this, and how should I answer it.
- *name withheld, Port Huron, MI*

A: You are right to be annoyed and find offense. Catholics are Christian, indeed the original Christians. We have been here all 2000 years, and are the Church founded by Jesus Christ himself.

It is sadly true, that there are some who polemically and rhetorically ask, "Are you Catholic or Christian?" as if the two categories were mutually exclusive. They are not. It would be like asking a certain man, "Are you male or human?" And of course the answer is both and the question as stated is offensive. And the same answer is true here, that Catholics are also Christians.

Unfortunately, not all Christians are Catholic. And this is a countersign, because Christ founded one Church, and has one Body, he prayed for unity, not endless divisions. He did not found tens of thousands of different disputing denominations. He established one Church which he founded, and unified around his vicar, Peter and his successors, the popes who are designated to unify and strengthen the others whom the devil would sift (separate) like wheat (*cf* Luke 22:31).

The word "Catholic," while often used as a proper noun, is also an adjective. The word catholic comes from the Greek, and means "according to the whole." And this is understood in at least two ways. First of all, the Church is Catholic, because we preach the whole counsel of Christ, not just certain favorite passages or popular viewpoints. We are called to preach the whole Gospel, whether in season are out of season.

Secondly, the Church is called catholic, because we are called to a universal outreach to all the nations. We are not just a church of a certain race or nation, we are called to go on to the ends of the earth, and make disciples of all nations. The Church has a "catholic," that is a universal, mission to everyone.

And thus, the Catholic Church is the Christian Church, and all Christians are called to be Catholic. It is for this unity that we must lovingly strive.

Q199: I don't think the Church teaches that the Saints are omniscient. Therefore my question is how are they made aware of our prayers, which are directed to them? – *Harold Whalen, Long Beach, CA*

A: Our communion with the Saints, is accomplished in and through Jesus Christ, who is the head of the Body, the Church. All the members of Christ's body, those here on earth (the Church militant), the Saints in heaven (the Church triumphant), and those in purgatory, the Church suffering), are members of the one Body of Christ, and are united by him, and through him who is the Head.

To use an analogy, my right hand has communion with my left hand, not because my hands have their own capacity to work together. Rather, my right hand and my left hand have communion and can work together only in and through the head of my body, which unites and directs them. And so it is with the members of the Body of Christ. In this regard, St. Paul teaches, when one member suffers all the members suffer, when one member is glorified, all the members are glorified (1 Cor 12:26). And there is thus a communion of the all the members in the one Body.

That the Saints are aware of us, and pray for us before the throne of God is attested in Scripture in Revelation 5:8 Where in the four living creatures present the prayers of the saints before the throne of God and where the incense, which is the prayers of God's saints are brought before the throne (Rev 8:5). There is also the ancient tradition of the church from apostolic times wherein the martyrs and heavenly Saints are invoked for help of every sort.

Let us be clear that such communion of the Saints does not occur apart from Jesus Christ, but rather, it is facilitated by him through whom and in whom all things are and subsist, and who is the head of the Body the Church uniting his members.

Q200: A priest wrote in our local paper that we should humbly accept that our church, whatever our denomination, does not have the whole truth. But I thought the Catholic Church was the pillar and foundation of the truth. – *Lucy Hart, Harper, TX*

A: Here too, the subtleties of language are important in understanding how questions are answered.

The Catholic Church maintains for demonstrable reasons, that we possess the fullness of revealed truth and the full means to salvation given by God. We hold this in distinction to other denominations and religious traditions, which may have elements of the truth, but are lacking the fullness of these and are usually admixed with error.

That said, we do not claim to know *everything* there is to know about God. God is more glorious than everything we could ever say or know about him.

It is perhaps in this vein that the priest wrote his remarks. Nevertheless, one might wish for greater precision from the good father, as your puzzlement demonstrates.

Q201: How does the Catholic Church reconcile the Catechism #841 which says, "The plan of salvation also includes Muslims" (who deny the resurrection) with 1 Corinthians 15:14 that says "If Christ be not risen…your faith is in vain. – *John Clubine, Etobicoke, Ontario*

A: God surely wants to save all and has set plans in place to do so through the preaching of the Gospel. That the plan of salvation aims for all, does not mean that all are in fact saved. If one were to knowingly reject Christ after having him effectively preached, they may well forfeit their salvation. However, not all have had Christ effectively preached, and the Church leaves the final determination to the Lord of how culpable they are of their seeming rejection of Christ.

Q202: Our Bishop is closing our parish. My grandparent were among those who built and paid for this parish. By what right does the bishop close what is ours? - *name withheld, Philadelphia, PA*

A: Canonically, there likely are some solutions that permit the lay faithful to take possession of building slated for closure, undertake its maintenance and keep them open as chapels etc. under the supervision of the local church. Frankly though, most congregations that have reached a critical state where closure is deemed necessary are not in fact able to undertake such solutions.

While there are legitimate canonical issues, and the lay faithful you have canonical rights at the closing the parishes, I am not a canon lawyer and would like to answer your question pastorally.

And from a pastoral point of view it seems evident that bishops do not close parishes, people close parishes. Some wish to explain the widespread closing of Catholic parishes, especially in the Northeast, as mere demographic shifts. And while there are demographic issues, the fact remains that with the Catholic population almost double what it was in the 1950s, many parishes filled to overflowing back in that era now sit increasingly empty.

This is a teachable moment, and we must accept some very painful facts. When only 25% of Catholics go to Mass nationwide, and when Catholics stop having many children, or effectively handing on the faith to their children, this is what happens.

The Church simply cannot maintain perishes and other institutions such as schools and hospitals when Catholics are largely absent. Pastorally speaking people, not Bishops alone, close parishes. Many parishes, schools, seminaries and convents, now sit largely empty. And as they begin to go empty bills are unpaid, maintenance is deferred, and the situation eventually becomes critical. Diocese do not have endless amounts of money, or priests and other personnel to staff and maintain increasingly empty, no longer viable parishes... Decisions have to be made.

Pastorally, one would hope that long before things go utterly critical, that bishops, working together with communities that are going into crisis, can speak honestly and work for solutions. But this is not simply the responsibility of the Bishop, it is the responsibility of all the people of God to have such honest discussions.

Thus, we are left with a difficult but teachable moment about what happens when the faith handed down to us is largely set aside by the vast majority of Catholics. It's time to Evangelize and make disciples, as Christ commands.

Q203: I hear the term "Evangelical Christians used a lot, but I am not sure to what or whom this refers. Can you enlighten me?
- *name withheld, via email*

A: Non-Catholic Christians have usually been termed Protestants in the English language, because they were collectively "protesting" something in Catholic teaching or practice. But of course, Protestantism is a very diverse group of tens of thousands of different denominations which span the theological spectrum: liberal to conservative.

Thirty years ago Protestant denominations were largely broken into two groups: the more socially conservative "Fundamentalists", and the more liberal, both socially and theologically "Mainline" denominations such as: Lutherans, Methodists, Presbyterians, Episcopalians, et al.

The Fundamentalist tended to draw their numbers more from the more conservative Baptist congregations, and a wide variety of independent and nondenominational groups.

What tended to divide Fundamentalist from Mainline Protestants was how the Scriptures were to be interpreted. Fundamentalist tended toward a more literalist adherence to the text that was more suspicious to applying historical context or other interpretive principles for understanding the text. The mainline denominations moved rather dramatically toward such interpretive keys, so much so that many of them have arguably move beyond the text itself, and, as such, have no problem permitting things which biblical texts unambiguously forbid. e.g. homosexual acts, homosexual marriage, women clergy, etc.

During the 1970s and 80s, there was a protracted campaign in the media and wider culture to discredit fundamentalism as rigid, pharisaical, and out of touch. Fair or not, the fundamentalists began to adopt the term "Evangelical" in response. While today's Evangelical Christians are not simply synonymous with the "Fundamentalists" of the past, the term "Fundamentalist" has largely been replaced by the term "Evangelical."

Today, despite theological differences between Evangelicals and Catholics, there is a lot of common ground on the moral issues. This has led to greater and one of the most fruitful sources of converts to the Catholic Church is from Evangelical Christian denominations today.

They bring with them a great love for the Lord Jesus, and a great love for Scripture and seek a more stable, historical, theological and sacramental framework of the Catholic Church in which to live their faith.

These closer relations have led to the description of "Evangelical Catholicism." This term expresses an emphasis on the Scriptural and Apostolic origins of our holy faith. At the heart of Evangelical Catholicism is the concern to avoid becoming too self-referential, to always remain centered on Christ.

Q204: I keep hearing that the Church is declining in numbers, but every year I see here that the number of Catholics in this country. Which is it, are we going up or down? - *Alfreda Johnson, Libertytown, MD*

A: To understand the numbers, it is helpful to make a distinction between nominal and practicing Catholics. Nominal Catholics are those who call themselves Catholic, but are not practicing or living the faith in any real sense. This number, is going up as our population continues to grow. And that growth is mainly from immigrants, the majority of whom are at least nominally Catholic. Thus the overall number of Catholics is growing.

But to be a nominal Catholic is not necessarily to be a practicing Catholic. And, though here in America, the overall number of Catholics is growing, the number of practicing Catholics does seem to be declining overall. Sadly, only about 25% of Catholics go to mass each Sunday (down from close to 80% in the 1950s). And even smaller percentage agree with all the teachings of the faith and practice their faith daily to a significant degree.

Q205: Why does the modern Church not have deaconesses? (Scripture and some of the Father's mention them). It seems they would fill a void, given the shortage of priests. – *Dolores Chauffe, via email*

A: The references to deaconesses in the early Church are complicated, and much debated. St. Paul does speak of certain women as having a ministry of service. And, in his discussion about deacons, in 1 Timothy 3:11, Paul does say, "The women too.... "

But what he means here is unclear. Does mean that women were ordained deacons? Or, is he referring to the wives of deacons? And even if they were deaconesses, did they receive the ministry by the laying on of hands? It seems not. Though Acts 6:6 mentions the first deacons having hands laid on them, there is no reference to this in terms of the women.

In the Greek text of the New Testament, the word *diakonia* can refer to the office of deacon (*diakoni*), or more generically to a ministry (*diakonia* = ministry) of service.

Some speculate that an essential task of deaconesses was to attend the baptism of women, since baptisms were conducted dis-robed. For modesty's sake women conducted the baptisms of women.

At the end of the day however we are left with a great deal of speculation, if we simply examine the scriptural text. But, we do not simply attend to the Scriptural text. We also look also to the practice of the early Church. And regarding this, there is no evidence, that the clerical office of deacon was ever conferred on women by the laying on of hands.

There is little doubt, that women can and do serve in many capacities in the Church today. It is true that women can provide great service (*diakonia*) to the Church. But it does not follow that they must be ordained the clerical state of deacon to do so.

Q206: What is the difference between a monastery and a convent?
- *Allen Eberle, Hague, ND*

A: Like many words, we can denote a strict sense, and a more relaxed colloquial sense. We can also note that the meaning of the words have changed a bit over time.

The word *monastery* originally came from the Greek word *monazein* "which means, "to live alone." In the earliest days monastics, (both men and women) went to the desert to live a largely solitary life, in separate dwellings. However, many of them in a local area came to share some common buildings for prayer, and eating. Over time many came closer together, and eventually were housed under one roof, though the monks and monastic sisters still tended to keep long hours of silence. Thus they lived in a relative, if not physical solitude, coming together also for communal prayers, meals and necessary community deliberations in the shared chapel, refectory, and chapter hall.

Today the word "monastery" has tended to be used only of communities of men, while communities of women have tended to have their dwelling denoted as a "convent" or "cloister." But, technically, there are women's communities whose domicile is most properly termed a monastery.

The main difference that the term "monastery" is meant to signify is that those who live there, live "alone" or apart from the everyday world. Their prayer is centered in the monastic community. Generally too, their work or apostolate is also centered there, rather than out in the community or world. Some enclosures are strict, others less so, but the concept of dwelling *apart* is key.

"Convents" and religious houses however, tend to house religious men and women who do not live and work in such isolation from the everyday world. Perhaps they work in education, hospitals or other external places during the day, but then return and live in community, sharing meals and prayer and other aspects of common life. The word "convent" comes from a Latin word which means "to convene, or gather," and is less inclusive of the concept of solitude contained in the word "monastery."

Historically, communities of men and women have used different terms to indicate "conventual" settings. Women's communities have use terms like convent, and nunnery, whereas for the men's communities terms like, priory, or friary have been used.

Nevertheless, and despite a variety of adaptations, the fundamental distinction to be observed is between communities (male or female) that live in some solitude (monastic) and those which interact more directly with the everyday world (conventual).

Q207: In the history show "How Sex Changed the World", they speak about the Church's role in prostitution and said that 20% of the "customers" were clergy. Is there any truth to this?
— *Susan Marron, Simi Valley, CA*

A: When one hears claims about Church history that are less than flattering, or shocking, two balancing perspectives are helpful.

On the one hand, one ought not to become to alarmed or defensive of claims that there has been sin in the Church. Any time there one human being in the room there is bound to be sin. And The Church is very big and very old. The "hospital" we call the Church includes many saints, but is also a hospital for sinners.

On the other hand, not all claims of sin the Church are fair, or presented in proper context. And some claims are outright lies, or exaggerations. Thus it is highly unlikely that 20% of the clientele of prostitutes were clergy. There are, and have been even great sinners among the clergy. But as recent scandals (sadly) show, the percentage of offending clergy is quite small, though even a small number is too many and can cause great harm.

Other claims against the Church regarding the Inquisition in the Crusades also tend to present these issues out of historical context and backload current sensibilities times that were far more brutal, and where stable governments and modern jurisprudence did not yet exist.

And so we must have balance. Jesus has always been found among sinners, to the scandalous of some. We do not make light of sin, we simply seek fairness.

Q208: A friend who grew up in the Russian Orthodox Church married a man from the Roman Catholic Church. They had a Catholic wedding and she now practices Roman Catholicism. She said she did not have to do anything to become Catholic. Is that correct?
— *Thomas Pohlen, via email*

A: No. She should speak to her pastor and request formal acceptance into full communion with the Catholic Church. There are also some protocols that are observed in receiving members from the Orthodox churches that will need some attention (see Code of Canon Law for Eastern Churches, Canons 35, & 896-901). While she would not need to receive sacraments, her formal reception into the Catholic Church is covered by these norms and protocols, which exist to show respect for the Rite from which she came. If she wishes to practice the Latin Rite, that can be done; but there are procedures to be followed.

Q209: My daughter says she loves Jesus but just doesn't like the Church (for lots of reasons). She doesn't see any problem with this and doesn't think going to Church is necessary. Is there anything I can say to her?
— *name withheld, via email*

A: The Church is the Body of Christ (*cf* Col 1:8; 1 Cor 12:27; Rom 12:4-6). Hence to declare love for Jesus but disdain for his body is inauthentic. We cannot have Jesus without his Body. How would your daughter feel if someone said to her: "I love you, but your body is awful, ugly, and I can't stand it." She would not appreciate this and discard any artificial distinctions between her and her own body. It is the same with Jesus. Perhaps if she can be taught to understand the rather insulting quality of her position, she will reconsider.

Certainly there are sinners and imperfection in Jesus' Body the Church. But even historically Jesus was found in the "strange company" of sinners. Many in Jesus' time were scandalized by the associations he maintained. But he is found where he is found, not merely where we want him to be. So if your daughter loves Jesus and really wants to find him, she needs to join the rest of us poor sinners.

Q210: I overheard a Baptist coworker explaining to his wife that the pastor was requiring him to submit his W-2 form so that his tithe could be properly monitored. Is this right? –*K. Tanty, Enterprise, AL*

A: Tithing, that is giving 10% of one's income to the church, is a commendable and rooted in Scripture. But, for a pastor to insist on tax documents seems far too intrusive. It is not something that would be tolerated in the Catholic Church.

Not only is the pastor intruding into private matters of a congregant, but it also manifests a lack of trust wherein a pastor ought to assume that a parishioner has discerned their proper level of giving with God. Accountability has its place, but intrusive investigations rooted in suspicion rather than trust seemed wholly out of place any Christian denomination.

Q211: Why does one see the names of Cardinals with their title between the first and last name, e.g. "Timothy Cardinal Dolan" et al? Sometimes I also see it the other way, "Cardinal Timothy Dolan" and so forth. Which form is more correct? – *Jim Perron, Indianapolis, IN*

A: The more correct in correct and common practice is the place to title between the first and last names, i.e., Donald Cardinal Wuerl. However, this is a matter related to pious custom, rather than a strict juridical requirement.

How the custom developed, is not fully clear. But, most interpret the practice as a form of humility. Those who acquire lofty titles in the Church, often like to remind themselves that, before God, we are all just his children. Indeed, of all the titles a clergyman could ever require, such as Reverend, Monsignor, Excellency, Eminence, etc. the greatest title he actually has is a title that he shares with every other baptized Christian: "Child of God."

Similarly, whatever leadership status anyone attains in the Church, one never loses the status of being a disciple. St. Augustine famously stated to his people, "For you I am a bishop, with you, after all, I am a Christian." (Sermon 340)

Q212: Why is the Society of St. Pius X (SSPX) consigned to obscurity? Why are they treated so harshly when they just want to worship in the traditional way? *–Dennis Yebba, Everett, MA*

A: It is more complex than that. The Church permits the Traditional Mass and the older forms of the Sacraments. In most dioceses these Traditional forms are celebrated in a few parishes regularly. I routinely celebrate the

Traditional Latin Mass and conduct sacraments in the older forms when requested to do so.

This issue of the SSPX goes more to a question of authority (bishops were ordained without permission, etc) and of their difficulty in accepting some of the Second Vatican Council's teachings that extend beyond Liturgy. These problems are too extensive to detail here. However, the Vatican has been working very consistently to restore the SSPX to proper canonical status. No less that Pope Benedict XVI took personal initiatives to canonically regularize the group. However, at the last moment negotiations broke down. Negotiations continue. Pray for unity!

6. CATHOLIC PRACTICES

Q213: We call our priests, "Father." But Jesus teaches in the Bible that we must call no man on earth "father" (Matt 23:9). How can I explain why we Catholics use this term for priests? - *name withheld*

A. If the purpose of Jesus were to banish the use of the word "father" in reference to human males, then it would seem the other New Testament authors, never got the memo. In the New Testament alone there are 195 uses of the word "father(s)" to refer to earthly human males. Hence, it seems clear that to understand our Lord's word as an absolute banishment of the term for any but God is not supported by the practice evident in Scripture itself.

The Catholic practice of calling priests "Father" has several meanings.

In one sense it is meant as an affectionate family term. Parishes are like a family and use family terms such as "brother," and "sister" for men and women religious, "mother" for the superior of a group of religious sisters, and "father" for priests.

Priests imitate biological fathers in a spiritual way. Just as fathers give life, food, encouragement and instruction, so priests give us these things in the spiritual order. They confer spiritual life by God's power at the baptismal font give food through the Eucharist and meet other spiritual needs through the other sacraments and by instruction and encouragement.

Thus, by analogy, we call priests "father." St. Paul referred to himself as a father: "...*you have many guides but not many fathers, for I became your father in Christ Jesus through the Gospel* (1 Cor 4:15). *For you know how, like a father with his children we exhorted and charged each one of you to lead a life worthy of God* (1 Thess 2:10). *Timothy...as a son with a father has served me in the gospel.* (Phil 2:22)

We can see how calling priests "father," in this sense, is not against Biblical principles. St. Paul himself makes use of the term in this way.

In saying "Call no one on earth your Father" Jesus is emphasizing that God is pre-eminent. No earthly father, biological or spiritual, can ever over-rule or take the place of the heavenly Father. God is ultimately the Father of all fathers, and we can never call any man "father" like we call God, "Father."

Q214: I read Msgr. Mannion's answer on angels a while back and was surprised to read "the practice of assigning names to the Holy Angels should be discouraged." Please explain this. What if I was told the name of my angel in prayer? – *Rose*

A: Msgr. Mannion is correct and seems to be quoting a document written in 2001 by the Congregation for Divine Worship entitled, <u>Directory on Popular Piety in the Liturgy: Principles and Guidelines</u>. It says, "The practice of assigning names to the holy angels should be discouraged, except in the cases of Gabriel Raphael and Michael, whose names are contained in Holy Scripture." (#127)

While the Congregation does not offer reasons for discouraging the practice, I would like to offer a couple.

First, there is the understanding of what a name is. For most of us in the modern Western world, a name is simply a sound we go by. But in the ancient, Biblical world, and even in many places today, a name has a far deeper meaning. A name describes something of the essence of the person. This helps explains the ancient practice of the Jews to name the child on the eighth day. The delay gave the parents some time to observe something of the essence of the child, and then, noting it, they would name the child. Indeed most Biblical names are deeply meaningful, and descriptive.

But it is presumptive to think that we can know enough of the essence of a particular angel, in order to be able to assign a name. Hence, assigning a name seems inappropriate.

The second reason is that assigning a name indicates some superiority over the one named. Thus, in the case of children, parents, who are superior over their children, rightly name them. However, in the case of angels, they are superior to us. And, even though we often speak of them as serving us, they do this on account of their superior power and as guardians. Thus, God commands us to heed their voice (*cf* Ex 23:20-21)

So, naming an angel does seem problematic, and to be discouraged. As for the name being revealed to you, let me respectfully offer that this is not likely the case, since it seems unlikely that an Angel, or the Holy Spirit, would act contrary to the directive of the Church, herself graced to speak for Christ.

Q215: If I can pray to God about anything I want, what is the purpose of praying to saints and Mary and asking them to pray for me?
— *Jason, Union Correctional Institution*

A: What if you could do both? It is not as though one sort of prayer excludes another.

Your question might well be applied to any number of scenarios. Why would I ask you to pray for me? Or, why do I often say to someone, "I will pray for you!" And why does scripture call us to pray for one another (e.g. Eph 6:18)? Why does Paul ask others to pray for him (e.g. Rom 15:31)? If Jesus is on the main line, and we can talk directly to him, why pick up line two?

And yet, it is our instinct to do exactly that. Both lines are important and Scripture commends both forms of prayer.

Sometimes God wills to answer us directly; sometimes he answers through another's prayer. At the Wedding at Cana (Jn 2:1*ff*), though Jesus surely knew the need of the couple for wine, mysteriously he chose to let his mother sway his decision. So why not pray both ways and let God decide?

Q216: What do we mean when we speak of "our exile" in the prayer "Hail Holy Queen". – *Dionilla, MN*

A: Biblically "exile" refers to the fact that, after Original Sin, Adam and Eve were banished from the Garden of Eden (*cf* Gen 3:24). Hence we are exiled from there and live in this "Valley of Tears," another expression that occurs in the same prayer.

Since the death and resurrection of Jesus we can also say that "exile" refers to the fact that we are not living in our true home. For Christ has opened the way not merely back to the Garden, but to heaven. Heaven is now our true homeland. This sinful and suffering world in not our home, and thus our time here can be considered a kind of exile as we await our summons to "come up higher" to our true and heavenly homeland.

Finally, speaking of this world as an exile, and valley of tears is a sober recognition that life in this world is often hard. And though we may ask God for certain relief, true and lasting joy can only come when we leave this exile for our true home with God.

Q217: I am confused by the admonition of the Church on burial and against spreading ashes in light of the practice of dividing the remains of saints and scattering them throughout the world. – *Jenifer, KY*

A: There are important differences between the practices. Relics usually involve small portions of the body, such as bone fragments to be reserved for veneration. Thus the entire body of a saint is not "scattered" throughout the world, or even scattered locally as with strewn ashes.

Secondly, the relic of the saint is retained for veneration as a kind of physical and visual memory, whereas scattered ashes are spread in order to disappear and return to the elements. And while some may find this meaningful, the result is that any physical reminder of the person is lost, quite different from a relic.

Thirdly, with a relic, the physical presence of a small portion of the body is treated with reverence, much as a gravesite would be, and prayers are often said in it presence in acknowledgment of the given saint. In the case of scattered ashes, neither the ashes nor the place of their dispersal receive the same kind of veneration, and may in fact be tread upon by human beings unaware of their presence, and by wild animals.

While it will be admitted that burial practices have some variance across cultures, the current practice of the Church, out of respect for ancient Christian practice and current sensibilities, is to insist that human remains of any sort be buried or entombed. The Order of Christian Funerals has this to say about the disposition of cremated bodies: *The cremated remains should be buried in a grave or entombed in a mausoleum or columbarium [a cemetery vault designed for urns containing ashes of the dead]. The practice of scattering cremated remains on the sea, from the air, or on the ground, or keeping cremated remains in the home of a relative or friend of the deceased are not the reverent disposition that the Church requires.*

Q218: Didn't Mary's consent occur before she conceived by the Holy Spirit? But in the Angelus prayer "She conceived of the Holy Spirit" comes before "Be it done unto me according to thy word..." Shouldn't the order be the other way around? – *Tim, FL*

A: Some theologians argue that Mary conceived in her heart before she conceived in her womb. Though this is not likely what is meant in the first strophe of the Angelus prayer.

More specifically, liturgical prayer accesses chronological time with reference to the fullness of time. Thus at Christmas, though referencing Jesus' infancy, we still gather with him in the upper room, and at the foot of the Cross, and celebrate him as risen, glorified Lord, at Christmas Mass. Though we focus on one aspect of his temporal work, we always have the whole in mind. Content and context trump chronology.

The same can be said for the Angelus prayer. We are not simply declaring the event of the Incarnation in a strict, chronological way, but in a way that theologically expresses all the components understood wholly: God's initiative, Mary's assent, and the fact of the Word becoming flesh.

Q219: Saying the Rosary and repeating the Mail Mary 50 times seems strange and irrational to me. Are we supposed to concentrate on the prayer we are saying and they mystery all at one time? Please help me understand. – *George Frohmader, Camp Douglas, WI*

A: The Catechism speaks of the rosary as an epitome of the whole Gospel (CCC # 971). In other words it is a summary or an embodiment of the whole Gospel, because it encourages the faithful to meditate upon the fundamental events of salvation history, and the life of Christ. Someone has called the rosary, the "gospel on the string."

These images help to emphasize that the central work of the Rosary is to meditate on the Scriptures and that Mary's work, above all, is to lead us to a deeper faith in Jesus.

There are some who find the Rosary a helpful way to pray. Others find it difficult and distracting. Thus the Church, while encouraging the Rosary, does not require it. It is a fact that people are suited to different prayer forms. Saying repeated Hail Marys, is appreciated by many as a kind of rhythmic background for the meditation on the gospel passages, which is the key point of the Rosary, and this aspect of it should be central in your thoughts.

Q220: My Pastor does not allow us to celebrate Christmas during Advent, tells us not to decorate our homes and forbids any parties on Church grounds until December 25. Is this right? - *Phil, NY*

A: The liturgical environment has stricter rules than Catholics are necessarily obliged to follow in their own homes. While it may be ideal that our homes perfectly reflect the liturgical cycle, practically speaking, many Catholics begin decorating earlier in the month of December.

As for celebrations on Church grounds, that is a matter of pastoral judgment. Frankly, most pastors are rather relaxed about this, understanding that cultural influences, even if less than ideal, can be respected out of regard for the legitimate wishes of people to celebrate conveniently.

I would encourage you to listen carefully to your Pastor's teachings, and strive to keep Advent as much as possible. But it does seem that some leeway in these matters is acceptable.

Q221: Why doesn't the Church have speak more about exorcism and have exorcists speak out more about possession? - *name withheld*

A: Major exorcism is a matter of supreme discretion and confidentiality. The identity of the diocesan exorcist is not generally made known, except to those who need to know.

While procedures in dioceses vary a bit, it is most common that the exorcist works with a team that includes at least one other priest, a medical doctor, and a properly trained psychotherapist who all assist in the assessment of whether a person is actually possessed.

If major exorcism is considered advisable, the exorcist proceeds with it, but only with the explicit approval of the bishop, who must concur with the judgment to go ahead with the major exorcism.

Here too, the exorcist should never work alone, but with at least one other assisting priest and an appropriate team. It is almost never the case that exorcism is a "one and you're done scenario." Generally exorcisms are conducted over a series of sessions, sometimes weeks or months apart.

If one suspects demonic possession, the first place to begin inquiry is always with the parish priest, or another trusted priest. If that priest has reason to suspect possession (rather than obsession or torment) then he should contact the Diocese and request consultation with the appointed exorcist.

Q222: An organization has been sending me what they term "relics" of Padre Pio. It is a small square of cloth encapsulated on a small plaque of the saint. I do not wish to receive these items, sent to solicit money, but I am reluctant to just throw them in the trash. How am I to treat these items which are now accumulating in my effects? - *Chris Wroblewski, Rutherford, NJ*

A: It sounds as though you were describing the third class relic. A first-class relic is some part of the body of a Saint, usually a fragment of a bone or perhaps a lock of hair. A second-class relic is some article owned by a canonized Saint, usually an article of clothing, or some other personal object associated with the Saint. A third class relic is something, usually a cloth of some sort, which is merely touched to a first or second class relic.

One may serenely dispose of third class relics. Most piously and properly, this is done by burning or burying it. Merely pitching such things in the trash is probably to be avoided, though there is no absolute Church norm related to the disposal of third class relicts.

The practice of mailing, or placing these third class relics in the hands of the faithful may, at times, seem annoying. But here too there are no absolute Church norms forbidding such a practice, or of mailing third class relics. This is quite different from first-class relics, wherein significant church Norms and laws are involved.

Q223: I don't think St. Joseph gets the recognition he deserves. We rightly speak a lot of mother Mary, and certainly of Jesus. But Joseph is often relegated to the background. Why is this so, and should it change? – *Jeannine Aucoin, Henniker, NH*

A: Yes, more should be said of St. Joseph, especially today when fatherhood is in such crisis. St. Joseph was a strong man, who was willing to sacrifice career and personal comfort to protect, and care for his family. St. Joseph listened to God, and do what he was instructed to do in the obedience of faith. Here is a powerful model for men and fathers today. I often preach on St. Joseph when I give men's conferences.

That said, the reserve in emphasizing Joseph extends to the Scriptures themselves. This is not due to any neglect of St. Joseph personally, but extends from the emphasis that the true Father of Jesus is God the Father. Thus, Joseph's role as foster father steps to the background after the early infancy narratives.

Nevertheless, your point remains valid. We ought not be overly forgetful of St. Joseph. Even if what we know of Joseph from the Scriptures is very limited, what we do know, is powerfully inspiring and should be emphasized.

Q224: The Church abolished most of the norms regulating "meatless Fridays" and declared Fridays outside of Lent merely as "A Day of Penance." Does the Penance have to be performed on Friday and are there any parameters to observe? – *Peter Stein, Roseville, CA*

A: Generally the penance should be performed on the Friday, though exceptions can be made due to other obligations such as attending family or civic celebrations. Strictly speaking one can work out deferrals or dispensations in regard to Friday observances with their pastor, but practically, most simply work through this on their own.

The thinking back in the 1970s when "meatless Fridays" were substituted with a day of penance was to offer other observances to people on Friday. Simply giving up meat and going to Red Lobster was hardly a penance for most, though the law was being observed technically. Hence it was thought to permit any range of penances, from giving up other things, to taking on special prayers or works of charity.

But as your question implies, it is difficult to follow an uncertain trumpet, and many Catholics simply drifted from any Friday observance with such wide open parameters. Psychologically it would seem that having a clear focus is necessary to assist in such practices. Hence, some Bishop's conferences are going back to meatless Fridays.

Here in America, that is not the case, though there is some discussion on going. For now, you are largely free to determine how to observe Friday, presuming it has a penitential character. It could be to abstain from something good, or to take on some pious or charitable work.

Q225: An Evangelical Christian in my office saw a holy card on my desk of the Blessed Mother. He was rather dismissive of it and my Catholic faith. Sadly I got angry. But I did not really know how best to answer him. He understands we don't worship her but still says we ought to focus only on Jesus. Any thoughts? - *name withheld, Rochester, NY*

A: In discussing such a matter with evangelical Protestants, it's best to stick with Scripture. While there are many scriptures we could quote, it seems the most fundamental passage to set the stage for the discussion is from the Gospel of Luke. There, Mary under the influence of the Holy Spirit, and rejoicing with her cousin, Elizabeth, says, *"From henceforth all generations shall call me blessed. For he that is mighty hath done to me great things; and holy is his name"* (Luke 1:48-49 KJV)

Now, if the Word of God is inspired, and it *is*, then we should be asking a few questions of our own to a good brothers and sisters in the evangelical tradition. Since Scripture says that all generations would call her blessed, aren't we Catholics fulfilling exactly what Scripture says? And if *we* are thus fulfilling Scripture, how are *you*, and why do you criticize us for doing it?

It is not to detriment of God to call Mary blessed, any more than it is a slight against an artist to praise a masterpiece by him. Mary is God's masterpiece, and as the text says, she is blessed because God who mighty has done great things for her. In calling her blessed, we bless the artist, who is the Lord himself.

At some point, we need to start answering questions by asking a few of our own in a kind of Socratic method. And thus, a simple and humble question to ask our critical Evangelical brethren is "How do you fulfill what Scripture says of Mary, "all nations will call me blessed"? We should ask this with humility, but in silence, await and insist upon an answer.

Q226: I have inherited a first class relic. Are there any norms for what I should do or not do with the relic? - *Kathy Keffler, Wellington, FL*

A: Other than a brief mention in Canon 1170 forbidding the sale of relics, there are surprisingly few direction on the care of relics.

Certainly they are meant to be reverently kept, and ought not be simply cast in a drawer or some forgotten place. Ideally they are put in an ostensiorium, a display vessel easily purchased in most Catholic bookstores, shrine shops or catalogues. Relics ought to be displayed in a suitable place of prayer in one's house. Ideally the place should be uncluttered with other more worldly things like souvenirs, collectibles etc. If the possession of relics is not conducive to one's spiritual life they ought to be given to another who might benefit or placed in the care of the local parish.

Relics are meant to remind us of the Saints, their stories, and what God can do even with weak human flesh. They should summon us to prayer and trust. But they ought not to be regarded superstitiously as if their mere presence could ward off all suffering or work independently of the will of God. The great wish and prayer of any saint is that we know and love God and be conformed to His will and plan for us.

Q227: No priest or Deacon could be at the burial of my husband at a National Military Cemetery, though he did have a Catholic Funeral Mass. Should the grave be blessed? – *Rose Belt, Kingsville, TX*

A: The priest or deacon at the burial should bless the gravesite. If for some reason this did not happen, it can be done at a later time. Hence, it may be good for you to ask a priest or deacon to come and pray the prayer of blessing with holy water.

This is especially the case in non-Catholic cemeteries and military cemeteries. In Catholic cemeteries the bishop has already generally consecrated the ground. But in non-Catholic settings this is not the case.
Be assured, that the grave was not blessed, in no way affects your husband's status with God. But it is our Catholic custom that burial sites should be blessed.

A related pastoral problem is that many cemeteries, especially national cemeteries, make it increasingly difficult for us to fulfill this custom. For it is often the case that people are not able to go to the actual gravesite, but are moved off to a separate chapel or pagoda somewhere nearby. This makes it difficult for the clergy to know where the gravesite is, and bless it.

Perhaps the National Conference of Bishops can most effectively address this problem since it is a national trend.

Q228: Is it true a guardian angel is assigned to every person? If this is so, do our prayers go right to God, or through our guardian angel?
- *Bob Penders, Burlington, VT*

A: It is taught by the Church that each believer has a guardian angel. The Catechism says "Beside each believer stands an angel as protector and shepherd leading him to life." (# 336). And this fact also flows from what Jesus says. "See to it that you do not despise one of these little ones, because I tell you, their angels always behold the face of my Father in heaven." (Matthew 18:10)

Regarding the second part of your question, it can reasonably and rightly be argued that angels do serve as intermediaries in our communication with God. The very word "angel" means "messenger," and it is clear that God often mediated his message to us through angels.

Regarding our prayers going to God, it is not unreasonable to presume that angels serve in some way to mediate these messages. However, it does not follow that God does not know or hear us if we don't tell our guardian angel something, or that the only way a message can reach God is through his angels. God is omniscient, knowing all things in himself.

Further, while Jesus does not forbid us to pray to our angels, when he teaches us to pray he tells us to pray to our Father who is in heaven. Hence, though angels may help to serve as intermediaries for these prayers, we ought to have our attention on God. Consider, for example that if we spoke to someone through a translator, we would not tell the translator to say something to the other person, we speak directly to other person and simply allow the translator to do his or her work.

Hence, exactly how the angels serve as intermediaries in our prayers to God is somewhat speculative, but the point is to focus on God and pray to him a natural way. To whatever manner and degree God has our angels serve as intermediaries is really not important for us to know. What *is* important is that God hears us, that he knows our needs, and what we say, and that he loves us.

Q229: Indulgences used to be designated by time value: 100 Days, 500 days, etc. Now, only the terms partial and plenary are used. Why the Change? – *Peter Stein, Everett, WA*

A: This change to "partial" or "plenary" occurred in 1968 when the Enchiridion of Indulgences was issued. There are several reasons this was done.

First, the designation of "days," did not originally reference that time in Purgatory could be lessened. The origin likely had more to do with the penitential practices of the early Church, which were often lengthy and somewhat severe. Given this, one could visit the Confessors of the Faith, in jail, or who had once been jailed for the practice of the faith. Given the esteem these confessors of the faith were held in by the Church, such a visit, and the promise to say prayers often resulted in time being knocked off one's penance by the Bishop. Where and when this designation of days weeks and years came to be applied to the souls in purgatory by the faithful is not exactly clear.

The second problem and designating a time values to indulgences is that we are not certain that Purgatory runs on an earth clock. How time passes there, or if there *is* time, or how time here relates to time there is all uncertain.

The third problem, is that the merit of a prayer or action, depends not only on the action done, but on the dispositions and state of soul of those who do them. Exactly how fruitful the saying of a rosary is, may not be something we can simply gauge by assigning a number.

Most prayers, are not sacraments, but sacramentals. Even indulgenced acts related to the reception of the sacraments, do not pertain to the sacrament itself, but to the fruitfulness of the reception of it, and the application of those fruits to another. Hence, we are not speaking of something that works automatically (*ex opere operato*), but rather something that depends for its fruitfulness to a large extent on the disposition of the one who does it (*ex opere operantis*).

Most people did find the old system of days, weeks and years to be helpful at gauging the general fruitfulness of certain acts or prayers. These days however the Church seems to prefer to leave matters such as this less clearly specified for all the reasons stated. And while common sense might value the rosary, above a brief prayer or aspiration, even here, it is sometimes best to leave things up to God who sees not only the appearance but looks into the heart.

Q230: I am told that on All Souls day if we make six visits to six churches and say designated prayers, the souls in purgatory for who we pray go straight to heaven. What do you think of this?
- *name withheld, via email*

A: There are many danger signs in the practices you describe. We ought to be cautious about various spiritual practices or exercises that have many different moving parts, or complex requirements. We ought to be even more suspicious of unqualified and overly certain promises of success.

At the heart of indulgence practices is a very proper notion that prayer has salutary effects. However, prayer should not be reduced to superstitious practices. We cannot force God's hand; neither should prayer be likened to magic which seeks to manipulate reality.

Every pious practice and prayer is always submitted to God's will; and through these things we commend ourselves to God's good graces, knowing that he will answer in ways that are ultimately best for all involved.

Q231: We have a priest at our church, who is a huge fan of Medjugorje. While he points out that it is not yet recognized by the church, his "the end is near" approach is not helpful to us who hope to make a difference. Any thoughts of what I can do? - *name withheld*

A: Priests should avoid preaching substantially out of material not approved by the Church. Balance is also necessary. Sober teaching on sin with hope rooted in grace in mercy is the basic meat and potatoes of the preaching task. Encourage Father with what he preaches well, but also request he focus his material on what is approved and less divisive.

Q232: Where did the practice of blessing ourselves with Holy Water on entering Church come from? In my parish they put sand in the stoops.
— *Karl Jones, Biloxi, MS*

A: In the ancient Church one usually entered the sanctuary through the baptistery and the custom of blessing oneself with the water naturally took up as a reminder of baptism. In later centuries as church buildings grew larger and doors multiplied, small fonts were placed near those doors and the tradition continued.

The practice of placing sand in the fonts for Lent is a tired aberration and not prescribed by any norms. At no point in the liturgical year is it appropriate to cease remembering our baptism.

Q233: Are Catholics bound to believe in the apparitions of Mary such as Lourdes, Fatima and Medjugorje? — *name withheld, via email*

A: No. When an apparition is "approved" by the Church it is simply proposed to Catholics by the Church as worthy of belief and for edification. But there is no requirement to believe it.

Lourdes and Fatima are approved but Medjugorje is not. Catholics are thereby cautioned to temper their devotion until such time as it is approved, but they are not forbidden from following or even visiting Medjugorje. Official Church sponsored pilgrimages there however are discouraged until approval may come.

Q234: A Protestant coworker, whom I think is anti-Catholic, says that we Catholics focus too much on the crucifixion and not enough on the resurrection; that we focus too much on our sins, and not enough on the new life Jesus gave us in the resurrection. How do I answer him?
— *name withheld, Tampa, FL*

A: Perhaps a first, and philosophical point, is that all of us should avoid setting up false dichotomies. The cross and the resurrection is not an either/or proposition, but a both/and reality.

Theologically, some also simplify salvation, which, while one reality, actually has two essential components: the forgiveness (washing away) of our sins, and the new life of the resurrection. In other words, Jesus did not only forgive our sins, but also offers us a new life. And these two aspects make up the salvation which Jesus wins for us.

St. Thomas Aquinas says, *The death of Christ…is the cause of the extinction of our sins; but his resurrection, by which he returns to the life of glory, is the cause of our justification, by which we return to the newness of justice.* (Commentary on Romans 4.3)

Therefore, the death of Jesus on the Cross is the starting point of our salvation and justification since it removes sin. In the resurrection, is the manifestation of the new life, which Jesus offers us, and which we are summoned to experience more deeply with each passing day.

Therefore, both the cross and the resurrection are essential in our salvation and justification: We die to sin, but we rise to new life.

I am going to guess that the co-worker is an evangelical Protestant. Traditional Protestantism placed a significant emphasis on the Cross, as any look at a older Protestant Hymnal will reveal.

Q235: Our priest seldom wears clerical attire. He often comes over to the church in athletic clothes. Is this right? — *name withheld, NM*

A: A priest should generally wear clerical attire. Canon Law says, "Clerics are to wear suitable ecclesiastical garb according to the norms issued by the conference of bishops and according to legitimate local customs" (Can. 284).

The USCCB here in the US says, "Outside liturgical functions, a black suit and Roman collar are the usual attire for priests. The use of the cassock is at the discretion of the cleric." (Index of Complimentary Norms, #3).

Thus, clerical attire ought to be worn. There can be common sense exceptions perhaps, e.g. when playing sports, at a picnic, or on a day off etc.

Q236: I noticed that Pope Francis is giving greater recognition to exorcists and exorcism. My own pastor however sees this as a problem and seems to be a critic of exorcism. Why would a priest be critical of this? — *name withheld, CT*

A: It is indeed a good thing that the Pope has given encouragement to the ministry of exorcism. It is proper that we recover an important part of our spiritual tradition, which was significantly lost, especially here in America in the past 40 years.

While I cannot read the mind of the priest critic you cite, we might do well to interpret his remarks as concerns rather than outright rejection. For, as in most areas of pastoral life, there are pitfalls and exaggerations to be avoided.

Those who practice deliverance ministry, to include the ministry of formal exorcism, are quite aware that demons often interact with a host of spiritual, emotional and mental struggles in people's lives. And many (not all) who approach the Church are often desperate for solutions and hope for something simple and quick. Alas, it is not usually simple or quick. Deliverance ministry, more often involves a lengthy and multifaceted approach which includes deliverance prayers, (and more rarely the prayers of major exorcism), along with the sacraments, spiritual direction, and in some cases psychotherapy and psychiatric interventions. To be avoided is a kind of magical thinking wherein it is supposed that the mere recitation of the prayers without undertaking other avenues of spiritual growth will bring quick results.

Another pastoral struggle involved in deliverance ministry is that many people today often describe exaggerated powers to demons, and at the same time, underestimate the power of angels, of sacraments, of prayer, of the Word of God, and the grace of Jesus Christ. Thus, someone might say "I was cursed by an ancestor and that is why I am locked in this mess." Okay, but what of the fact that you have been baptized, claimed for Christ, and blessed on countless occasions in the liturgy and by the reception of sacraments?

Thus, those who seek deliverance ministry (to include exorcism) must seek to grow in faith in the power of the sacraments, and of the steady growth in the spiritual life. All of us must lay hold of the truth that Jesus Christ is more powerful than any demon, including Satan himself, and not give way to exaggerated or superstitious fears.

Hence, like most other things in the spiritual life, growing in faith and holiness is at the heart of the solution. The prayers can help, and should be offered. Cynicism about exorcism and ascribing it to the "lunatic fringe" of the Church is neither healthy nor true to our spiritual tradition. But exorcism is not magic; it is a journey in faith.

Q237: I just returned from a pilgrimage to Quebec City and visited the Shrine of St. Anne de Beaupre. In the Basilica there is a reliquary containing the forearm of St. Anne. I have faith and believe, but I wonder how we could have such a relic and know that it is authentic. Is there some light you can shed on this?
- *Jeannine Aucoin, Henniker, NH*

A: The veneration of relics is both commended by the Church and regulated by her in Canon Law (#s1186-1190).

Among the practices of the Church in more recent centuries is to insist that relics be authenticated. Various persons within the Church do this, for example, the postulator of the cause for sainthood of a man or woman, or the General Superior of a Religious Congregation who has custody of the body of a saint from their community. They supply a modest amount of relics from the body of the Saint or Blessed, and attest to their validity. Proper evidence is submitted to one of various Roman curial offices, and a certificate of authenticity is issued from there. In addition, the reliquary in which the relic is placed has a wax seal affixed to it which also has a stamp of authenticity.

In this way the church seeks to both authenticate the relics in question, and protect the faithful from fraudulent claims. The system works reasonably well for the relics of more recent saints. However, it is obvious that relic of Saint Anne, the mother of Mary, would predate any such system.

Clearly the Basilica of Saint Anne, has ecclesiastical permissions to display the relic, but how can we be certain of its authenticity? In a direct sense we cannot, if by certainty is meant direct physical and documented evidence of the origin of the bone, traced directly to the known burial site of the saint. No sort of evidence exists for a relic like this.

However, indirect evidence may exist in the documented handing down of the relic from antiquity. Another indirect evidence of authenticity is the healings, and conversions that the relic brings by God's grace. Indeed, there is a long history of numerous healings taking place at the Basilica of St. Anne in Quebec city. Many crutches, and other testimonies of healings are found in the Church. And in this sense, many, especially older relics, are validated by the experience of the faithful.

While the faithful are not required to believe in relics, the veneration of them is both permitted, and commended by the Church. Many testify to the consoling presence, and healing power that relics bring, much like a mother who lost a child, who is consoled by the presence of a lock of that child's hair and feels somehow connected to that child.

Q238: I don't bless myself with holy water when I enter the church; the water looks dirty. Is this wrong? – *name withheld, Chicago, IL*

A: No, you are not required to bless yourself with holy water as you enter the church. It is a reminder of baptism and a request for purification as we enter the holy place of God's house. You are encouraged to spiritually ask mercy and recall baptism, but the water is not necessary.

For obvious reasons, the holy water in the stoops at the church doors needs to be changed frequently. You might wish to speak to your pastor or an usher about the problem. Also, in the past, blessed salt was often mixed with the holy water, to keep down bacteria levels etc. This practice is still permitted and should be encouraged.

Q239: I am a person exploring different faiths and where I belong. In the OSV August 17, 2014 edition there is an article about "U.S. nun's cause for sainthood opened". The article of people who have prayed to her". Yet the Bible says you shall have no other Gods before me. Since we have a personal relationship with God - why would I need a go between? Why do Catholics see praying to saints as more effective than us praying to God directly?- *Katy Hinsch, via email*

A: Part of your concern is the understanding of the word "pray." Pray, like all words in the English language has undergone some change in meaning in emphasis over the centuries. Most modern people in hearing the word pray think of an act of worship, and worship of course is directed only to God.

However, originally, the word "pray" simply meant "to ask." Even today, in the world of law, lawyers will often conclude a legal briefing with request "The defendant prays that the court will do such and so...." Many older Catholic prayers stretch back centuries, and Catholics frequently use the word pray in this older sense. To pray to a saint is to ask him or her something, not to engage in active worship.

As for your wonderment about going to anyone other than straight to God, it should be clear that we are always able to go to God, and should do so. However, there is also the human instinct that we all have to ask one others to pray for us. St. Paul often ask others to pray for him, or for the Church, or for world leaders etc. St. Paul, and the Holy Spirit speaking through him do not consider asking others to pray for us to be a futile or a pointless thing to do. Communal prayer helps to build up the body of Christ and to grow in mutual charity.

Biblically it does seem, there are some who have special influence with God. While this is mysterious, it is illustrated in Scripture. Moses for example as well as Abraham and others were able to specially intervene and get God to "reconsider" or delay his plans for punishment. Mary too, at the wedding feast at
Cana was able to get Jesus to make wine for the young married couple, though he seemed reluctant at first to do so. Scripture says that *the prayer of the righteous availeth much* (James 5:17). So, while our personal prayer is

effective because God loves us, it does seem that God also wills that we seek out others to pray as well, especially those noted for holiness.

Q240: When does a person receive his guardian angel, at birth, or when one is baptized. – *Michael Missaggia, Bayonne, NJ*

A: The Catechism of the Catholic Church teaches of the guardian angels, *From its beginning until death, human life is surrounded by their watchful care.* (336). Hence an angel is assigned from the moment conception

That the unbaptized also have an angel assigned seems likely as well and is deduced from the fact that the Old Testament (e.g. Ps 34:7; 91-10-13; Job 33:23-24; Zech 1:12 and Tob 12:12) speaks of the unbaptized Jews as having or being in the care of the angels.

Q241: There are many relics of the true cross about. Where did they come from, how do we know they are true, and is there a large chunk of it somewhere? - *Joseph Vasut, Nashville, TN*

A: The largest relic is said to be in The Monastery of Santo Toribio de Liébana, Spain, and it is 25 x 15 inches.
Relics of the true cross originated when St. Helena (the Mother of Constantine) was shown the hiding place of the wood and nails. From there, tiny slivers were eventually spread throughout the world.

The authenticity of each relic is hard to directly verify. Usually the authenticity is indirectly given when the relic exhibits power to heal, or over demons in exorcisms and so forth. As such they self-authenticate. But very ancient relics such as the true Cross us ultimately be accepted with faith, rooted in evidence of their power.

Q242: Our Diocese is held a procession in Honor of Our Lady of Guadalupe on Sunday Dec 7. Is not Sunday reserved to our Lord? In Years when Marian Feasts fall on a Sunday they usually moved to Monday. Will not non-Catholics perceive this as Mary-worship?
– *Daniel Barth, Houston, TX*

A: Outdoor processions and devotions do not have to follow the same strict calendar norms as the Mass. I suspect the procession was timed to be when many did not have to be at work.

It is unlikely that our Lord is offended by our honoring of his Mother and there is nothing inherently disrespectful in celebrating Mary whom God himself chose to work with, and whom Jesus honored and revered as his mother. A non-Catholic offended by this practice might be reminded that Catholics fulfill the Scripture, which says, "All generations shall call me blessed, for God who is mighty has done great things for me." (Lk 1:48)

Q243: It is my understanding that we do not know the time or circumstances surrounding St. Joseph's death. However in my children's religion textbook shows St. Joseph in bed surrounded by Jesus and Mary and mentions an angel calling him home to heaven. What do really know about the death of St. Joseph? *—Lori Yarsky, Rosenburg, TX*

A: Your initial observation is correct. We know nothing about his death. The depiction you describe of St. Joseph in bed and Jesus and Mary there is a common one. However, it is merely an imagined scene. It is likely given in the children's book merely as a plausible answer to the sorts of questions children ask. One may ponder the prudence of "making things up" but it seems harmless enough.

There is a fairly consistent tradition that Joseph was an older man, perhaps a widower, when he was wed to Mary. If so it makes more sense that he simply died of the effects of age, rather than by some dramatic cause, This may be why the Scriptures do not record what was a normal occurrence.

The story about the angel is not something I have ever heard. Here too one can hope it is presented more as what might have happened, rather than as a factual account. It seems clear enough that the angels do have a role in escorting us to judgment, and we pray eventually to heaven. But here too, there is no factual account of such an event.

Q244: My friends and I debated the culpability of falling asleep in adoration. Is it acceptable to fall asleep accidentally? How about intentionally after we have finished our prayers.
—Teresa Fenn, Fredericksburg, VA

A: Something done accidentally is not matter for sin, unless it is the result of woeful neglect. To intentionally choose to nap is not the purpose of adoration. Adoration implies an attentive, loving and conscious worship of the Lord. To the apostles who slept in his presence he said, *So, you could not watch with me one hour? Watch and pray that you may not enter into temptation* (Mat 26:40-41).

The Lord knows our weakness but counsels us to be sober and watchful.

Q245: At a Friday funeral in Lent the visiting priest told the faithful that, since food had been prepared that contained meat for the luncheon after the funeral, we could be dispensed from our obligation and eat it. But pastor came to the reception and publicly reprimanded the visiting priest for doing this. We all wondered if we had done something wrong by eating it. – *Sandy Vignali, via email*

A: From a juridical point of view it does not pertain to a visiting priest to dispense congregants from observing specific aspects of the precepts of the Church. When dispensations can be granted (such as in a case like this), that is usually the prerogative of the bishop or pastor. Hence, the visiting priest was wrong to do this.

However, one is left to wonder as to why the pastor chose to publicly indicate his irritation, especially at particularly awkward moment when the very meal is being enjoyed. One might wish he had discussed his concerns discreetly with the priest who transgressed the proper jurisdictional norms.

As for the assembled people of God, they did nothing wrong, they acted in good faith presuming they had the dispensation needed.

Q246: It is said that Adam and Eve had preternatural gifts. What does preternatural means and what were these gifts?
–*Robert Bonsignore, Brooklyn, NY*

The term "preternatural" in traditional theology refers to something that is rare but nevertheless happens by the agency of created beings. It is a distinct from what is supernatural. The term "supernatural" refers to acts of God. Today preternatural acts are sometimes called marvels.

The word preternatural comes from the Latin *praeter* (beside) + *natura* (nature). The word "supernatural" comes from the Latin *super* (above) + *natura* (nature). And thus theologians emphasize that only God has the power to disregard the laws of nature that he has created; so He can do supernatural things. Demons, however, and more rarely humans, may be able at times to manipulate the laws of nature but not supersede it. They cannot really move from the preternatural to the supernatural and work genuine miracles.

That Adam and Eve are said to have had preternatural gifts refers specifically to three gifts they had: bodily immortality, integrity and infused knowledge. They are called *preternatural* because they are not strictly due to human nature but do not necessarily surpass the capacities of created nature as such.

Bodily immortality means that they would not have died. Integrity meant that there was a harmonious relation between flesh and spirit since their passions were completely subordinated to their reason. Infused knowledge refers to the fact that their intellects had knowledge granted them by God immediately, rather than in the usual way through the senses by learning and experience. Hence they knew of God and his laws more intuitively since the knowledge was infused (poured in).

Q247: I get confused about the various uses of the words continence, chastity, and celibacy. Are they the same thing?

— *name withheld, via email*

A: The words are related but also have distinct meanings.

Continence in the wider sense simply means "self control," especially related to the body. It comes from the Latin *continentia* which means "a holding back." And thus when one is ill or elderly and has trouble holding their bowels, they are said to be "incontinent."

However, over the years the word "continence" has also developed the more specialized meaning of sexual restraint or of the complete abstaining from sexual intercourse. In this case it is similar to state of living celibately.

Celibacy too has a strict and wide meaning. Its wider meaning refers to anyone who lives in an on-going state of refraining from sexual intercourse. And in this sense, anyone who is unmarried should live "celibately." However, a person could eventually marry, and the celibacy would cease. More strictly "celibacy" refers in the Church to a vowed, perpetual state of refraining from sexual relations that religious and priests undertake. Here, of course the celibate state is on-going and expected to be maintained for life.

Chastity is the virtue whereby we refrain from all unlawful sexual activity and intercourse. It is a virtue all are called to have, but its manifestation will vary based on one's state in life.

Q248: What is the rule about eating meat on Fridays? Is it only a Lenten requirement? —*name withheld, Bordentown, NJ*

A: Currently Roman Catholics in the United States are directed not to eat meat only the Fridays of Lent (and Ash Wednesday). On other Fridays of the year Roman Catholics in the U.S. are free to substitute other observances to commemorate the Lord's passion and the requirement to refrain from meat (under pain of sin) no longer binds.

The Bishops still encourage abstaining from meat on all Fridays and direct that if that is not chosen, some other abstention or practice be observed. Here too this is not directed under pain of sin, but rather by way of encouragement so that Catholics freely undertake an observance of the Lord's that best suits them and avoid scrupulosity in their own case or harsh judgments of others.

Note that that Catholics in other parts of the world may have other norms from their bishops, and that Catholics from Eastern Rites also follow norms set by their bishops. Among Roman Catholic Bishops in the US, some find the current norms too vague and lament the loss of more common Catholic practice. Future years may see more specific norms such as recently were restored in England.

Q249: What is the meaning of candles that people light in Church when they put in an offering? — *Adelaide Murphy, St. Joseph, MO*

A: These are referred to as votive candles and people purchase and light them to symbolize their prayers or devotion. The candle continues to burn for some hours or days (depending on the size) and thus signals the prayer and love of the person who lit it, long after they must go.

Biblically the root of this practice is the notion of a "burnt offering." In the Old Testament things of value, (usually sacrificed animals) would be burned and thereby offered to God. The smoke was a symbol of the sacrifice of praise ascending to God.

Catholics who light candles are making an offering to God or prayer and praise. The fire of the candle symbolizes ardent love. The consuming of the candle symbolizes the oblation (offering) of something of value to God: our time, our praise, our resources and so forth. The lingering quality of the candle symbolizes the fact that our prayers, praise and concerns continue in our heart even when we must leave the Church. The flickering light also seems to say "Remember me Lord, remember my prayer and those for whom I pray."

Electronic votive candles do not as clearly show these symbols but the idea is still the same.

7. VARIOUS OTHER TOPICS

Q250: Why do animals suffer? It is apparent that nature has always featured death even before the Fall of Man. Therefore, I don't see how "the Fall" could explain why animals suffer. – *Pat*

A: If one draws simply from the Book of Genesis then the answer is that death; violence and chaos in nature all resulted from Original Sin. Not only were Adam and Eve affected by what they did, but all creation, too. God told Adam, "Cursed be the ground because of you…." (Gen 3:17) In other words, paradise is no longer; death has entered the world, and sin is its cause.

So, Scripture links suffering and upheaval in creation to sin, but the relationship may not be simple as cause and effect. Perhaps it is enough to say that our sin intensified the chaos of creation, but was not its only cause. As you observe, scientific evidence is strong that long before man or Sin, there were great upheavals in creation, and that animals, such as dinosaurs, killed each other for food, and that there was death, even mass extinctions.

Thus, that animals suffer is linked to sin, but mysteriously to other things, too. Consider that there is a circle of life that seems apt for the world. God fashions and refashions using this cycle. Last year's leaves serve as nutrients in the soil for this year's growth. Hurricanes distribute heat from the equator toward the poles. Animals feed upon each other, but also keep their populations in proper balance. There is a genius in the system that must be appreciated, even if it shocks some of our sensibilities.

And while it does seem clear that they do suffer physical pain and experience fear, it may be that a lot of the suffering we impute to them may be a projection. Much of human suffering is rooted in our sense of self and our awareness of death. An animal does not necessarily go through all this. They may instinctually respond to danger in the moment and have little or no emotional feelings at all other than fear which stimulates fight or flight. It is hard to say.

Ultimately, in matters like these, it may be best to admit that we do not have all the answers and are summoned to reverence the mystery that is before us. And suffering, be it human or animal, is a great mystery.

Q251: I read a quote by St. Augustine, which says, "Beauty is indeed a good gift of God; but that the good may not think it a great good, God dispenses it even to the wicked." Could you please explain further what this means? – *name withheld*

A: St. Augustine states this in The City of God, XV,22. Essentially what Augustine is teaching is that we can become too focused on lesser goods and, thereby, neglect higher goods.
Physical beauty, though somewhat differently defined, does exist, and is a pleasant gift of God to behold. But we can esteem it too much, failing to realize that spiritual beauty; truth, goodness, holiness and God Himself, are far greater gifts. Hence, God signals the limits of physical beauty by often bestowing it on those who may seem undeserving of it, to teach us that physical beauty is a limited good.

St. Augustine continues, "And thus beauty, which is indeed God's handiwork, but only a temporal, carnal, and lower kind of good, is not fitly loved in preference to God..." The problem is not with beauty, but with us. So Augustine adds, "When the miser prefers gold to justice, it is through no fault of the gold, but of the man; and so with every created thing."

Q252: If God made us to know him, love him and serve him, why did he make some of us who will never be able to do this because they do not have all their faculties? – *Thomas, PA*

A: Your question seems to define "knowing" in merely intellectual terms. Yet knowing, in terms of faith, is something richer than a mere intellectual grasping of God.

Further, we cannot know fully the inner life of the mentally disabled. The same can be said for infants and very young children. I have a small memory of my very early childhood when I was perhaps five years old and that memory is of great intimacy with God, who spoke to me simply and with love, and I to Him. As I grew older, and my brain grew "bigger" my heart also seemed to diminish and I lost that experience of intimacy with God. I have spent these, my later years trying to recover than early intimacy.

I do not offer this memory as proof that little children, or, by analogy, the mentally disabled, all have this intimacy, but only to indicate that there are mysteries in how God relates to us that cannot be simply reduced to high intellectual knowing.

It would seem rather that God relates to us in ways appropriate to our state. It would also seem we should at least be open to the possibility that the mentally disabled may have an even intimacy with God than we of "able mind" can only admire as we seek to become more "like little children, so as to enter the Kingdom of God" (*cf* Mark 10:15).

Q253: I was taught that, once mankind was put out of Paradise due to original sin, two distinct impediments to his return existed. First, he needed redemption, and this was supplied by Jesus on the Cross. Secondly, he needed sanctification, and this is supplied by man in this life. A priest recently told me I was wrong. Am I, and how?
—David Bearss, Harrison, MI

A: Your terminology and theology need a bit of refinement. You are correct in asserting that we were put out of Paradise due to Original Sin. You are also correct in saying that Jesus has redeemed us, that is, he has purchased our salvation, by his once and for all perfect sacrifice on the cross.

However, man, does not supply sanctification. Only God can sanctify so as to save us. It is true, that works *do* accompany the gift of our faith. But these works are not so much the source of our sanctification, as the result of it. Our works are God's gift to us. Scripture says, "For we are God's workmanship, created in Christ Jesus unto good works, which God prepared in advance for us to do" (Ephesians 2:10). So, for us, all is gift, all is grace. Sanctification is a work of God in which we cooperate, and our merits are due to grace, not to our nature (Trent, VI, cap. xvi).

Finally, it is not God's will that we merely return to some earthly paradise. Rather, in his immense love, and despite our grievous fall, God has now willed to open heaven itself to us. Thus our redeemed state, is greater than even our original state, before the fall.

Q254: How does one properly dispose of old and worn priestly vestments? One lady in the altar guild took the vestments and made throw pillows. This does not seem right.
— Julia Sullivan, Moorehead, MN

A: No, making pillows isn't right. Once something is dedicated to sacred use, it should not then be converted to ordinary use.

Older vestments are often sent to missions. But if they are too worn, they ought to be burned, and their ashes collected and buried in an out of the way and appropriate place.

This is a general rule for all sacred, blessed objects and sacramentals. Sacramentals, such as scapulars and prayer books, should be burned and then buried. Larger sacramentals that don't burn should be altered so that they no longer appear to be a sacramental. For example, a statue can be broken up into small pieces and then buried. Broken rosaries can be further disassembled and burned or buried. Objects made of metal can be taken to a sliver-plater and melted down and used for another purpose.

Some hesitate to break up or burn sacred things. But it is generally held that items lose their blessing if they are substantially worn, such that they can no longer be used.

Q255: The Church teaches that lay Catholics share in the priestly, prophetic, and kingly offices of Christ. Can you provide a fuller understanding of these offices, and what limits or distinctions are in order? *— Mary McCarthy, St. Augustine, FL*

A: Yes, as a Catechism affirms, *The anointing with Sacred Chrism… signifies a gift of the Holy Spirit to the newly baptized, who has become a Christian, that is, one "anointed" by the Holy Spirit, incorporated into Christ who is anointed priest prophet and king* (no. 1241)

The common priesthood of believers and the ministerial or hierarchical priesthood, while being ordered to one another differ in essence. It is not simply a difference in degree, but a difference in kind.

Biblically, priests are those who offer sacrifice to God. Thus in the common priesthood of all the baptized, believers are to offer their own life as a sacrifice to God, serving God and caring for all God's people. The whole life of a believer should be a sacrifice pleasing to God, as we offer our time, talent, and treasure. All the faithful are also called offer a sacrifice of praise by taking part in the sacred liturgy, and in prayer in vivid and conscious ways, exercising roles in the sacred liturgy that are proper to the laity.

Prophets are those who speak for God, who are God's voice in the world. As prophets, believers must first hear and heed the Word of God and, having done so, proclaim the authentic Word of God to this world by what they say and do. Clearly the prophet must proclaim only that which befits sound doctrine, only that which the Lord has revealed to his Church, in the Scriptures and Sacred Tradition.

Kings are those who exercise authority. And thus the baptized believer must first of all take authority over his or her own life. Believers must rule over their unruly passions, over disordered drives of the soul and body, and so forth.

Having gained self-mastery, Christians are also called, exercise lawful authority in this world. Of course this must begin in the family with parents. But the royalty of the baptized must extend beyond merely the family, into the whole world, as believers seek to extend the kingship of Christ, throughout the whole social order.

Q256: A Member of my family is an atheist hostile to faith likes to challenge me to explain how a loving God permits suffering. Is there an answer I can give? - name withheld, *MI*

A: It is perhaps too absolute to say the Church has "an answer" to suffering, and why God permits it. The full answer to this is ultimately mysterious, and has many aspects, which are hidden from our view.

To be sure, we do have elements of an answer, which God reveals to us, or which human reason can supply. One element of an answer is the existence of human freedom. One way God could prevent a lot of suffering would be to cancel human freedom whenever it was abused. But God, it would seem, does not usually see fit to do so, and his respect for our freedom, is very consistent.

Another aspect of an answer is that suffering often brings growth and opens new possibilities. Perhaps God sees these fruits and thereby allows some degree of suffering.

But again, these insights are *part* of an answer. They do not constitute a full or complete answer to the great mystery of suffering and why God allows it. These insights tend to bring up even more questions. Fundamentally we must accept that we do not have an absolute answer the problem of suffering.

While it is fine that atheists raise this issue, (for it is a valid question we all have), the demand by them for an absolute answer is not reasonable. We must also ask them to consider that not everything has a simple answer.

Thus, if they will demand that I must absolutely answer the question, "Why is there suffering?" then I would also like to ask them to give an absolute answer to the question, "Why is there love? Why is their generosity or a passion for justice or self-sacrificing heroism?"

If you and I must account for negative side of suffering, then perhaps too our critics must account for the existence of love. If they are honest they will perhaps admit that while they can give a partial answer, they cannot fully account for these things.

The bottom line is, not everything can be absolutely answered. To unreasonably demand answers from others, when they cannot supply them either, is not itself a rational or adequate reputation of the existence of God.

Q257: Jesus drove out some demons into a herd of swine, which ran down the bluff, into the water and drowned. Could not such an action be construed as cruelty to animals? – *Peter Tate, Long Beach, CA*

A: Well, the pigs are not really the point of the story, and we ought not to get too focused on them. More to the point of the story is the authority of Jesus Christ to cast out demons.

Thus, one might respond to the cruelty charge, that the Lord God has the capacity and authority to do this to the pigs, just as you and I might go to our garden, uproot withered tomatoes and replace them with corn. Further, having authority over animals, we also lead pigs to slaughterhouses.

One might still argue that driving the demons into the pigs was an arbitrary and unnecessary act by Jesus. But perhaps the Lord has reasons. For example, he may have wished to inspire a holy fear in those who saw the action. It was surely a memorable action, and while the townsfolk initially reacted with fear, it would seem they later welcome Jesus back with faith

(Mk 5:17-20; 7:31). Hence, Jesus makes use of the animals to bring blessings to human beings, which is fitting.

Culturally, pigs were considered by the Jewish people to be unclean animals. Thus, the pigs also help to fittingly illustrate the uncleanness of demons, and the fate of those persisting in uncleanness.

Q258: My daughter-in-law, was watching "The Bible" on TV, said she did not understand why Jesus had to suffer so much. I am not sure how to answer why His Father made him go through so much. - *Rose Haynick, FL*

A: One of the difficulties in understanding why Jesus suffered for sinners is that many of us, especially in the modern world, tend to think of sin only in legal terms as the breaking of some abstract rules. But sin causes real harm, and has real effects, and these must be healed. Something actually has to happen.

For example, let us say that you see me near the edge of a cliff and I warn you to take three steps to the right. But let us also say that, out of rebellion, I take three steps to the left, and slide down a great cliffside into an abyss. I lie there, injured and utterly incapable of ever rescuing myself. Let us then say, in my humiliation and pain, I cry out and ask you to forgive me. In your mercy, you say yes. And that is forgiveness. But in order to be healed and restored, you will now have to expend great effort to come down the Cliffside, care for my wounds, and carry me out of the abyss.

As I hope you can see by this analogy, my sin was not simply the breaking of rule. Deep and devastating effects happened in my life, and I was incapable of restoring myself. And this was our state; we were dead in our sins (Col. 2:13). We were incapable of ever restoring or healing ourselves.

Jesus therefore, not only brought us God's forgiveness, but also extended the effort and agony to come down, heal our wounds and lift us up. This was a great, and painful effort. Our sinful disobedience had brought us suffering and death. Jesus took up that suffering and that death in order to restore us, even elevate us to a higher place.

The horrible suffering of Jesus, shows us very clearly how awful sin really is, how it disfigures, wounds, and even brings us death. These are realities, and Jesus takes them up in order to heal them and carry them away for us. We tend to make light of sin today. It is no light matter, and to remember that we do well to look to any crucifix and see what love cost him.

Q259: I have to be honest that I get a little annoyed sometimes by the rather constant refrain of "The New Evangelization." What is new about it and why use the word "new? For an ancient faith?
- *name withheld, via email*

A: Irritation of this sort is perhaps understandable, when a phrase gets picked up and used widely in multivariate ways, and thereby comes to seen more as a slogan, than as informative.

That said, the New Evangelization is officially used to mean several rather specific things. First it is new, in the sense that we, as a Church, cannot afford to do business as usual. We must behave in new ways. We can no longer be content to sit within our four walls and talk about the faith among ourselves; we must go out. We cannot simply think that evangelization is opening the doors and hoping people come. If there ever was a kind of inertia that brought people to church, that is not so now. It is clear that we must go into the community, into the culture, and re-propose the gospel. In this sense, "everything old is new again." For the new evangelization seeks to go back to Christ's initial Instruction, "Go unto all the nations and make disciples..." (Matthew 28:19).

New evangelization, also appreciates, and we cannot simply say what we believe, we must explain *why*, and show it's reasonableness. Perhaps in previous times, it was sufficient to argue from authority, but these days, people want to know why, not just what.

Thirdly, evangelization is "new" in that we must vigorously engage in all the new ways of communicating that have exploded on the scene today. We must creatively engage all these new forms of communication, along with the traditional modes of communication, such as writing, cinema, radio and so forth.

Q260: Can you cite a scriptural reference it supports tithing?
- *Norbert Gorny, Altamonte, FL*

A: Yes, Malachi 3:8 says *Will a man rob God? Yet you are robbing Me!...In tithes and offerings......Bring the whole tithe into the storehouse, so that there may be food in My house, and prove Me herewith," says the LORD of hosts, "if I will not open for you the windows of heaven and pour out for you a blessing until it overflows.*

Further, in the New Testament Jesus References tithing when he says, *Woe to you, teachers of the law and Pharisees, you hypocrites! You give a tenth of your spices--*

mint, dill and cumin. But neglect weightier matters of the law--justice, mercy and faithfulness. You should have practiced the latter, without neglecting the former. (Matt 23:23) Note that in this text, while the Lord speaks of weightier matters than tithing, he says regarding tithing, that we should not neglect it.

The Church does not require an absolute adherence to the biblical tithe, (i.e., giving one tenth of income to the church), nevertheless, there is a precept that Catholics contribute to the mission of Church. While details are left to the individual conscience, tithing is a long and ancient tradition. As Malachi 3 says, tithing is not merely an obligation; it also opens the doors to many blessings.

Q261: I have read prayers that ask blessings for healing of body, soul and spirit. I always thought that soul and spirit is the same thing. Are "soul" and "spirit" different or are they the same? - *Jo Hadley, Claremont, CA*

A: The terms "soul" and "spirit" are often used interchangeably in modern English, and also to some extent in the Scriptures. They are synonymous, in the sense that they are not describing two separate realities. The human spirit is not some third part of the human person, separate from the soul. Rather, as an aspect of the soul, the human spirit (as distinct from the Holy Spirit), is that aspect of our soul that opens us to God. Some theologians speak of this openness of our spirit as giving us *capax Dei* (a capacity for God). That is to say, since our souls are spiritual and rational, we have the capacity to know and interact with God. And thus, the spirit is that aspect of our soul, which most distinguishes us from the animals.

In this distinction of soul and spirit, the Catechism says the following: *Sometimes the soul is distinguish from the spirit: St. Paul for instance prays that God may sanctify his people "wholly" with "spirit and soul and body" kept sound and blameless at the Lord's coming (cf 1 Thess 5:23). The church teaches that this distinction does not introduce a duality into the soul. "Spirit" signifies that from creation man is ordered to a supernatural end, and that his soul can gratuitously be raised beyond all it deserves to communion with God.* (Catechism # 367).

Q262: A Jewish friend insists that, according to his religion, there is simply no afterlife. Is this true and consistent with the Old Testament?
- *Charley McKelvy, via email*

A: The views of the Jewish people regarding the afterlife vary to some degree. Unlike the Catholic Church, there is no central teaching authority among Jewish people. Thus, in a short answer like this, we cannot fully treat what all Jewish people believe about the particulars of the afterlife. But it is fair to say that most believing Jews *do* believe in an afterlife. It is also fair to say that the concept of the resurrection of the dead developed in Judaism over the centuries, and became clearer in the later books as God brought the ancient Jews to a deeper understanding of what He was offering.

But for your friend to say that there is nothing in the Old Testament about it requires the dismissal of a good number of texts from the prophets, Psalms and the Wisdom tradition that speak quite vividly of the dead rising (e.g. Is 26:19; Job 19:25ff; Daniel 12:2; Ezekiel 37:12; Hosea 13:14; 1 Sam 2:6, among many others).

At the time of Jesus, the Sadducees did reject the resurrection of the dead, and held that, at death one simply ceased to exist. Part of the reason for this was that they only accepted the first five books of the Bible, and claimed that in them, there was no mention of the dead rising. Jesus sets aside their view by invoking the encounter of God with Moses at the burning bush in the book of Exodus, one of the first five books of the Bible. There, God called Himself the "God of Abraham, Isaac, and Jacob." But if God is a "God of the living, and not the dead" as the Sadducees would surely insist, then somehow, to God, Abraham Isaac and Jacob are alive. (see Mark 12:24-27)

And while your Jewish friend is not likely accept the authority of Jesus, this text of goes a long way to show that declaring there's nothing in the Old Testament about resurrection, especially in the first five books, is not an interpretation immune from critique. It further illustrates that at the time of Jesus, while the Sadducees rejected the resurrection of the dead, most other Jews such as the Pharisees and also followers of Jesus and others *did* accept, teach and expect the resurrection of the dead.

Therefore, it seems safe to consign your friend's remark as the opinion of one Jew, or some Jews, but not all Jews, then or now.

Q263: Does Satan have any access to the Souls in Purgatory?
– *Kathy Cain, Yampa, CO*

A: No. The souls in purgatory are not accessible to the devil or demons. They are safe in God's hands, in what amounts to the "vestibule" of heaven. There, they undergo final purifications, which only lead to heaven (*cf* 1 Cor 3:13-15).

Further, at death, our final disposition for or against God; and for or against his Kingdom is final, it is definitive. This places the souls in heaven, and also in purgatory beyond the reach of the devil. Sadly, it also places heaven beyond the reach of those who have finalized their decision against it. At death the judgment, or verdict is in and is irreversible. (see Luke 16:26; Heb 9:27; Jn 8:21; Jn 10:27-28).

We do well today to be more sober about this definitive aspect of death, and to realize that our cumulative decisions build toward a final disposition by us that God will, in the end, acknowledge.

Q264: Our Priest in his homily referred to the Angels as "reflections of God" and made the comparison to the facets of a diamond, God being the diamond, and the angels his facets. Does this sound right?
- *name withheld, via email*

A: No, it does not. Angels do reflect God's glory, as do all creatures to some degree. But angels are creatures, distinct from God, they are not a part (or facet) of God.

Some sympathy for the preacher may be order however. Sometimes analogies go wrong in live preaching. I suspect what Father meant to say was that angels reflect God's glory in different ways. The Seraphim are the "burning ones" before the Throne of God, manifesting God's fiery glory and love, the Cherubim manifest God's glory and will toward creation, and so forth.

I rather doubt Father thinks of angels as part of God. I think his analogy slipped or morphed and that by facets he does not mean to imply the angels are of the same substance as God, but rather, that they reflect his glory differently as facets or a gemstone reflect different qualities.

Q265: A fellow Catholic maintains that at some time in the past the Catholic Church believed in reincarnation. Is this true?
— *Maria-Luisa Berry, via email*

A: As regards the matter of so-called reincarnation (the belief that we have had previous lives in other bodies, or will come back in other bodies or forms), the view is clearly excluded in Scripture and by Christian Anthropology.

Scripture says, *It is appointed unto men once to die, but after this the judgment* (Heb 9:27). "Once" is pretty clear, there are no previous deaths or lives, nor shall we face death again. "Once" cannot mean many.

Further, Christian anthropology, rooted in the Scriptures, excludes the notion of reincarnation. This is not the place to set forth a full anthropology, but it is here sufficient to state that the soul is the form of the body and it does not pertain to the same soul to "form" different bodies. I am my body, it is not a mere appendage or container that can be shed or exchanged.

Finally, whenever some claims the Catholic Church once taught something, a good follow-up request is "Show it to me in writing." For, many make unsubstantiated claims and the pressure should not be on to defend against something that never happened, but for them to demonstrate clearly the truth of their charge.

Q266: Do you have any suggestions or a person who is guilty of sloth and laziness? On account of it, I am often sluggish and this keep me from many of my responsibilities and duties to be a good and prayerful Catholic. - *name withheld, Baltimore, MD*

A: Sloth, which is one of the Seven Capital Sins, is sorrow or aversion to the good things that God is offering us. And thus, one who has sloth, and hears that God can save them from sins and enable them to do many good works, instead of being happy and eager to embrace these gifts, has a kind of sadness or aversion to them. Perhaps they like their sins and would rather not be free of them. Perhaps the thought of good works seems burdensome. So, the slothful person becomes avoidant of God and the gifts that he is offering.

While this is often manifest through a kind of a laziness or inattentiveness, sometimes the opposite is true. And thus, some slothful people immerse themselves in worldly activities such as business and career, and claim they are far "too busy" to pray, to think about God, or go to Church.

Therefore, at its heart, sloth is a problem about desire; namely, that we do not ardently desire God and the things he is offering.

I might encourage you to pray out of the beatitude, "Blessed are those who hunger and thirst for righteousness, for they will be satisfied." (Matt 5:6). In other words, we ought to ask for the desire for God and what he offers, if we don't even have that.

Secondly, I would counsel that while praying for greater desire, some small and initial steps be made toward God. Look for something you can reasonably do, which may not be highly desirable at first, but still can be reasonably accomplished. Before I was a priest, I worked in downtown Washington, and I made a Lenten resolution to go to daily Mass at my lunch break. At first, this seemed difficult and irksome. But gradually, I grew to like it, and when Easter came, I just kept going to Mass almost every day to experience its peace and the nourishment of God's Word and his Body and Blood. Often life works like this. We ask for deeper desire, and step out on our request by small actions which build.

Q267: Our Archbishop is closing the one and only Catholic Church near the airport. Isn't there a requirement that there be a church in or very near an airport? – *name withheld*

A: No. It is of course a very nice convenience for travelers in larger airports that Mass might be offered, at least on Sundays. But given the shortage of clergy, and also the nature of modern airline travel with shorter lay-overs, both the ability of travelers to attend, and the capacity to provide this service is less.

Canonically, travelers who cannot reasonably attend Mass to fulfill their Sunday obligation, may be exempted by their pastor from the Sunday obligation.

Q268: Should priests, organists, altar servers, and sacristans be paid for participating in a funeral? - *name withheld, via email*

A: It varies according to each. Priests are not "paid" for celebrating funerals. And while it is customary for many families to give the priest a donation or stipend, Church Law does not require such a donation. Such donations are generally small or tokenary since priests are well cared for by the parish already. And while priests can and do accept such donations, any notion that what they receive is a "fee" is to be avoided. Priests must be willing to celebrate liturgies and sacraments even when no stipend is offered. This is especially the case when working with and caring for the poor.

Organists and Church musicians are another story. They can and should be paid. They have spent years in preparation and practice, and the monies they receive area a usually part of their livelihood. Often they must leave other obligations to cover funerals and may have travel expenses. If families wish to engage their services, musicians and organists should be compensated. In cases where there is poverty and a family cannot afford to cover even basic music, the parish can help. But since elaborate music is not required for funerals, the requested help should be reasonable.

As for servers and sacristans, the practice of donations is less common. In some places it is customary to give the servers a small donation; in other places not. Sacristans are seldom given donations. Severs and sacristans are generally presumed to be volunteers, and while a young server may appreciate a $20 dollar bill, it is generally not expected. This is even more the case with adult servers who would likely be embarrassed by receiving a donation.

Q269: Since God knows all the harm that wicked people and demons cause, why does he permit them to exist at all, or at least knowing the evil they would do not destroy them before or at least after they do it?
- *name withheld, via email*

A: While a brief column such as this cannot possibly plum the depths of the questions you raise, a few observations should be made.

First, it does not pertain to God to annihilate any rational creature he has made. Thus, angels and men have an immortality that pertains to their souls; and for humans, one day, to our bodies as well. Having given the gift of life, God never withdraws his gift. While it is true that demons, and the human souls in hell have definitively rejected his love, God does not thereby cancel the love he has extended to them. He continues to sustain the life even of his enemies, though they choose to live apart from him and what he values.

Secondly, your question tends to put God within serial time, where time passes incrementally from future to present to past. And thus the question occurs to us, "Why would God at some time in the past, knowing what a person would do in the future, bring them into existence today?" But God does not live in or relate to time in this manner. For God, past present and future are all equally present. And thus, while God's inner life is mysterious, it is clear to us that God does not deliberate in the manner we do. Time does not unfold for God like it does for us. So, to some degree, even the way we phrase our questions is invalid. God does not ponder "A", look forward to "B", and then do "C".

But let us for a moment, assume God did act temporally in this way, and that at some point in the past, God, knowing that a person would do horrible things in the future, considers their existence today. Let us say, that seeing the bad things they would do, he simply vetoes their existence.

But what does this do then to human freedom? In effect it cancels it. Why? Because if in knowing that a person will choose badly, God preemptively vetoes their existence, then the whole process of choosing God and his kingdom values is "front-loaded" and none of us who do exist are really free. Freedom would only be theoretical since no existing person actually can or ever did say "no." If we are not free to say no, we are not really free to say yes to God and love Him.

Many more things related to the questions you raise could be said. But for now, let it be enough for us to say that the answers are caught up in the mysteries of God's love, time, and human freedom.

Q270: I recently read that Pope Francis has said that many Catholics are sacramentalized but unevangelized. What does this mean? It seems to me that it denigrates the Sacraments. – *Thomas Keene, Miami, FL*

A: I am unaware that Pope Francis has used this phrase. However, it is a rather common expression today among priests and theologians. It describes the unfortunately common reality of many Catholics in the pews who have received all their Sacraments, and may even faithfully attend Mass each Sunday and go to confession at least once a year, but they have never really met Jesus Christ or encountered his presence powerfully.

Sadly, many Catholics, often due to poor catechesis, reduce the sacraments to rituals, rather than to living and real encounters with the Lord Jesus, who himself is the true celebrant of every Sacrament. The purpose of all the Sacraments is to sanctify us and in particular ways to lead us deeper and deeper into a life changing and transformative relationship with Jesus Christ. They are to put us in living, conscious contact with Jesus, so that we see our lives being changed.

But the all too common experience of many Catholics is that Sacraments are only vaguely appreciated in this way. Many see them as tedious rituals, rather than transformative realities. Too many seek the shortest Mass almost as if it were more like a flu shot, a kind of "necessary evil," to be dispensed with as quickly and painlessly as possible. Confession too is avoided.

Very few Catholics come to Mass expecting to be transformed. In a way, people put more faith in Tylenol that the Eucharist since, when they take Tylenol, they expect something to happen, they expect the pain to go away and healing to be induced. But too many Catholics do NOT expect anything like this from the Holy Communion with Jesus.

This is what is meant to be sacramentalized, but unevangelized. It is to be faithful to the pew and to the Sacraments but to lack the evangelical zeal, joy and transformation one would expect from a more fruitful reception of the Sacraments. It is to go through the motions but not really get anywhere. It is to receive Jesus but not really experience him any meaningful manner.

Pastors, parents and Catechists need to work to overcome what amounts to a lack of deep faith in and experience of Jesus. Far from denigrating the Sacraments, the phrase seeks to underscore the truer and fuller reality of the Sacraments, which are not mere rituals, but powerful realities if received fruitfully.

Q271: In the sermon the other day, the priest said Satan hates us. It occurred to me to ask, why does Satan hate me, what did I ever do to him? - *John Smoot, Bayonne, NJ*

A: To be sure, there are very deep mysteries involved in the motives for Satan's hatred. We struggle to understand our own human psyches, let alone the psyche of a fallen angelic person.

However, an important clue to Satan's hatred is contained in the third temptation he makes to Jesus in the desert. Showing Jesus all the kingdoms of the world to Jesus he says, *All these I will give you, if you will but fall down and worship me.* (Matthew 4:10)

Here we see the curtain pulled back, and we glimpse for a moment the kind of inner torment that dominates Satan. He seems desperate to be adored. He cannot bear that he is a creature, and that there is another, other than himself, who is God, ever to be adored.

Thus, in his colossal pride he hates, first of all, God. And, by extension, he hates everyone, and everything that manifests the glory of God. Even more, he hates those who seek to adore God, rather than him. In his venomous pride, he seeks to destroy the Church, which declares the glory of God and reminds us that God alone is to be adored. Surely he hates, and seeks to destroy those who even try to adore God, and who do not accord him, Satan, the worship and pride of place he ravenously hungers for.

Hence, as the text from the temptation in the desert suggests, Satan is tormented by pride, and his torment is filled with deep hatred for all who worship God or and all who draw others to the worship of the one, true God.

Q272: A friend at work says Catholicism cannot be reconciled with evolution. What is the teaching here? - *Arthur Johnson, Covington, KY*

A: There is no formal church teaching which requires Catholics to except or reject the scientific theory of evolution, namely that present and more complex forms of life may have evolved from simpler or more basic forms of life.

However, there are some aspects related to evolutionary theory that tend to run afoul of certain Church and Scriptural teachings. First, many evolutionists insist upon a type of "blind evolution" wherein genetic mutations happen as completely random acts. This form of evolution rules out any intelligent or intentional cause behind the evolutionary process. Such an insistence runs contrary to Scripture's assertion that God intelligently and intentionally creates all things and guides whatever evolution does take place.

There really isn't a reason that evolutionists must insist the process behind evolution is utterly blind and random. It is possible to simply observe evolution, without rendering an opinion as to the exact cause of it. The cause, currently unknown to science, is frankly beyond the realm of what science is designed to study. To insist that evolution is an unguided and blind process is actually a metaphysical claim. But physical sciences study only the physical world, they are not designed study the metaphysical. Frankly, there's a lot of evidence that things evolve in this world in an orderly, not random, way.

The second problem related to evolution is more technical and complex. It is the problem of polygensim versus monogenism. Polygenism emphasizes that human beings emerged from some group of hominids. Monogenesim would hold that we all emerge from one set of parents (who the Bible names Adam and Eve). While Catholics are not absolutely forbidden from holding polygenism, the Vatican has warmed over the years that it is difficult to square this teaching with the doctrine of Original Sin. That doctrine teaches that Original Sin comes from one man, Adam; not from a tribe of early human descendants of hominids who erred.

The bottom line of all this is that, while Catholics are free to accept or reject the fundamental scientific theory of evolution, we cannot accept the theory uncritically and with no distinctions it all. There are aspects related to the theory such as those described above, which require critique.

Q273: A co-worker of mine who claims to be an atheist is dismissive of anything beyond modern science and claims that there is no scientific evidence for the soul and that we are really just advanced apes. What can I say in answer to this? – *Jason Reid, Ft. Collins, CO*

A: It sounds like the co-worker is a proponent of something called "scientism" which holds that the physical sciences can now, or one day will, wholly explain all reality, and there is no reality beyond physical matter. The problem with such a claim is that it breaks the very rule it announces. For to say there is no reality beyond the physical world is a metaphysical claim; it is a philosophical stance that the physical sciences cannot prove. In other words he or she is using a non-scientific premise to try and prove that physical science gives a comprehensive explanation for all things.

That there are non-material realities is not difficult to demonstrate. Justice, mercy, humility, beauty, and forth are not physical, but they are real. And while these concepts surely interact with our physical brain and register there, they themselves are metaphysical, that is non-physical. We would not be able to see justice and humility out having lunch together.

That we can grasp things beyond the physical world and discuss them, points to the existence in us of a non-material and rational soul. For, since action follows being, that we can apprehend non-material concepts and make use of them, points to a reality and faculty about us.

That Human beings are different from animals (by having a rational soul) is demonstrable by mere observation. Though we physically resemble animals in many ways, there are dramatic differences. Animals do not built cities, form bi-cameral legislatures and debate the common good, they do not write poems, collect their accumulated knowledge in libraries; animals do not invent or show ingenuity, and they show no appreciation for beauty, truth, or concern about death. Apes, do not debate matter and form, they do not write on the topic of causality and engage their co-workers non-material topics. They do not appreciate a Beethoven sonata or ponder an impressionistic painting. There is no "life of the mind" evident in them at all. And even if one may wish to show some rudiments of this in higher animals, the human person is so dramatically beyond these rudiments that we cannot reasonably conclude that the differences between human beings and animals is anything but vast.

All these differences point to the existence of the rational soul. In other words we are more than merely advanced apes, we clearly have different faculties altogether. Perhaps your co-worker is making a claim and thus bears some burden of proof. Perhaps he might be asked to prove that the soul does not exist, using science.

Q274: Did people 10,000 years ago have a soul, or did it just start with Adam and Eve? – *Francis Phielx, Pine City, NY*

The wording of your question presents a couple of difficulties in presenting an answer. First of all, we're not sure exactly when Adam and Eve lived, it may have been a good bit longer than 10,000 years ago. The shorter time frames for human history often emerge from a very literal reading of biblical dates and time frames, which is not necessarily required of a Catholic.

Nevertheless, whenever Adam and Eve lived, your question still stands. But here too the wording of your question presents the need for a distinction. We would not speak of the hominids that existed before Adam and Eve's as "people" or persons. According to widely accepted Catholic and philosophical tradition, a person is an individual substance of a rational nature. Hence human beings who have a rational soul, are persons; so our angels, and so are the three members of the Blessed Trinity. Animals however, to include primates, are not persons, for they have no rational soul.

Thus, if it is true that we in some way physically emerged from prehistoric primates (a widely held scientific theory) we could not speak of them as having a rational soul until God acted to directly create Adam and Eve, infusing them with a rational soul. Even if our animal or physical nature may be said to have evolved, the human soul is directly created by God, and we are now dealing with a new reality: no mere advanced primate, but the creation of the human person Adam and Eve.

With these distinctions in mind, the answer to your question is, No, the primates who existed prior to Adam and Eve had no rational soul. However they may, like all living things, be said to have had a non rational soul. This is because, philosophically, the soul is the animating principle of a living thing. Hence animals have a soul.

What makes humans different is that we have a rational soul, sometimes referred to as the spirit. On account of this we are able to think and grasp metaphysical concepts like justice, beauty, meaning and truth. It is the spiritual aspect of our soul that makes us capable of relating to God.

Q275: With regard to long adopted traditions within Christianity like Santeria in the Latin Americas, would it be safe to say that charismatic-Pentecostal dancing can also be traced back to Black Slavery voodoo practices and Santeria. – *Robert Morales, Mountain View, CA*

A: No. Dancing is widespread in all cultures. We cannot narrowly attribute dancing, even in liturgical settings, as simply due to voodoo, Santeria or to pagan or even demonic roots.

It is true that different cultures ascribe different meanings to dance and thus have different tolerances for it in liturgical settings. In the West dance is more usually associated with romance and secular entertainment. In Africa, and some places in the far East however, dance is also used for praise and has sacred meanings too.

The Church generally frowns on dance within the sacred liturgy. There are however exceptions made for liturgies that take place in Africa and certain other settings.

Santeria and voodoo, though tacitly ignored by most Catholic prelates (due to racial and cultural complexities), cannot be equated with or "adopted" to the proper practice of Catholic Faith. That the practitioners of these borrow from Catholicism is not evidence they are Catholic any more than Protestants (who also borrow from Catholicism) should considered Catholics.

Q276: You recently wrote that Adam and Eve are (theologically) considered the first human beings. And though God gave them rational souls, He may have developed the physical aspect of man through evolution. However it seems interesting that some of the hominids that precede Homo Sapiens seem to have some rational tendencies, such as burying the dead and fashioning tools and the like. Does this mean their brains were developed enough to know more values such as writing wrong? *–Steve Brestic, Merrionette PK, IL*

Exactly what they "knew" is somewhat speculative. Even some non-rational animals today show some signs of social behaviors such as organized hunting etc. Reward and punishment can also condition animal behavior.

However, this does not mean they are engaging in moral reasoning or accessing metaphysical concepts such as justice, right and wrong. Further, moral reasoning and accountability presuppose freedom. Be we do not presuppose freedom in non-rational animals and thus we do not hold them morally accountable for their actions.

It was probably the same with these early hominids. Anthropologists will properly debate the "emergence" of the rational intellect and moral reasoning within their field, but the theologically we posit the beginnings of this with the direct creation of the rational souls of Adam and Eve prescind from matters of brain development etc.

Q277: On the Feast of the Guardian Angels I was wondering how the angels can know what we are thinking, and if they are able to read our minds? Also, how do we hear them? – *Charles Genaro, Des Plains, IL*

A: As for angels reading our thoughts, it is not likely they can. In the field of demonology a similar question exists, and most demonologists conclude that demons, while very intuitive and good observers, cannot actually read our minds. I presume the same basic thing about the angels too. However, angels might have the additional advantage that God reveals to them our thoughts on some or all occasions. But all this is speculative. No scriptural or dogmatic statement on the matter comes to mind.

There is also the great mystery of how angels (or demons) can "hear" or "see" us. "Talking" and "hearing" are usually terms that refer a physical process of vibrating air being perceived by our eardrum. Seeing involves photons touching our retina. But angels do not have bodies, and thus have no ears or eyes. So even if we talk out loud, how can they "hear" us, or for that matter how can they see us? This is mysterious.

Perhaps then, our thoughts can be projected in some manner, such that a being that is pure spirit can "perceive" them.

An analogy comes to mind. Even we humans, possessed of physical senses, do not "see" everything physically. For example, we do not see sub-atomic particles, even with a very powerful microscope. Rather we come to know their existence by the use of our intellect and reason. We may see some their effects (e.g. by math), but fundamentally we "see" them by reasoning to their existence and developing an understanding of them based on what we already know. The same thing is true for metaphysical concepts such as justice and mercy. We do not "see" them physically, though we may see their effects. Rather we "see" these concepts by reasoning to their existence. They are real, though metaphysical and we "see" through our intellect and our spirit, (which supplies our ability to grasp metaphysical concepts).

Further, how can we hear and listen to the voice of our angel as God clearly tells us to do in Scripture (e.g. Ex 23:21)? Since angels do not have bodies, we cannot hear their voice in a physical sense. Thus, somehow they are able to interact with our soul (I suspect they do this particularly through our conscience) in a way that reaches our intellect.

It is clear that Scripture and Tradition take for granted that angels can and do interact with us, but how they do so is mysterious.

Q278: Why does the Lord's Prayer ask God not to lead us in temptation? Why would God do that? I have also read texts in the Bible about God hardening people's hearts. Again why would God do that?
- Gerald Phillips, Omaha, NE

A: Part of the problem in understanding biblical texts like these comes down to the philosophical distinction between primary and secondary causality. Primary causality refers to God's action in creating, sustaining and setting into motion all things. From this perspective, God is the first (or primary) cause of all things; even things contrary to his stated and revealed will.

Thus, if I hit you over the head with a bat, I am actually the secondary cause of this painful experience. God is the primary cause because he has made and sustains all things in the process, such as me, the wood of the bat, and the firm resistance of your skull.

As such, God is the first or underlying cause, without which nothing at all would be happening or existing. God is surely opposed to my action, and even has Commandments against it. However, given his establishment of physical laws, and respect for human freedom he seldom intervenes by suspending these.

So to be clear, in my horrific little example, God is the primary cause since he is the cause of me and the bat, but I am the secondary cause to my shameful act of violence.

The biblical world was more conversant with and accepting of primary causality. Biblical texts often more freely associate things with God, because he is the first cause of all things without excluding the human agency that is the secondary cause.

However, with the rise of the empirical sciences and secularism, we moderns are far less comfortable in speaking to primary causality (God's world) and focus more on secondary causes (our world).

When the Lord's Prayer says *lead us not into temptation,* it is not asserting that God would directly and intentionally lead us into temptation but is averting to the fact that God is the first cause of all things. We are thus asking that God's providence will allow fewer opportunities for us to be led into temptation by the world, the flesh and the devil.

Likewise, texts that refer to God hardening hearts, employs similar thinking. God hardens hearts only insofar as he is the first cause of all things. But it is usually we who harden our own heart. God only permits the conditions and sustains our existence (primary causality) but it is we as secondary causes who directly will the sins that harden our hearts.

Q279: On the Cross Jesus said, "Father forgive them, they know not what they do." Does his plea absolve all who took part in the crucifixion?
– *Cliff Journey, Fairhope, AL*

A: The Lord is certainly offering forgiveness and absolution. But as with any offer of absolution or forgiveness, we must also receive the gift by accepting it with contrition for our sins. In a certain sense absolution cannot simply be granted (by way of an imposition or a mere declaration of sorts), since this does not respect human freedom. If I were to stand before you and say, "I forgive you and absolve you of the terrible things you did to me," you might react with relief and joy. Alternately you might react with anger since you think you did nothing wrong. Hence the offer of absolution is one thing, the reception of it is necessary to complete the act. Jesus is surely offering absolution. If they received it is up to them.

Q280: I cannot understand why a just and holy one like Jesus had to die on the cross instead of God just doing away with Satan and evil.
-*Roy Roberts, Union Star, MO*

The approach undertaken by God in addressing sin is one that is respectful of human and angelic freedom. Were God simply to come and do away with the choices made by angels or humans that he did not like, then we are not really free, since God simply overrules choices.

Adam and Eve, were warned by God of great suffering and death that would come from indulging of the Tree of the Knowledge of Good and Evil. Nevertheless, tempted by the fallen angel Satan, they rejected what God said.

But God, accepting that they opted for the way of suffering and death, instead of canceling their decision or its consequences, Himself takes up suffering and death. Jesus, by his obedience to the Father, and though sinless, endures the full fury of suffering and death and never ceased saying yes to his Father. In so doing, he opened a way for us that does not cancel original choice but actually uses its consequences as a way back for us, through way of the Cross.

Q281: Why has Mary never been given the title "Co-redemptrix?" Answer: Mary is not divine. She had to be a very special person since from her physical body Jesus came, but she is not divine.
– *Jean McKinney, West Burlington, IA*

A: Usually I get the question, and am supposed to give the answer. But I see you have done both! However, your answer needs distinctions.

The title "Co-redemptrix" (redemptrix is a feminized form of redeemer) has been used of Mary, even by popes in the past. It can be understood of her in a proper theological sense that does not "divinize" her or make her an equal partner in the work of redemption.

The problem in understanding the term emerges in the changing meaning of the prefix "co" which, to most modern ears, indicates an equality of status. Thus a co-president, co-commander, or co-chair, would usually indicate two people who equally share in an office or function.

However the prefix "co" does not always indicate equal status. Thus a co-pilot is not equal to the pilot, he is subordinated to the pilot. If I tell you to cooperate with God I am not indicating you are equal to God but rather that you should submit to God's work (or operation) in your life.

In this second sense, Mary can rightly be called a co-redemptrix, since the Lord chose to work very closely with her in the work of redeeming us. Thus, as you point out, he took his Sacred Humanity from her, was nourished and cared for by her; he allowed her to signal the beginning of his public ministry (John 2:1*ff*), and she was with him at the foot of the Cross, having the title "Woman." The title "Woman" is a reference to Genesis 3:15 where God indicates that Satan and the Woman would be enemies and that she would be instrumental in his defeat, since her seed (Son) would crush Satan. The same theme is developed in Revelation 12.

Mary does not save or redeem us; Jesus does. But the Redeemer Jesus so closely associates her in his work that she can be said to co-operate, in the work of redemption. Thus the title Co-redemptrix, properly understood, can be properly ascribed to her. "Co" here does not refer to an equal partner, but a subordinate partner.

The reason the title has not been formally declared is likely due to the very misunderstanding of the term your question illustrates. Too many would think "co" meant equal, not subordinate.

Q282: Why does the Catholic Church think the spiritual gifts (e.g. Apostle, evangelist, speaking in tongues healing, miracles, etc) ended with the Apostles? —*Steve Kwilos, via email*

A: It is not taught by the Church that the charismatic (spiritual) gifts ended. Vibrant praise, speaking in tongues and even words of prophecy are evident. These gifts, and others, still exist and are often manifest in the Church, especially in "Charismatic Masses" or prayer services. There are many "healing Masses" and prayers of deliverance.

The title "Apostle" did give way and seems to have been restricted to those who had seen and walked with the Risen Christ. Perhaps out of deference to the apostles, the term shifted to "bishop" but the office remains the same. Though the Apostle St. Paul did not walk with Christ, he did see him in risen glory when he was struck down on the road to Damascus. The title "Evangelist" was used only of the four Gospel writers in any formal sense. And since no new gospels are to be written that title is restricted in Catholic circles.

Q283: I bless myself with holy water when I enter and leave the Church. Several people said I should not bless myself more than once a day, since I am already blessed. Is there a rule about this. — *name withheld, Sarasota, FL*

A: No there is no rule in this regard. It is a matter of personal piety, and you are free to follow the practice you describe.

Perhaps those who say this to you have some liturgical principles in mind but are over-extending the norms or absolutizing them.

Generally speaking, there were some efforts when the Ordinary Form of the Mass was introduced in the 1970s to downplay or eliminate extra signs of the cross that had come into the Mass by custom. For example, there was the tendency to make the sign of the cross after the Confiteor, and many priests began and ended the sermon with the sign of the cross, etc. There was a conscious effort by some liturgists to emphasize that the Mass began and ended with the sign of the Cross, and that other merely customary introductions should be eliminated to give emphasis to those prescribed moments of blessing.

Further, some liturgists thought that other pious customs such as the priest giving a blessing to the servers or others in the sacristy after Mass should cease. After all, they reasoned, had he not just blessed them at the end of the Mass? Did this request for a blessing in the sacristy not suggest that the blessing at Mass was inadequate?

It was also this premise that made some think that, while blessing oneself with holy water on entering was a proper and even necessary sanctifying action, yet to do so on leaving gave the impression that the blessings received in Mass were not adequate or that people had actually lost sanctity during the Mass.

While such concerns are not without some merit, as you can see there is also the possibility that we think a little too much about some things, and can end up getting fussy or even pharisaical.

A gentle teaching is good that seeks to elevate the understanding that the blessings at Mass are real and powerful blessings, not mere ritual actions. This may in a constructive way lessen the *felt* need for extra blessings after Mass. However to assume that people are denying the efficacy of the Mass by the pious customs described here, is a stretch. You remain free to bless yourself any number of times a day so long as superstitious notions are avoided.

Q284: If we teach that life begins at conception, why do we account our age from the day of our birth? – *Victor Bunton, Elkhorn, WI*

A: We should recall that our modern understandings of fetal development have come a long way. So has our capacity to account for time in a more accurate way.

Yet even with our more developed understanding of conception and fetal development, and our more accurate calendars and timepieces, it is not always easy to fix the exact day of our conception (and it might be a little rude to ask a lot of questions to do so).
I was born July 10 1961, but all I can say is that I was conceived sometime in early October 1960. Birth however is a pretty clear demarcation. It is the day when everyone could see me, and refer to an agreed upon calendar on the wall.

Thus, while not denying that life begins at conception, fixing our age by the day of our birth is currently more practical and certain.

Q285: Given the harm that alcohol causes, I find it strange that the otherwise strict Catholic Church allows for Catholics to drink. Call me an old-time Protestant, but I find your silence on this scandalous.
– *name withheld, VA*

A: Strict prohibition of alcohol is hard to maintain given the biblical data. The Bible, and cultural mores have generally steered a middle course between prohibiting drunkenness but also allowing, even praising the "gift of wine."

Thus, St. Paul advises Timothy, "Stop drinking only water, and use a little wine because of your stomach and your frequent illnesses." (1 Tim 5:23). The context of advice like this was that water was seldom pure in the ancient world. And though the ancients knew little of bacteria, they knew by experience that wine (likely the alcohol in the wine) could assist in avoiding illnesses. Surely the alcohol assisted by killing at least some the bacteria that thrived in impure water sources such as wells and dirty streams. Frankly, by modern standards, the ancients drank significant amounts of wine for these health reasons, though they often mixed or diluted it with water.

However, the same Paul also warns of not indulging in too much wine or being given over to drunkenness (1 Tim 3:3, 8, Titus 1:7; 2:3). In Ephesians 5:18 he says, plainly "Do not get drunk on wine which leads to debauchery." So we are pretty clearly dealing here with a call to moderation and sobriety, but not a total abstinence. And if the Catholic Church is strict in matters, she is strict in what God's word says, not in mere human prudence.

Note too that Jesus made wine in abundance (over 60 gallons) at Cana, and used wine at the Last Supper as one source (or matter) of the Sacrament of Holy Communion. Psalm 104:15 says "God gives wine to make man's heart glad." And Proverbs 31:6 advises: "Let strong drink be for those who are perishing, and wine for those who are in anguish!" So there is a medicinal and "cheering" effect that God's word permits and encourages, at least in certain settings.

But again, none of this should be taken to advise drunkenness which is a sin of gluttony, and which robs us of our most important faculties of intellect, judgment and even our will.

Q286: How is the Dallas Charter not against Canon Law, which affirms the right to a good reputation? But the Charter seems to presume guilt.
— *Cathy Andrzejewski, via email*

A: The "Dallas Charter" is more of an agreed-upon framework and policy statement set up by the Conference of Bishops, than a legal document, per se. As such, a lot unresolved canonical and civil issues relate to it. How, for example, does one interpret what are "credible" accusations? A lot depends on the local Bishop and his advisors. Generally, because of the perception of laxity by bishops in the past, and advocacy groups which keep an eagle eye on the Church, many diocesan panels, which review accusations, are quick to presume they are credible and recommend removal.

And therein lies the problem you describe. Due process and the presumption of innocence is alleged to be violated frequently. And while each case must be considered individually, there are many who argue that the civil and canonical rights of priests are in fact violated frequently in the way the Charter is interpreted and applied.

Canonically, of course, priests can appeal any removal or censure. Priests have done so, and some have won and been exonerated. But usually the process is long, and meanwhile the reputation of the priest is questioned and his ability to minster as a priest is largely non-existent.

The Charter, like any framework, needs some revisions and Canon lawyers and others are already in vigorous discussions about how to do this.

As you might imagine, there are some of a different view than yours who think the Charter isn't vigorous enough since it allows local bishops to decide how it is applied in particular cases. They also argue there are too many loopholes and not enough accountability required of the Bishops, nor any mechanism to punish bishops who fail to apply the norms, other than to hope Rome will do so.

And thus the balance of the Charter is always teetering between the need to protect children and also to protect the civil and canonical rights of accused clergy (and laity) who may in fact be innocent of the charges.

Q287: I was having a friendly debate with a family member over whether or not the unbaptized have a guardian angel? Is there a teaching on this? – *name withheld, Chicago, IL*

A: The traditional (but not unanimous) teaching from many of the Fathers of the Church (e.g. Clement, Tertullian, Eusebius, Origen) and also St. Thomas Aquinas is that every human person has a guardian angel assigned at birth. However, after Baptism the angel plays a new and richer role.

Prior to Baptism, and for all non-Christians, though an angel is assigned, they have little power over them other than to protect from the most savage attacks of demons, and to provide some influence.

But at Baptism the Angel is now able to tap into the power and grace of Jesus Christ. Origen adds, "If I belong to the Church, no matter how small I may be, my angel is free to look upon the face of the Father. If I am outside the Church, he does not dare." (Homily on Luke, 35).

So baptism unlocks the greater powers of the angel to help. One can also see that a human person rescued from Original Sin and increasingly healed from its effects by grace is someone with whom a Guardian Angel can work more richly.

Q288: I am having difficulty in resolving the teachings of the saints and the subject of Islam . The Saints say that no one can be saved apart from the Church and they call Islam superstitious and refer to their prophet as antichrist and so forth. I cannot square this with the Catechism # 841 which says God's plan of salvation includes Muslims.
- *David Pair, via email*

A: The text of Catechism # 841 reads , The plan of salvation also includes those who acknowledge the Creator, in the first place amongst whom are the Muslims; these profess to hold the faith of Abraham, and together with us they adore the one, merciful God, mankind's judge on the last day.

It remains the teaching of the Catholic Church that no one who knows the Church and Christ are necessary for salvation and who rejects them can be saved. However, when and how a person "knows" enough to be blameworthy of this sin of unbelief is not always clear.

There is a distinction made between vincible and invincible ignorance. Invincible ignorance is ignorance that cannot be reasonably overcome, given the circumstances. As such one is not fully culpable for acting contrary to what they did not know. Vincible ignorance is ignorance that could have been overcome with a reasonable effort but was indulged anyway. This sort of ignorance is more blameworthy and brings forth varying degrees of punishment depending of the degree of resistance to the truth.

Church teaching therefore recognizes that there are sometimes obstacles that keep the Muslims from recognizing the need for Christ and the Church. Many are taught from youth that Christians are blasphemers for our teaching on the Trinity. In certain areas it is unlawful to practice the Christian faith etc. Such Muslims can be saved if they sincerely seek God but remain in substantial and invincible ignorance as to the need for Christian faith.

This does not mean that they are automatically saved or even likely saved, only that salvation is possible for them, since we know God to be just and not the sort who would condemn others for what they could not reasonably know. Surely they would have to undergo purgation and enlightenment after death and acknowledge it was only through Jesus that they could enter heaven.

As for the Saints, we cherish their lives and example. However they are not the Magisterium. Thus we are not required to square Church teaching with them. Rather their views need to be squared with Church teaching. Further, the Saints often lived in and spoke to situations more specific than what the general norms of the Church address.

Q289: As I understand it, Catholic teaching tells us that when Adam and Eve fell, creation also fell. But if nature had no say, why did it fall at all. – *Peter Tate, Long Beach, CA*

A: St Paul indicates that creation was indeed affected by the fall of man. *For the creation was subjected to futility, not of its own will but by the will of Him who subjected it in hope; because the creation itself will be set free from its bondage to decay...* (Rom 8:20-21).

This was indicated also by God when he spoke to Adam, *Cursed is the ground because of you; in toil you shall eat of it all the days of your life; thorns and thistles it shall bring forth to you;* (Genesis 3:17-18)
So, creation was indeed affected by our fall, God himself thus affected it. We are living in Paradise Lost; a created world that still manifests God's glory, but also, the unruliness of sin by its chaotic and painful qualities.

However your question seems to point more to the "fairness" issue: Why should nature be affected poorly by the sin of Man?

At one level let us be clear, it does not pertain to creation to "decide" one way or the other. Neither does it pertain to creation to merit reward, deserve punishment, or perceive injustice and be harmed in such manners. The earth was given to us, and thus it is part of *our* punishment that our surroundings were affected by our sin.

In this sense, it is a simple ecological fact that our bad behavior can and does affect our world. Human sin can affect the world in any number of ways to include pollution, the squandering of resources, the loss of beauty, and the ruination of local ecosystems.

That said, theologically, creation is affected by our sin foremost because we are the pinnacle of material creation. To us God gave the mandate *Be fruitful and multiply; fill the earth and subdue it. Have dominion over the fish of the sea, the birds of the air, and all the living things that crawl on the earth.* (Gen 1:28). And thus, having a degree of dominion or headship, man affects everything under him. Where the head goes, the body follows.

8. THE LAST THINGS: DEATH, JUDGMENT, HEAVEN & HELL

Q290: Where do our souls go after we die? Do all go to heaven?
— *Audrey*

A: The first destination is the judgment seat of Christ: *It is appointed unto men once to die, and after this the judgment* (Heb 9:27). And again, *For we must all appear before the judgment seat of Christ, that each one may receive what is due him for the things done while in the body, whether good or bad.* (2 Cor 5:10)

From here are three possible destinations. Many *do* go to Heaven, the ultimate destination of all who believe in the Lord and, by his grace, die in love, and friendship with him, and are perfected.

But most of the heaven-bound likely first experience Purgatory where those who die in friendship with God, but are not yet fully perfected in His love, are purified and then drawn to heaven (*cf* 1 Cor 3:12-15).

Finally, some go from judgment to Hell, for by their own choice they rejected God and the values of the Kingdom. It is wrong, as some do, to dismiss Hell as an unlikely possibility since the Lord Jesus taught frequently of it, and warned that many were on the wide road that led there.

Q291: Does the Church teach that in heaven we will recognize and communicate with each other? If so, what will an infant or aborted baby have to say? Will they be a fetus or infant eternally?
- *Fred Matt, West Chester, PA*

A: In answering questions about what our state in heaven will be like, it is important to recall that we are dealing with mysteries beyond our experience. We cannot simply transpose earthly realities to heavenly ones. We must also recall that we are engaging in a great deal of speculative theology in these matters.

With these cautions in mind, we do well to use a basic rule employed in the final section of the Summa by St. Thomas, (or one of his students) in speculating on these matters. In pondering what our bodies and other aspects of our inter-relatedness will be like, we can reason that most perfection has neither excess, nor defect.

Age is one of these aspects. In terms of physical life, we can speak of being young, and immature physically, and thus we manifest sort of defect of age. And we can also speak of being past our physical prime, and thus we speak of an excess of physical age. Thomas thereby speculates that we will have resurrected bodies that will appear to be of about age 30, an age, which manifests neither defect nor excess, and also, is the same approximate age at which Christ died and rose. It is His resurrected quality that models our own (*cf* Phil 3:21).

Hence, it would seem that in heaven, when our bodies rise, we will not see infants or elderly among us, but we will all manifest the perfection of physical "age."

Similar reasoning can be applied to other aspects of our physical bodies, such as disease, or missing limbs, or other certain defects. It seems, that these defects will be remedied. However, one might speculate that some aspects of our physical sufferings might still be manifest, though not in a way that would cause us pain. For we see in Christ's resurrected body the wounds of his passion. But now they are not signs of his pain, but rather, of his glory, and so too perhaps for some of our wounds.

As regards our inter-relatedness, this too would be perfected. We will not only recognize and communicate with each other, but we will do this most perfectly as members of Christ, since our relationship to the Christ the head of the Body will be perfected.

Q292: If no soul may see God unless it has been totally purified, which is why we must go to purgatory before Heaven, and since Purgatory ends on the Day of Judgment, what happens to the souls of the people who are still alive on Judgment Day? How are their souls purified?
— *Amy O'Donnell, Silver Spring, MD*

A: This level of detail, is not supplied to us by the biblical texts. Nor are such details defined in the magisterial teachings of the Church. Hence, we are in the realm of speculative theology when it comes to such matters.

We ought to begin by saying that the Day of Judgment will not be a day like any other. There are many unknown factors, especially related to the mystery of time, that underlie our speculations. For example, is Judgment Day, really a day of 24 hours? Or is it a moment in time that happens like a flash? Perhaps it is a longer period of some indeterminate length? Does time even exist, as we know it now, at a moment like that?

There is also a premise in your question, which is not unassailable. Namely, that Purgatory ends on the Day of Judgment. We do not know this. Perhaps Purgatory, or the process of purgation, may exist for a time after the last judgment. But here too is another question. What does it mean to say that something exists "for a time," if time as we know it no longer exists?

Perhaps the best we can do with a question like this is to say that it is not for us to know such details, and that God will accomplish the purifications and purgation necessary in ways known to Him.

It would certainly seem that such purification would in fact be necessary based on Scripture, which says of heaven, *Nothing impure will ever enter it* (Rev 21:27). And thus, while Purgatory, or the process of purgation is set forth in Scripture for us who die now, how God will accomplish this for souls in the rarefied conditions of the Great Second Coming is known to Him, but not revealed to us with enough specificity to answer your question without speculation.

Q293: The Catechism (# 1023) states that faithful who die after receiving Baptism "... already before they take up their bodies again .... will be in heaven ...." Could you please explain and elaborate on just what this means? - *Jim Grady, Marion, MA*

A: Currently, prior to the Second Coming, when we die our bodies lie in the earth, but our soul goes to God. Those deemed worthy and capable of heaven, after any necessary purifications, are admitted into heaven.

Only at the Second Coming, will our bodies rise, when, as Scripture attests, the trumpet shall sound and the bodies of the dead will come forth (1 Cor 15:52). Our body which rises, will be truly our body, but gloriously transformed as St. Paul details in the same place in Scripture (1 Cor 15:35ff)

What this most fundamentally means is that Christ did not come to save only our souls but the whole of us, soul and body. One great dignity of the human person is that we unite both the spiritual and material aspects of God's creation in our very person. This glory will be restored to us at the Second Coming.

An additional meaning of this truth is that we must reverence both our soul and body through the spiritual and corporal works of mercy and we must fulfill the mandate to glorify God in our body as well as our soul.

Q294: We learn that God loves us unconditionally. But then why is there Hell? That doesn't seem unconditional. —*Peter Smithers, via email*

A: Perhaps you would agree that if someone loves someone else, that love would not include him forcing his will on the other. And while it is certainly true that the Lord wills to save everyone, he does not force us to accept his. God is not a slave driver, he is Love and love invites us to freely accept his offer of an eternal relationship.

While some think that everyone wants to go to heaven, generally they have a heaven in mind of their own design. But the real heaven is not merely a human paradise; it is the Kingdom of God and all its fullness. In heaven is celebrated: Charity, worship of God, truth, chastity, forgiveness, esteem of the poor, humility etc. And yet there are many, who reject so or all of these values. Why would a loving God force people to enter into the eternal place which celebrates things they reject?

Hence, the existence of Hell is not opposed to God's love. It is in conformity with the respect necessary for our freedom to accept or reject the relationship of love. Mysteriously, many come to a place in their life where they definitively reject God, and the values of the Kingdom he offers.

Q295: In our Catholic faith we believe in the resurrection of the body. The Scripture states that in the kingdom there is neither male nor female. Does this mean that our body will not be resurrected in its full earthly form? - *Dion Hankinson, New Baltimore, PA*

A: It seems that you're referring to what Paul writes in Galatians 3:28 *There is neither Jew nor Gentile, neither slave nor free, nor is there male and female, for you are all one in Christ Jesus.*

Here St. Paul is indicating that there is no difference in terms of dignity. In other words, whatever distinctions there are between us, even essential distinctions, there remains the truth that we are all equal in dignity before God, whose children we are.

But this equality in dignity does not mean there is no difference in essence. Clearly, being male or female is a distinction that goes to the very depths of our being, including our soul. And thus, when our body rises, we will indeed be male or female.

Perhaps, in the context of your question, it is also good for us to reflect on a common modern error that reduces sexual distinctions to a merely incidental, surface quality about the physical characteristics of the body. But this is not so. The soul is the form of the body. That is to say, it is the identity of the soul and it's capacities that give rise to the design of the body. Hence, a person's sex is not simply an incidental quality of their body, but is an aspect of their person that extends from the depths of their soul. Human persons do not just *have* a male or female body, they *are* male or female.

The most extreme form of reducing sex to a merely incidental quality of the body, is illustrated in those who engage in so-called "sex change" operations, as if simply altering the body surgically could change a person's sexual identity. It cannot. Scripture says, *God made them, male and female He created them.* (Gen 1:27). Our identity as male or female extends to our inmost being, and cannot simply be shed like clothing is.

Hence, when we rise, we will indeed be male and female. Further, even before the resurrection of the body, our soul remains male or female.

Q296: I want to be sure I go to heaven when I die. What exactly should I do? - *John Hahn, Woodbridge, VA*

A: A short biblical answer to your question is supplied by Peter in Acts. Having heard a sermon that he preached on Pentecost, many were struck to the heart and cried out what shall we do? *Peter replied, repent and be baptized every one of you, in the name of Jesus Christ for the forgiveness of your sins. And you will receive the gift of the Holy Spirit.* (Acts 2:38)

But this is not simply to be understood is a ritualistic observance that we fulfill on one day, but is meant to usher in a whole renewal of the human person. And thus we ought to look at all three things that Peter indicates in some more detail.

The word translated as "repent" is *Metanoia* which means more than to clean up our act. It means to come to a whole new mind, rooted in what God teaches and reveals, with new priorities and able to make better decisions.

To be baptized, is not only to be cleansed of our sins but also to see our old self put to death, and for Christ to come alive in us. Baptism ushers in the beginnings of a lifelong healing process that must continue by God's grace. Baptism also points to all the sacraments of the Church. For, having been brought to new life, we must also be fed by the Eucharist and by God's word, we must see the wounds of sins healed in confession, we must be strengthened for a mission by confirmation. Baptism also makes us a member of the body of Christ. And thus, we are called to walk in fellowship with all the members of Christ's one body, The Church.

St. Peter also speaks of receiving the gift of the Holy Spirit. And thus we are taught that our dignity is to be swept up into the life, love, and wisdom of God. We are called to be sanctified by the Holy Spirit to see sins put to death and many virtues come alive.

Finally, something needs to be said about your use of the word "exactly" which might imply there is some very simple formula for getting saved. But as can be seen, there are many dimensions to the work of God in saving us. Thus, we are to walk in a loving covenant relationship with the Lord and His body the Church. And like any relationship, this cannot simply be reduced to a few things. We must trust the Lord, and walk in a relationship of love and obedience to him. We are to do this in fellowship with His Church, through the grace of the Sacraments, obedience to the Word of God, and prayer (*cf* Acts 2:42).

Q297: A Jewish friend insists that, according to his religion, there is simply no afterlife. Is this true and consistent with the Old Testament?
- *Charley McKelvy, via email*

A: The views of the Jewish people regarding the afterlife vary to some degree. Unlike the Catholic Church, there is no central teaching authority among Jewish people. Thus, in a short answer like this, we cannot fully treat what all Jewish people believe about the particulars of the afterlife. But it is fair to say that most believing Jews *do* believe in an afterlife. It is also fair to say that the concept of the resurrection of the dead developed in Judaism over the centuries, and became clearer in the later books as God brought the ancient Jews to a deeper understanding of what He was offering.

But for your friend to say that there is nothing in the Old Testament about it requires the dismissal of a good number of texts from the prophets, Psalms and the Wisdom tradition that speak quite vividly of the dead rising (e.g. Is 26:19; Job 19:25ff; Daniel 12:2; Ezekiel 37:12; Hosea 13:14; 1 Sam 2:6, among many others).

At the time of Jesus, the Sadducees did reject the resurrection of the dead, and held that, at death one simply ceased to exist. Part of the reason for this was that they only accepted the first five books of the Bible, and claimed that in them, there was no mention of the dead rising. Jesus sets aside their view by invoking the encounter of God with Moses at the burning bush in the book of Exodus, one of the first five books of the Bible. There, God called Himself the "God of Abraham, Isaac, and Jacob." But if God is a "God of the living, and not the dead" as the Sadducees would surely insist, then somehow, to God, Abraham Isaac and Jacob are alive. (see Mark 12:24-27)

And while your Jewish friend is not likely accept the authority of Jesus, this text of goes a long way to show that declaring there's nothing in the Old Testament about resurrection, especially in the first five books, is not an interpretation immune from critique. It further illustrates that at the time of Jesus, while the Sadducees rejected the resurrection of the dead, most other Jews such as the Pharisees and also followers of Jesus and others *did* accept, teach and expect the resurrection of the dead.

Therefore, it seems safe to consign your friend's remark as the opinion of one Jew, or some Jews, but not all Jews, then or now.

Q298: If no soul may see God unless it has been totally purified which is why we must go to Purgatory before Heaven; and if Purgatory ends on the Day of Judgment, what happens to the souls of the people who are still alive on Judgment Day? How are their souls purified?
- *Amy O'Donnell Silver Spring, MD*

A: Actually, we don't know if purgatory ends of Judgment Day. It could, arguably continue for some "time" there after. Then again, maybe not, perhaps the Last Judgment ushers in a quick searing purification and purgatory passes away with the current heavens and earth.

But perhaps a more fundamental "answer" to your question is to say that there are just some things we don't know. Good Theology must recognize its limits, being content to accept that there are many things God has not revealed. And even in those things He has revealed, we must humbly admit that the mysteries about God, and creation have depths beyond our capacity to fully comprehend.

Q299: How can we be happy in heaven knowing that some of our loved ones did not make it there? - *Sandy Vignali, Iron River, MI*

A: The happiness of heaven cannot be equated with earthly categories and pre-requisites. Exactly how we will be happy in heaven cannot be explained to us here. Scripture describes heavenly happiness as: *What no eye has seen, what no ear has heard, and what no human mind has conceived"* -- *these things God has prepared for those who love him* (1 Cor 2:9).

Jesus also cautions the Sadducees, who tried to project the earthly realities of marriage and family into heaven. He said *You are in error because you do not know the Scriptures or the power of God* (Matt 22:29). In other words, and for our purposes here, we have to admit that our grasp of what Heaven is, and how it will be experienced, cannot be reduced to, or explained merely in terms of how we are happy now.

That said, some have speculated (and it *IS* just speculation) that the happiness of heaven, even despite missing family members, will be possible in light of the deeper appreciation of God's justice that we will have there. Surely we will concur in heaven with all God's judgments and in no way incur sorrow on account of them.

Hence, we will see that those excluded from heaven are excluded rightly and have really chosen to dwell apart, preferring darkness to light (Jn 3:19). And while it may currently be mysterious to how this will not cause us sadness, God does in fact teach us that he will wipe every tear from our eyes (cf Rev. 21:4).

Q300: What is the Catholic view of the "rapture" which is held by some Protestants? - *Terry Morrison, Platte City, MO*

A: The Catholic view would reject the notion of the rapture as held widely by certain Evangelical Christians. The word rapture (from the Latin rapiemur) means to be caught up or snatched away. Those who hold the view claim First Thessalonians as their source where St. Paul writes:

The dead in Christ will rise first; then we who are alive, who are left, shall be caught up together with them in the clouds to meet the Lord in the air; and so we shall always be with the Lord. (1 Thess. 4:16–17)

The problem is that St. Paul clearly applies this "being caught up" to the definitive and final Second Coming of Christ. Scripture also teaches that the period just before the Second Coming will include a great deal of tribulation and suffering both for the faithful (e.g. Mat 24:9-14), Then Christ will come in glory and the final Judgment will take place at once (cf Matt 24:31ff).

But those who hold the Rapture remove it from this context and insert a lot of views that the text does not support and St. Paul never taught.

Thus many Evangelical Christians insert into the First Thessalonians text a notion (not taught by St. Paul) that unbelievers will be left behind on earth and that a 1000 year period will ensue, which will be kind of earthly golden age during which the world will become thoroughly Christian. Thus they separate the Second Coming and the Last Judgment by a thousand years and teach that Christ will physically reign on earth.

To hold this view they make questionable use of other biblical texts, mainly from the Book of Revelation. They also use many dubious notions referred to as premillenialism, and complex brew of pre, mid and post tribulationism which are too complicated to detail in a short article. So complex are all these interwoven theories that the rapture enthusiasts hotly debate the details among themselves.

The Catholic approach is to rest on the more firm ground of Sacred Tradition (current notions of the "rapture" are less than 150 years old) and a more plain teaching of the Scriptures. These unite as one event the Second Coming, the Last Judgment and the faithful being caught up into heaven to be forever, with God and the unfaithful departing immediately to Hell.

Q301: Was heaven not available to the human race until Jesus died on the cross? —*Teresa Thompson, Des Moines, IA*

A: You are correct, there was no access to heaven until the work of Jesus to reconcile us to the Father. Without this sanctifying grace from Jesus, we could not endure the holy presence of God. It would be like wax before fire.

Prior to Jesus the dead were understood to go to Sheol, a shadowy place where the dead slept and were only vaguely aware, as they awaited the coming of the Messiah. After dying on the cross Jesus went down to the dead and preached to them (1 Peter 3:19), gathering the righteous to him. And as he ascended to heaven led them there (Eph 4:8)

While there are stories of Enoch and Elijah, and possibly Moses being caught up to heaven, it is unlikely that the highest heaven is meant in those passages.

Q302: If the condemned in Hell are there for all eternity, why is Satan allowed to run amok in the world out of hell. Isn't he supposed to be suffering in hell along with his minions and other condemned? It seems as though he is having a good time creating havoc and not suffering one bit. - *Robert Flint, Merced, CA*

A: While some texts in Scripture speak of Satan and the fallen angels as being cast into Hell (e.g. 2 Peter 2:4, Jude 6), other texts speak of the fallen angels (demons) as being cast down to the earth (e.g. Rev 12:8, Job 1:7). Thus, though consigned to Hell it would seem that some or all the demons have the capacity also to roam the earth. However, Satan is described as being "chained" and in prison (Rev 20:1-3). This is likely a way of indicating that his power is limited in some sense. But it is not a denial that he still exerts considerable influence through other fallen angels which can and do roam the earth.

Near the end of the world Scripture says that Satan will be wholly loosed and come forth to deceive the nations for a while, and after this brief period he and the other fallen angels will be definitively cast into the lake of fire and their influence ended (Rev. 20:10).

Why God permits freedom to demons to wander about the earth is mysterious. We know that God permits evil as a "necessary" condition of freedom for the rational creatures he has created. Angels and humans have free and rational souls and, if our freedom is to mean anything, it must be that God allows than some angels and men abuse their freedom, and even become a source of evil and temptation for others.

As such, this life amounts for us as a kind of test wherein God permits some degree of evil to flourish, yet not without offering us the grace to overcome. Further, there is the tradition implied in the scriptures that for every fallen angel, there were two angels who did not fall (Rev 12:4) . Thus our lives are not merely to be accounted as under the influence of demons, but also under the influence and care of angels.

It is also clear that, on account of temptations and trials, our 'yes" to God has greater dignity and merit than if we lived in an essentially sin-free zone or paradise.

It would be too strong say, as you have, that demons and Satan do not suffer at all. Demons, like human beings, suffer defeats as well as victories. They have things, which delight them, and things, which disappoint and anger them. Anyone who has ever attended an exorcism can attest that demons DO suffer great deal, especially when the faithful pray and make pious use of sacraments and sacramentals such as holy water, relics, blessed medals, rosaries and so forth. Faith and love are deeply disturbing to demons.

Q303: You said in a previous answer that purgatory operates outside of space and time. Does that mean that, for the millions of souls that may be there, they don't require any space? Also, if there is no time in purgatory, why was I taught as a child that I could pray and get a person 100 days indulgence etc.? – *Philip Hoos, Muskegon, MI*

A: I don't recall using the expression "purgatory operates outside of space and time." However, regarding the need for physical space, it does not follow that purgatory would require this. Why? Because there are souls in purgatory, not bodies. Our souls are not physical, and do not occupy physical space anymore than a thought occupies physical space. This does not absolutely mean that the Lord does not have purgatory in a certain location. But where that location might be, and how large etc. is not revealed to us. The point is, physical space is not per se required for Purgatory.

Regarding time in purgatory, it would seem there probably *is* time in purgatory. Why? Because there is the change of purification occurring. One understanding of time is that it is a measure of change or "movement" in the philosophical sense. However, whether time is experienced in Purgatory as it is here, or how time here relates to time there is mysterious.

As for the old system of giving prayers a sort of ranking based on the number of days of indulgence granted (e.g. 100 days, 500 days etc), that was not a reference to the number of days in Purgatory. Numbers like that go back to an early period in Church history when penances are often quite lengthy. The prayers of certain fellow Christians (especially confessors of the faith who had suffered imprisonment etc) could be used to reduce the length of certain penances for other Christians. The system of days and years than came to be used as a kind of gauge of the relative merit of certain prayers and pious actions, but were not a reference to days in purgatory. The system of assigning numbers (such as 100 days indulgence) was set aside in 1970, in favor of simply declaring an indulgence to be partial or plenary. This change was made in large part due to just this sort of confusion about the true meaning of those numbers.

Q304: I heard a priest who gave an orthodox description of purgatory say, as he concluded, "Purgatory will end when the world ends." I have not read this before. Can you clarify? – *Jim Flynn, via email*

A: Part of the answer is wrapped up in the mystery of time. We cannot be sure that time in purgatory, and certainly in heaven is experienced the way it is here. Likely it is not. And if there is time in purgatory, how does it relate to time here? And what the "end" of the world means in temporal relation to heaven and purgatory is unclear.

What we do know is that some sort of purgation is necessary for anyone who dies in sanctifying grace but is not yet perfected with the holiness necessary to see God. (see Heb 12:14)

Even if the world ends today, it does not seem reasonable that no purgation would be necessary for those still on earth. So some means to accomplish this would seem necessary. In this sense purgatory, (as a process) would exist even if the world ends. But we need not assume that such a purgation will go on for "years" in time as we know it now. The biblical data implies a finished quality to all things on Judgment Day, and this is probably what Father meant. Yet, God will surely accomplish any needed purifications in a way known to him.

Q305: The descriptions in the Bible seem to describe a vast amount of people and the paintings I have seen from the Renaissance make it look rather crowded and busy. Frankly I hate big cities and crowds. Are these descriptions accurate or am I missing something? *–Doris Leben, Wichita, KA*

The danger to avoid when meditating on heaven is taking earthly realities and merely transferring them to heaven. Whatever similarities heavenly realities have to things on earth, they will be experienced there in a heavenly and perfected way, with joy unspeakable.

The more biblical way and theological way to understand the multitudes in heaven is not as some physical crowding, but as a deep communion. In other words the Communion of Saints is not just a lot of people standing around, and perhaps talking or moving about.

St Paul teaches: *So we, who are many, are one body in Christ, and individually members, one of another.* (Rom 12:5). And though we experience this imperfectly here on earth, we will experience it perfectly in heaven. As members of one another we will have deep communion, knowing and being known in a deep and rich way. Your memories, gifts, and insights, will be mine, and mine will be yours. There will be profound understanding and appreciation, a rich love and sense of how we all complete one another, and really are one in Christ.

Imagine the glory of billions of new thoughts, stories and insights that will come from being perfectly members of Christ and members of one another. Imagine the peace that will come from finally understanding, and being understood. This is deep, satisfying and wonderful communion, not crowds of strangers. Therefore, the biblical descriptions of heaven as multitudes should not be understood as mere numbers, but as the richness and glory of the communion. The paintings showing "crowds" should be understood as an allegory of deep communion, of being close in a way we can only imagine now.

St. Augustine had in mind the wonderful satisfaction of this deep communion of us with God, and with one another in Christ when he described heaven as Unus Christus amans seipsum (One Christ loving himself). This is not some selfish Christ turned in on himself. This is Christ the head in deep communion with all the members of his body, and all the members in Christ experiencing deep mystical communion with him and one another, together swept up into the life of the Trinity. Again, as St. Paul says, *and you are Christ's, and Christ is God's.* (1 Cor 3:23)

ABOUT THE AUTHOR

Msgr. Charles Pope was ordained in 1989 for the Archdiocese of Washington, DC, after attending Mount St. Mary's Seminary in Emmitsburg, Maryland. There I received both a M.Div. and a Master's Degree in Moral Theology. Prior to entering the Seminary I received a Bachelor of Science Degree from George Mason University in Virginia and worked briefly for the Army Corps of Engineers. During those years I was also a cantor, choir director and organist in two Catholic Parishes.

I have served in five different parishes in my 24 years as a priest, 14 of those years as pastor in two different parishes. I am currently the Pastor of Holy Comforter–Saint Cyprian Parish. I am also a Dean of the Archdiocese, have served on the priest personnel board, the Priest Council, and as one of the Consultors for the Archdiocese. Pastorally, I have served as the coordinator for the Legion of Mary and currently the coordinator for the celebration of the Latin Extraordinary Form of the Mass. I have given numerous retreats and talks for laity and clergy around the Archdiocese and, when time rarely permits, elsewhere in the country.

I have authored the Blog for the Archdiocese of Washington (http://blog.adw.org) for the past four years which covers and discusses a very wide range of topics. Of special focus at the blog is the intersection of faith and culture. As our culture continues to manifest some very problematic trends, it is essential for us to understand how our faith and the teachings of the Church have wonderful and healing remedies for what ails us.

Made in the USA
Monee, IL
01 August 2022